HEAT
IN
THE
VEGAS
NIGHT

HEAT
IN
THE
VEGAS
NIGHT

A TRUE STORY BY
JERRY REEDY

COMPILATION AND RESEARCH BY
SKOOKUM MAGUIRE

atmosphere press

*I would like to dedicate this book to Steve Kammeyer,
AKA the Boss.*

The man was a genius, a mentor, a friend and a brother.

CHAPTER ONE

It was 1988. Over the course of the last two and a half years, I'd come to reflect on the past, and had begun to rely on our experiences for guidance. We'd been working as the Kammeyer Group for nearly eight years, and we'd come to know exactly what we were up against—and that history had become a beacon for the future.

I was mentally processing some of our past experiences as the crew and I made our way into downtown Las Vegas. We were headed for the Mint, an older casino that was considered by old-time residents to be situated in mob territory. It certainly was in our eyes. It didn't matter much, though, whether it was a mob-controlled casino or not. We were scared to death of these places, and for very good reasons. The casino management teams, the civil and private authorities, and the mob bosses themselves all knew that we were still out here—and they were desperately trying to catch us. But just the thought of playing in a mob-related casino made the old adrenaline flow that much faster, and it kept us at the top of our game.

We were on our way to the Mint Casino. It was a large, single-story affair in Old Las Vegas, sporting an eye-catching marquee that took on the shape of a huge gold coin that rose up out of the desert floor under a shower of massive red lights. The casino itself was backed up by a multi-story hotel and parking garage structure, obstacles that could limit a fast-moving fellow's means of egress if he needed to leave in a hurry—which was something we did often.

But today we were coming in during the daylight hours. The allure of the Las Vegas lights was subdued by the sun, making our entrance less dramatic—a good thing.

Research told me that the Mint was the brainchild of one Milton Prell, a man who had gotten his start running a bingo parlor in California. In fact, when he moved to Vegas he started with bingo. And Prell did well. He ended up owning both the Sahara and the Mint. He eventually sold his holdings to Del Webb—a fellow who, himself, started out as a foreman on the crew that built the Flamingo Hotel and Casino for Bugsy Siegel—the original high-stakes venture that started Las Vegas on its march to gambling prominence.

So the rumor was true. Las Vegas was indeed the ultimate city of dreams, and once in a great while, those dreams would come true. But the real beauty of the place was this: Nobody ever talked about the losers—and there were a whole lot of losers. The trick, of course, was simply not to be one of them. And in order to avoid ending up on the losing end of things, a guy needed some kind of an edge.

The original purveyors of Las Vegas had connections to organized crime, an edge that had limitless boundaries. The mob was always looking for ways to clean up their money, and Las Vegas was the perfect venue. There were other players, of course, with other kinds of edges—some with political connections, some with old-money connections, some with Wall Street connections, and some who wanted their edge to remain hidden.

We fell into the latter group. We had an edge—we were in possession of *the perfect way to cheat at blackjack*. We called our edge the *gaff*, though if you happen to show it to any passing tourist on the street they'd say that you were simply holding a small piece of mirror. It's a matter of perspective, I suppose, but it worked for us, and at that moment we were on our way to take money from the Mint.

It was just after shift change on Saturday afternoon when we got there, and as per our protocol, we didn't want to be seen together, so we each passed into the casino through a different entrance. At that point we began to look for a playable dealer. As we carried out our search, we would pass each other from time to time, but we never showed any signs of recognition. We had a script to follow, a script that had been written some years earlier by the Boss, and we'd been well trained not to deviate from that script.

Once we'd worked our way over to the blackjack pit, Skate spotted something. He quickly rubbed his nose to let me know he'd found a dealer.

I acknowledged with a wipe to the forehead, a response that had become habitual through repetition. Then I headed in his direction.

We wanted to get in and out of this place as quickly as possible, so I moved to the playable dealer's table and carried out my routine. I could do it in my sleep by now, though it hadn't always been that way. Then I took a moment to force myself into the present. I didn't want to be dwelling on the past with so much at stake right now.

I sat down, got a stack of chips for a $100 bill, and casually looked around as I reached under the table and into my pocket for my gaff. Then I deftly set it up on the table, using a bottle of Guinness Extra Stout beer for cover. The extra stout came in a very dark bottle, and that was good for shielding the gaff.

I checked with Skate—all was well—so I gave him the signal to bring in Tailsman.

This dealer was easy by my standards. She kept the cards higher off the table than most dealers. And the high-roller seat was open, so I didn't need to have someone hold it. The tourist on third base decided to leave the table so I signaled to the new screen, Re-K, to take that spot for protection on my left side.

Then, without turning my head, I watched in my peripheral vision as Tailsman waltzed up to the table and threw down $500. The money landed in the circle on the table, making it a viable bet. Then he simply said, "Play it."

"Money plays five hundred," the dealer announced, loud enough for the pit boss to hear.

At that point, the pit boss moseyed over and introduced himself to Tailsman. "Hi, I'm Gus Stamata," he said, sticking out a hand to shake.

As Tailsman reached for the hand, he replied, "Hello, I'm J. J. Simplot."

Small talk continued for a few minutes, which gave Skate enough time to get a read on the rapport between the pit boss and Tailsman—something he monitored every play to determine if there were any signs of deterioration in the pit boss's demeanor.

After a few preliminary hands, things seemed to be going Tailsman's way—which could be either a good thing or a bad thing. Good because we were winning, bad because winning early in the play would bring attention from the higher-ups.

As things progressed, it was becoming obvious that the relationship between Tailsman and ol' Gus was beginning to deteriorate. Gus got on the phone and dialed a three-digit number, which meant he called someone in-house.

Then down the stairs came the shift boss, and he began to watch from a short distance to the left of me. Skate had concern on his face and rubbed his chin, telling me that things weren't so good. The shift boss watched a few more winning hands. Then he disappeared in the same direction from which he'd appeared. Skate gave me the rub to the forehead, letting me know things were cool again. But in my experience things don't go from cool to not-so-cool and back to cool again that quickly.

The next hand that was dealt left Tailsman tending to three hands of $500 each. The dealer had an eight up and an ace in the hole—*nineteen*—and I knew this would be our last hand. I had to play the hand out while preparing to leave.

After that, Tailsman picked up an ace-six. I signaled him to hit. He drew a four, which gave him *twenty-one*. At that point, he went to his second hand, which also had a two-card count of *seventeen*. I looked around to see if any of the pit bosses were watching. They weren't, so I signaled him to hit again. He drew a three—for a total count of *twenty*. Taking a hit with a two-card seventeen, of course, is not advisable in the casino world.

By the time Tailsman reached for his third hand, I was getting up from the table to leave. But I noticed that he had a two-card count of eighteen. I signaled him to hit as I started to leave the table.

I had taken two steps away from the table when I looked in the direction in which the shift boss had disappeared just a few moments earlier. At that same instant, the shift boss was returning to the pit with two security guards. He looked right at me, pointed his finger, and yelled, "Grab that guy!"

The chase was on.

I took off in the manner in which I was trained. I ran around the end of a bank of slot machines, and I was moving as fast as I could. But as I turned the corner, my head was about three feet off the ground, and I discovered a cocktail waitress right in front of my face. Her chest was eye-level for me. My forehead hit her right between the tits.

I knocked her to the floor and the tray of drinks she was carrying flew into the air. I certainly didn't want to hurt anyone, but I had to keep running. I could hear cocktail glasses shattering into shards behind me.

I hit the doors at full speed, and then I was out of the casino—which in my business is the best thing possible, especially in that place. But I still had work to do.

I continued to run in the direction of a freeway overpass in North Las Vegas. Then I noticed I'd picked up a pursuer. The valet parking attendant had taken up the chase. He looked to be about six-two and probably weighed 150 pounds soaking wet. I was six-feet even and crossed the scales at about 230 pounds. I knew I probably couldn't outrun him—it was the classic matchup, a linebacker against a wide receiver. I would have the advantage if we were running at each other, but...

As I rounded the corner of the next block, I still had the gaff in my hand. I didn't want to get caught with it, so I opened the palm of my hand and swung my right hand into a steel light pole, hoping to break the gaff all to hell.

But in all the excitement, I'd forgotten to take the tape and the paper clip off the back of the thing. When I hit the pole, the mirror came out of my hand and fell to the ground in a heap of taped-together glass.

I was moving fast, but I had to stop and turn around and go back for the incriminating evidence. We didn't want the casino to know that we'd used a mirror to cheat them. It was explicitly forbidden in Las Vegas. But just as I started back, here came the parking attendant. He managed to scoop up the gaff on the run. Just as he grabbed for that little piece of evidence, though, he lost his balance and fell to the ground.

I hurried over to the skinny dude, as he lay flat on his back, holding the gaff out to the side as far as his arms could stretch. Then he put his left foot up into my chest as I leaned over him and yelled, "Give me that fucking mirror!"

It turned out that he'd been told I'd stolen some lady's necklace. In fact, that's what he thought he had in his hand.

A look of terror crossed his face. "Why don't you just run?" he asked.

I didn't hesitate and said, "Good idea."

I took off for the back entrance of the California Club and went immediately to the gift shop. I bought a khaki denim bucket hat and an extra-large T-shirt. Then I slipped off into a maze of slot machines, took off my bluish-green shirt, wiped the sweat from my face, and put on the white T-shirt and the hat. I stuffed my discarded shirt into a slot machine tray and started walking casually in the direction of the front door of the casino.

I immediately encountered two security guards. They were coming right at me, both looking from side to side to detect any fast-moving or suspicious-looking person in a blue-green shirt. But I kept my cool, as I was trained. I was hidden in plain sight as the guards passed without incident. We'd been trained so well, I knew that the security guards were on the lookout for a man desperately running.

I didn't panic, and maintained a slow, leisurely pace back out to Fremont Street. When I stopped at the curb, I could see security buzzing all over town. I also saw Skate and the new screen, Re-K, standing about fifty yards away. They were staring in my direction. Skate had his hands on both collars of his shirt, which meant the heat was on. Of course I knew that, so I moved across the street and started to walk away from the trouble. I went right past City Hall and on into a residential neighborhood.

I concentrated on a fast but casual pace to distance myself from the heat. When I'd gone about a mile, I stopped at a pay phone, called the Peppermill—the backup joint—and asked to have Skate McCloud paged.

I got no salutation or small talk from the anxious field marshal; he simply said, with his New Jersey accent, "Red, that was fucking awesome. Where in the hell are you?"

"I'm at the corner of Charleston and Rancho Drive. Come and get me."

Then I leaned back against the glass wall of the phone booth and let out a big, long sigh of relief.

CHAPTER TWO

It all started during spring break of 1980. I was playing college baseball for Portland State. A road trip landed us in San Diego at the Sunlight Classic, and that's when I first met Steve Kammeyer. His brother, Spanky, and I were former teammates, and Spanky was playing ball for USC in the same tournament. The two brothers were both in attendance at the game I was pitching in against San Diego State. After the game, I met up with Spanky, and he introduced me to Steve.

After a short visit, Steve announced that he had some business to tend to, so Spanky gave me a ride back to my hotel. On the way, he happened to mention that his brother was a professional gambler.

"Wow, that's a unique occupation." I said, in a surprised tone, but after that evening I never thought much about it.

Eight months later, though, in late November—after getting weathered out on the logging show where I'd been working—I was sitting idly around my dad's house in Oregon. The logging side had been down for a while, and my money was running low. I was searching for something to do. Then one afternoon, the phone rang. It was Spanky.

"Hey, Spank," I said, glad to hear from my old friend. "What's up?"

"What are you doing, Red?" he wanted to know. *Red* was my nickname from college.

"Just training for the spring," I said. I told him I was

broke and didn't have a job.

"How'd you like to come down to Lake Tahoe and learn how to gamble?" He giggled.

Spanky and I had been on the same baseball team two years prior. We were selected by a bunch of Northwest college coaches to play on a handpicked semi-pro team. We sat on the bench together when we weren't pitching, and we hit it off pretty good for the rest of the summer. I knew that giggle, and also knew it meant that he was up to no good.

I was stunned into silence. I didn't know what to say to that offer. It wasn't exactly what I expected to hear from my old friend.

"Here, talk to Steve," he said, breaking the silence.

When Steve came on the line, he mentioned our get-together in San Diego. I told him that I recalled that meeting. Then he proceeded to explain to me that he was training a new crew, and asked if I was interested.

I thought for a moment and told him I was definitely interested. I was actually excited at the time for an opportunity.

Then he asked me if I knew anything about playing blackjack.

"No," I said.

"Good," he replied. Then he went on. "I want you to pick up a couple of books about gambling," he said. "The titles are *Playing Blackjack as a Business* and *Turning the Tables on Las Vegas.*"

I wrote down the names of the books.

"Read them cover to cover," he said. "Pay special attention to the chart on page 25 in *Playing Blackjack as a Business.* I'll get back to you in a couple of weeks or so."

So, I did what he'd asked, and three weeks later he called back. He asked me if I'd read the books. I told him that I'd read them cover to cover.

"Great," he said. "Be at the Harrah's Club in Lake Tahoe on the day after Christmas."

By the time Christmas rolled around, I had only a $100 to my name. It was painful to spend sixty-six bucks on a Greyhound bus ticket to Lake Tahoe. But I was a twenty-one-year-old white male—no job, no car, no money, and no home. I had no option but to take a chance on this opportunity.

The bus left my hometown of Grants Pass, Oregon, at 2:13 on a Friday morning.

I'd traveled by Greyhound before, and I'd found bus riders to be different than the folks a guy will meet on airliners. There are the temporary down-and-outers, like me. There are the habitual drifters, and parolees from federal and state prisons. There are those folks who hadn't found a way to fit into the social fabric of the country and probably never would. And then there are the sad souls who have accepted that they have very little future at all.

Being an outgoing sort, I tried to engage the folks around me in conversation—the weather, the election, the recent eruption of Mt. St. Helens—but talk on a Greyhound bus is sparse and erratic. My attempts were mostly greeted with blank stares.

I was left to reflect on other things, as the bus ground its way up the long grade over the Sierra Nevada Mountains. The first big snow of the season had come a week earlier, and the highway had been plowed. The snowbanks along the road were steep and solid, but they stood way off to the side. Plowing would leave the snowbanks closer to the edge of the pavement the next time—and then the next, and the next. By April, the highway would be reduced to a narrow trail between two huge, imposing banks of snow.

As we approached the Donner Pass, I thought back to what I knew of the Donner Party. With nothing to look at but snow, I couldn't stop thinking of that harsh, fateful winter they suffered through in 1846-1847.

The Donner Party was originally composed of eighty-seven people, but only forty-eight of them lived to reach California. Of the thirty-nine who perished, many were eaten.

I knew a lot of folks were religious back then, which made me wonder how the survivors managed to deal with what must have been some very gruesome memories—memories that probably stayed in their heads for the rest of their lives.

As the bus driver continued to downshift, the Jimmy diesel engine struggled mightily to pull the grade. Our progress got slower and slower. But then a strange thought came to me. Say you were a member of the Donner Party, and you were one of the forty-eight who'd survived—and you were religious. It would naturally seem proper and fitting that you would want to say grace before each meal.

So, say you're seated at a table with other survivors, and you have a nice piece of boiled human backstrap, steaming on a plate in front of you. Of course, everyone in the room would naturally assume it to be appropriate to say grace before eating. But that brings up a question—*who would you thank for the food?* Would you thank the Lord who had provided for such a delicious bounty, or would you thank the poor, unlucky fellow who you're about to eat?

It was a question I hadn't totally resolved when the bus pulled into the station in Tahoe. I had no money for a hotel, so I went to a pay phone and called Spanky to come and pick me up.

CHAPTER THREE

The bus station in South Lake Tahoe was located immediately behind the Harrah's Casino. Steve must have known that when he told me *Be at the Harrah's Club*. I went into the casino to check it out. I had never been in a big casino before. I walked in and immediately noticed the banks of slot machines; they were all over the place. They were set up in a uniform manner, row after row. There were people putting coins in the machines and pulling on a lever situated on the right side of the machine. The machine would make noise, bells and some sort of ringing sounds, as the inside of the machine would begin to display a rotating tumbler in a glass window in the front-center of the machine.

I stood behind one of the players and watched. She was sitting on a stool with coins in a tray that received the payoff right in front of her below the glass window. When the machine stopped tumbling, I could see that there were actually three tumblers inside the window, and each one had an image on it. The tumblers I was watching displayed several images of fruit—lemons, cherries, bananas, apples, and oranges. If three of the same fruit images lined up in a row in the center of the machine, the player would win. If not, the player would reach into the tray and feed more money into the coin slot.

I watched for a few minutes, listening to the dings of the bells and the *thunk thunk thunk* of the images on the tumblers lining themselves up. Then I decided to head deeper into the casino, noticing the establishment's fancy décor, the flashing lights, and hordes of people. The actual casino area was huge. As I walked, I noticed an area with a circle of other casino games. It turned out to be the blackjack pit area. There must have been fifty blackjack tables, along with several other casino games.

The first one I stopped at was a game called roulette. It had a red felt table with numbers from one to thirty-six in uniformed squares in the middle of the table; half of them were black and half were red. There were two green squares, one with a zero and one with a double zero, at the end of the table. There was also a roulette wheel that possessed all of the same numbers as the table. It appeared as though the players would put money in the square on the table and then the attendant would spin the wheel and roll a little ball around the top. The wheel would spin for about thirty seconds, slow down, and then stop with that same little ball resting at the bottom of the wheel on one of the numbers. If one of the player's numbers matched the number that the ball rested in, that player would win.

The attendant would then pay that player thirty-five-to-one on their bet, and then take the money of the losers. There were other rules to the game, but I didn't stick around to figure out the rest of them.

I then noticed a game called craps. I watched for a few minutes, but that game seemed too complicated to me, so I moseyed over to the blackjack tables.

I wanted to sit down and play a few hands, but I didn't have much money, so I just watched. The table was shaped like a half moon. The dealer stood inside the circle of tables. I remembered from the books that I'd read that this area was called *the pit*. The pit had several casino employees in it, called *pit bosses.*

The pit bosses wore suits and ties, and the area was roped off so that tourists could not enter. The dealer stood on the straight side of the table. The rounded side was on the outside of the pit and had seven painted circles on the green felt, and seven seats for the players. There was a rack of casino chips in front of the dealer, used to store chips in several increments. The dealer would delve into that rack of chips to pay the winners, and to restore the chips of the losers who wanted to continue to play.

The game of blackjack is also called *twenty-one,* because the object of the game is to have a card value higher than the dealer without going over twenty-one. Before each hand can begin, the dealer shuffles the cards and then makes sure every player at the table has their bet properly placed in the circle.

At that point, the dealer distributes the cards, one to each player who has a bet in the circle. The cards are dealt facedown, meaning no one can see that card, except the player. Then the dealer deals his/her first card faceup. That way, each player can see the dealer's *upcard.* The second round of cards is also dealt facedown, but the dealer's second card is slipped under the *upcard,* so that the players cannot see it. The dealer's second card is called the *hole card.*

By that time, everyone around the table has two cards. The only difference is, the dealer has one card up and one card down.

In the game of blackjack, players base their strategy on the value of the dealer's *upcard.* The value of the cards was as follows: the face cards had a value of ten, the ace can be either one or eleven, and the numbered cards are taken at face value.

A player has several options once viewing his/her cards. He can *stand*, by placing the two cards under the chips in the circle, or he can take a *hit,* by scratching the table with the two cards. This is done by holding the cards and making a scratching motion toward the player.

If a player takes a hit and goes over twenty-one, his/her hand is considered *busted,* and the player lightly tosses his cards faceup towards the dealer. The dealer then scoops up the cards and chips and goes to the next player.

If a player has two cards of the same value, it's considered to be a pair. When that happens, they have an option to *split* the cards into two hands. They do this by placing the two cards faceup, side by side, in front of their bet, and then placing an equal bet next to the original bet. After that, each hand is played separately, by either hitting or standing. A player doesn't have to split a pair—though aces and eights are often split in the game of *twenty-one.*

The last option is to *double down*. A player can double his bet by placing an equal amount next to the original bet. To double down, the player places the two cards faceup out in front of the bet. At that point, the dealer gives the player one card down. This is typical if the player has a total of ten or eleven, for a ten-value card gives them a good hand.

If a player is dealt a ten-value card and an ace on their first two cards, they have what is called a *blackjack.*

When all of the players are finished, it's the dealer's turn. The dealer has certain rules to follow. They have to hit if they have less than seventeen. The dealer has to stand once they reach seventeen, with one exception: The dealer has to hit what is called a *soft seventeen,* which is a hand with an ace and a six. Once the hand is finished, the dealer turns over and exposes the player's cards to see if the dealer's hand is better than the player's.

This is done one player at a time, and the dealer pays the winners and takes the money of the losers. If the player and dealer have the same total, the dealer taps the table twice, and leaves the bet alone. This is called a *push*.

Half an hour had passed, as I stood there watching, and when I raised my gaze to look around, I saw Spanky. He motioned with his head, so I headed over to greet him. We shook hands and headed for the car.

We drove for a few minutes, and ended up at an upscale vacation chateau in the Tahoe Keys. "Steve owns this house," Spanky said, "along with a number of others."

We made our way to the stoop at the front door. It was a heavy door laden with thermal-pane windows. Once inside, Spanky showed me to a room upstairs where I could stow my gear and take a shower.

I'd just finished dressing when Steve came by to reintroduce himself. "Hi, Red," he said. "Remember me?"

"I sure do," I replied as we shook hands.

Steve was dressed in clothing that spoke of fine taste and quality, keeping up with recent trends in fashion—slacks, polished dress shoes, button-down collared shirt, open at the neck, no tie. He was tall, a couple inches taller than Spanky, who I knew to be six-foot-three.

He carried himself with a great deal of confidence, and while we talked, he maintained a businesslike demeanor. "When you're ready, come on downstairs. I have some guys I want you to meet."

I knew from my earlier conversation with Spanky that Steve was twenty-eight years old, and while he didn't look any older than that, he seemed and acted much older.

A few members of the crew were present when I came downstairs. Wall was the first one I met. Steve introduced us. Wall was a few inches shorter than me, with curly, light brown hair and a medium to muscular build. He was wearing a T-shirt under an unbuttoned flannel, 501 shrink-to-fit Levi's, and riding boots. The boots had block heels—more for walking than riding. Wall told me he was from Idaho, and he looked like a country boy. He also told me that he and Steve had gone to school together. I assumed they were the same age.

Then Wall introduced me to Bird—a man who sported a shiny bald head and a slender build. He was dressed pretty much like Wall, but his cowboy boots were a little fancier—with red-leather inlays.

After meeting Bird, Wall had me shake hands with Cirk—a larger man, six-foot-two maybe—a good-looking fellow who was attired in a dress shirt and slacks. It turned out that Cirk lived in Boise, where he was in the process of opening a business. He looked more like a city boy than the others.

All three of these guys were different, one from the next, but they all had a number of things in common. They were all from Idaho, and each of them came across as down-to-earth, commonsense, country-type folks.

They were talking about meeting up with the other crew members in Vegas for New Year's Eve. I wasn't part of the conversation, and Steve was quick to let me know that I'd have to finish a basic training course before I could participate in the action. I was beginning to understand that there was a lot to know about this operation, and I needed to get up to speed as quickly as possible.

The guys were all gathered in the living room to watch a football game on television, but I sat down in the kitchen with Spanky. After all, Spanky was the only person here who I really knew. The other fellas were engaged in reliving past events that had taken place in Vegas. They didn't put much stock in entertaining a new trainee, but I felt welcome anyway. Spanky and I had known each other for several years, though, so he felt compelled to fill me in on his brother's system.

There was some leftover pizza from the night before. We heated a few slices in the microwave, grabbed a couple of beers from the fridge, and Spanky started in. He began by telling me that there were additional members of the crew who weren't here at the present time.

"You won't meet them until we get to Las Vegas," he said. Then he launched into an explanation of how his brother's operation actually worked.

"Steve has developed a system to win at blackjack," he said, and after saying that he held an odd, all-knowing look on his face, like he was expecting me to react in some way or another.

But I was a naïve, small-town country boy, fresh out of college. I really didn't have a clue as to what he was talking about, so I sat and listened. Frankly, I was beginning to feel a little overwhelmed with what I thought might be shaping up to be a life-changing adventure.

"The Boss has names for each position," Spanky continued. "Steve is the Boss, of course, and there's the brain, the arm, the field marshal, the screen, and the runner."

At this point, nothing Spanky said was making a lot of sense to me, but I was determined to get the most out of it.

I figured I'd attempt to put the pieces together later.

"The brain is the key to the operation," he said, "and all of the others are there to protect the brain."

We sat and chewed on the pizza for a few minutes. I finished off a piece of pepperoni and went on to a Canadian bacon and pineapple. Spanky got up and retrieved a couple more bottles of Michelob beer from the refrigerator.

"The arm," he said, "is actually an extension of the brain. The arm bets the money and he gets his signals from the brain. The brain tells him when to hit, when to stand, and when to double down or split.

"The arm also plays the part of a shill. Besides betting the money and taking signals from the brain, he is trained to distract the pit boss at the exact moment that the cards are being dealt. The point is to keep the pit boss's eyes off the table at those critical times—that allows the brain to do his work.

"The field marshal is there to monitor the table and the pit bosses. It's his job to make sure the crew doesn't get caught while they're playing Steve's winning strategy. The field marshal stands back a little. He is always on the lookout for heat."

I made a mental note to myself to ask somebody what they meant when they spoke of *heat*.

"The screen," Spanky went on, "is instructed to do whatever the brain tells him to do. The brain might have the screen fill an empty seat, or bribe someone out of a needed seat, or," Spanky shrugged his shoulder, "what have you. And the runner, he is just that. His job is to take the gaff from the brain when it looks like trouble is about to start. His mission it to get the gaff out of the casino as quickly as possible—hopefully without drawing any heat to himself."

Spanky stood up and began to pace around the kitchen.

"The gaff...?" I asked.

"We call it a gaff because it snags the hole card," Spanky told me, "just like the gaff a fisherman would use to snag a big fish and pull it into a boat."

I looked at my beer—it seemed to be a standard Michelob. But there was something here that I wasn't getting. *Maybe it's the Tahoe altitude,* I thought, *along with a severe lack of sleep.*

"Let's back up a minute," I said. "What is a gaff, exactly?"

He proceeded to explain that the gaff was a little piece of mirror supported by a paper clip that was taped to the back of it. He stepped out of the kitchen for a moment, and then came back in holding something in his hand. When he got a little closer, I could see it was a little piece of mirror that looked like it had been cut out with a glass cutter. He placed the contraption on the table and began to explain.

"You set it up on the blackjack table in front of you," Spanky explained, "and then you adjust the paper clip so you can read the dealer's hole card when he, or she, pulls it off the deck to place it underneath the upcard. That way, you know what both of the dealer's cards are."

I was a little bit stunned. I stood there with my mouth hanging open, trying to digest exactly what it was I'd just heard.

"Isn't that cheating?" I wondered aloud.

"The casinos have these games rigged so the odds are in their favor," Spanky said. "The gaff just evens up those odds a little. And everything works out just fine, as long as you don't get caught with it."

I sat with a blank look on my face.

Spanky started giggling.

"So, it is cheating," I said, "and it's the most important thing in the world for the runner to save the brain's ass by getting the mirror out of the casino."

"And that's where you come into it," Spanky replied. "Steve wants to start you out as a runner. If something goes wrong—a pit boss looks nervous, or the dealer starts doing something a little quirky—the field marshal will flash the signal and the brain will grab the gaff off the table and give it to you. Then you will run out of the casino."

"And that's my job?"

"That's your job for now," he said. "There are several positions that have to be manned in order for this operation to work. The brain and the runner are two of them. Then there's the arm and the field marshal—and Steve kind of oversees the entire operation from a distance. I'll explain the other positions later."

We had one more beer, and then I went up to my room to get some badly needed sleep. It had been a really long day.

When I started to slowly climb the stairs, I began to wonder—*What have I gotten myself into?*

I thought back to that day several months earlier, the evening when I first met Steve Kammeyer—the night when Spanky told me that Steve was a professional gambler. But by the time I reached the top of the stairs, I realized that these guys were more than professional gamblers—they were professional card cheats.

I was so nervous by the time I got to my room, I couldn't sleep much.

CHAPTER FOUR

I spent most of the next day in my room studying blackjack strategy, trying to get up to speed on what the crew had christened *The Kammeyer System for Winning at Blackjack.*

I learned one very important rule on my first night here, thanks to Spanky. The brain was the key to the entire operation, and every movement that the crew made was designed to protect the brain. As a runner, it was my job to get the mirror from the team's most valuable player and remove that evidence from the premises. I was to do whatever it took to make that two-inch-by-one-and-a-half-inch mirror go away. The most important thing I had to do was keep the gaff away from the cops. I'd have to outrun casino security and any other agents on the streets of Las Vegas who were trying to catch us.

I discovered that when Steve first put his operation into action, he didn't have a runner, but the runner provided the final advantage that his precisely tuned machine needed in order to remove the evidence from the casino. The other protective measure was the field marshal. The field marshal would be stationed in a position to sense an oncoming attack. When he saw something that didn't look right, he would sound the alarm—and when he did, the runner would take the gaff and run like hell.

In a way, it was a little like playing football. The offense knows where they're going—who will carry the ball, and who will be the decoy—but it was really much better than that. On a football field, the defense at least knows who the offensive players are. With the Kammeyer System, the defense knows only the player—or maybe players—at the table. Other members of the offense simply look like unconnected casino patrons milling around in the crowd.

If everyone executed the system perfectly, there would be no evidence at the table at all, keeping the casino authorities confused. They couldn't detain or hold anybody. In most cases it would come down to mere seconds. The brain simply needed someone to run the gaff out, and run it out fast.

I sat back for a moment to reflect on my studies. I opened an ice-cold soda pop that Spanky had brought in and set on the table. Then there was a rap on the door and Steve stepped in with a little box under his right arm. "How's it going, Red?" he asked.

"Oh, pretty good," I said. "There's a lot to get your arms around."

He simply smiled, placed the box on the table, grabbed a straight-back chair, turned it around, and sat so his arms were draped over the back. "It takes a little getting used to," he agreed. Then he went on to explain, "This is a high-stakes operation, and everything has to click just right."

"I can see that."

"Do you know what you're up against here, Red?" he asked, as his face took on a more serious look.

"No," I replied, "not really, Boss." I'd come to realize by this time that everyone referred to Steve as *the Boss*.

He stood up and walked over to the window. Then he turned back and said, "Good answer." Then he went on. "Here's the deal, Red. We're cheating against the mob. There's no other way to put it, and no sense in trying to sugarcoat it either."

I nodded and gulped at the same time. I struggled to keep my composure, not wanting to show any weakness—though I might have unwittingly demonstrated a little ignorant pride. After all, I too was a proud, small-town country boy.

"And there are rules that we all have to follow," he continued. "The consequences for failure in this business are so extreme, we don't even like to think about them. There isn't room in an operation like this for a guy who can't follow the rules."

Again, I nodded by way of answering. Steve seemed even more businesslike now than when I'd talked to him before.

He went on to explain a few of the basic rules. "Rule number one," he said, "is this: The Boss is always right. Rule number two: If the Boss is wrong, see rule number one."

And that was all there was to it. He only needed to say it that one time.

"That's the way it is," he said, "and that's the way it has to be."

"I understand," I said. What I didn't say was—*I'm beginning to understand, and it's scaring the bejesus out of me.*

Then he went on to explain. "The Boss dictates every move: who carries the money, who is working and where, who talks and who listens. Trust is paramount. The Boss has to trust the crew; the crew has to trust the Boss; and crew members have to trust each other."

I nodded again. I was beginning to feel like a bobblehead doll.

"If you think you can deal with all of that," he said, "you need to familiarize yourself with some of the basics of the game. The basics will help you learn the overall objectives of the team."

He sat back down and began to recite a little spiel that sounded like he'd memorized it long ago. "Playing cards well is only one part of the game," he said, very matter-of-factly. "But when I say *the game*, I mean *the game that we are playing here*. We all need to learn to play cards well, and that's an artful skill, but it's only the basics of the game we actually play, only the beginning. Winning, the way we play, will take care of itself. Getting the money out of the casino is the hard part."

We sat for a moment. The Boss had one more thing to say. "Red, let's talk man-to-man about this cheating-the-mob thing."

"Sure, Boss," I replied.

He continued. "We are a blackjack cheating crew. These casinos hate our guts and they are trying to catch us with the mirror with every ounce of energy that they have. If they catch you with or without the mirror and they know you are one of my crew, they will threaten you with rides to the desert, billy clubs, hammers, and baseball bats. You need to hang tough, and don't tell them anything. The protocol in the back room is as follows: Always have an ID on you, it's the law. Never drop your chin below level with the ground. Never show disgust in your current situation. When they ask for your ID, give it to them. When they ask you a question, you look them in the eye and say, 'I don't know what you're talking about, sir,' and then look back at the wall in front of you. Always be polite no matter what. Show respect; no smart-ass comments. If they ask about anything else, you say, 'I'm not making any statements, sir, and I would like to consult an attorney.' After that, do not say another word. At that point they will read you a notice barring you from the premises. In most cases they will walk you off the property and tell you to never come back. Do you have any questions?"

I sat there for just a moment looking up at the Boss with a relaxed look on my face. "I think I can deal with that, Boss," I said.

"Well, Red, if you don't ever get caught you won't have to deal with it. Good luck."

"I'll do my best not to get caught, Boss."

At that point, Steve stood up from his chair and pointed at the small box he'd placed on the table—I could see it contained files. "Go through those files and study the basic strategy. After that, go through the flash cards."

Then he asked, "Do you have any money?"

I shook my head and said, "No."

Steve reached into his pocket and pulled out a small handful of $100 bills. He handed the bills to me and said, "Here, put this money in your pocket. It's yours for coming down on such short notice."

"By the way," he said, pointing at the box. "Before you can play, you'll be required to have these formulas memorized and internalized." And with that said, he left.

I sat for a few moments and reflected on what had just happened. The Boss had given me $500. *Was it really for just coming down? Or was it an investment—the proceeds of which were to be cashed in later?* I really didn't know, but I thought it was pretty cool. Steve had been all business during the time he'd been talking to me, but that gesture at the end meant a lot to me—a whole lot.

Going through the files, I discovered that Steve had pored over every strategy chart on the subject of blackjack that was known to man. He'd finally picked the one that made the most sense for his application. After that, he'd translated these formulas into flash cards, one card to represent each possible hand in the game of blackjack. Instead of simple arithmetic, which Steve felt was too theoretical and wouldn't prove to be graphic enough, he'd constructed some very professional, adult-level flash cards. These cards tested recognition and comprehension at the highest levels. A typical flash card would show the dealer's upcard on top and the two cards of the player on the bottom. The proper play, according to the formulated strategy, was printed on the back of the card.

For instance, there are only four options to choose from in blackjack: *hit,* which was designated by an "H"; *stand,* designated by an "S"; *double down,* which was a "D"; and *split,* which was indicated by the letter "P." There was both single-deck and double-deck variations to the formula, but there were only a total of sixteen different moves between the two approaches.

With all the support elements and intricate communication techniques the crew needed to employ, it was essential for each man to have a basic understanding of the mathematics behind the game. It turned out that the strategy Steve had selected had been based on calculations extracted from a composite of nine million computerized hands of blackjack. These calculations formed the foundation for everything each new member would have to learn.

Each and every member of the crew was required to know the basic strategy. The brain needed to know exactly what each player at the table was going to do with their cards. Since everyone at the table knew basic strategy, the brain would automatically know if a player was going to hit, stand, split, or what have you. That way the brain could always play the winning strategy.

In all, there were 290 cards to memorize and Steve had established an exacting standard for testing. Any new recruit would have seven and a half minutes to go through every card, and he would only be allowed three mistakes in that time. It was made abundantly clear to me that no one would ever play live with the crew without clearing that initial hurdle first.

I'd become embroiled up to my neck in this stuff, when there was another knock on the door. Then one of the fellows I'd met the day before stepped in. It was Wall—at least, that's the only name I knew him by. Spanky called him Wally Gator.

I knew Wall to be an old childhood friend of Steve's. They both hailed from the same small town in Idaho. He was a strong, muscular sort of fellow, and he gave off the impression of being quiet and observant. He stood about five-foot-ten, and he seemed like the serious type. He also seemed like a fellow who might loosen up a bit once a guy got to know him. His curly hair was messed up, like he'd been outside in the wind.

"How's it going?" he asked.

"Oh, pretty good," I said, a little apprehensively.

"That's a big load of shit to learn all at once," he said with a grin.

"It sure is." I could feel the tension receding.

"When Steve unloaded all that stuff on me," he said, "I felt like dumping it all in the garbage and going back to

Idaho."

I laughed.

"Just take it slow and easy," Wall told me. "It'll come to you."

"I hope so," I said, feeling a little lack of confidence in my own voice.

"I had to do it a little bit at a time—not sure I've got it all yet," Wall said.

I smiled and nodded.

"Well, good luck with it," he said. Then he ducked back into the hall and closed the door.

It was quite a confidence booster, that little visit from Wall. I thought maybe it was one of his strengths for the team—a kind of a Yogi Berra sort of a guy—keeping everyone's spirits up.

I went back to work—and work it was. I felt like I was cramming for a final exam in college, and I had only a few days to do it. I'd never studied so hard in my life.

Then, too, I'd developed a funny feeling that there were a number of things going on around here that I didn't know about. But I didn't worry about that. I had plenty to do at the moment.

CHAPTER FIVE

I never really got used to the way it gets dark when there's snow on the ground. If there's any light at all—a distant farmhouse, the sliver of a moon, headlights on a remote highway—that light seems to be amplified by the snow into a great crescendo, but when the light goes away, a total darkness is instant. I was watching the snow through the window of my room, and the light was about to fade, when someone rapped on my door and said just one word, "Dinner."

But I discovered it wasn't really a dinner at all—at least not in the sense where one might expect to find people sitting at a table, passing things around, each anxious to tell the others the highlights of their day.

Here, one of the guys went into Tahoe, picked up some Chinese food to go, and everyone sat wherever they wanted in Steve's large, luxurious house. Some sat at the bar or the counter in the kitchen. A couple of guys sat at the table with the Boss. He sat at the head of the table with a large, freshly made salad. He didn't eat fast food. He was really into nutrition and all he ever ate was wholesome, healthy food.

Little was said. Nothing at all was mentioned that seemed important, but that all changed once the food was consumed and fellas began to discuss methods and maneuvers, refreshing their memories as they talked, going through the basic strategy and actually playing cards. There were several sets of cards lying around downstairs.

I had been studying all day and I needed a break, so

Spanky and I went to the local gym to get a workout. We did a little cardio work and some weightlifting, light weight—full range of motion—exercises that helped our flexibility, strength, and speed for baseball training. Spanky was heading for USC for his final year as a college baseball player. We were both college pitchers; consequently, we were used to training in the same manner.

After we showered Spanky said, "We're heading for Harrah's, Red. I'm going to show you the ropes." He giggled like a child, as he often did—it was a character trait that he had in common with his brother.

On our way to the casino, he began by going over some hand signals that the crew used to communicate in a casino. He taught me three hand signals, a scratch to the forehead, which meant *acknowledgement or okay,* a scratch to the chest, meaning *cash out and go to the car,* and a scratch on the back of the leg that flashed the message *follow me.*

I had very little experience in a casino, so I paid very close attention. Spanky knew this, and he decided to have some fun with me.

He said, "Red, once we're in the casino we absolutely cannot talk to each other. We can only use hand signals or the intercom. If I lose you, I'll get on the white courtesy telephone and page Phil King. That means go to the car. I want you to keep track of me at all times, but stay at a distance that's comfortable."

"Are we going to play any cards?" I asked.

"No."

We headed into the casino and it was crowded. We went to the blackjack pit area and I stayed across the pit from Spanky as we walked along. I was a little nervous about not having been in a casino very much. In fact, it wasn't five minutes before Spanky managed to lose me.

I looked around for him, in a mild panic. I went around and around, trying not to look worried, even though I was a little alarmed. I headed back to where we'd entered the casino, and there was Spanky, leaning up against a slot machine, shaking his head and giggling.

He turned away from me and scratched the back of his leg, signaling me to follow him. So I did. We were almost back to the car, when I said with a smile, "You ditched me, didn't you?"

"It's a fast-paced game, Red," he said. "You'll have to get used to it. Anyway, let's go to Caesars."

As we drove the short distance to Caesars Palace, he continued to give me pointers on how to keep an individual in sight in a crowded casino. It wasn't easy.

"Let's try it again, Red," he said, as he jumped out of the car and headed for the entrance.

I had to hurry to keep up. He was already inside the building by the time I made it through the door. Then I spotted him over by the pit area. I kept a close eye on him for about ten minutes, but somehow he managed to lose me again.

The next thing I knew, somebody grabbed my arm from behind, while a harsh angry voice said, "Come with me, sir."

I was startled for a second, and then I realized it was Spanky. He had snuck up on me from behind.

As I tried to calm my nerves, he signaled me to follow him again. We made it outside before I said, "You son of a bitch."

Again, he was giggling. As we got into the car, the giggle

turned to laughter. "The Boss told me to do that, Red. He wanted you to get used to it. That's how things are going to happen when the shit hits the fan."

As we headed back to the house, Spanky's demeanor changed. "I need to fill you in on a little background, Red," he said in a serious tone. "We had a bad experience recently, a monumental setback. It happened a few months back. The crew was busted at Caesars Palace in Vegas.

"I know you don't know much about the game yet," Spanky continued, "so if I say something that you don't understand, let me know."

"I will," I replied.

"A standard play for the crew," he said, "would be to go into a casino and scout for a dealer. We normally do that while the high roller sits at the bar. When a crew member finds a dealer who he thinks can be played, he lets the brain know with a rub of the nose." He demonstrated how they did that—it was similar to signals that we would use on a baseball diamond.

"Once the brain takes his seat at the table," he went on, "everyone gets into position—the screen on third base, the runner behind the brain, and the field marshal across the pit so the brain can see him.

"When the brain signals that he's ready, the field marshal goes to the bar and signals the arm to the table. Then he gives him the 'follow me' sign and leads the arm to the table. At that point, the play begins. The goal is to play as many hands as possible before we have to leave. Sometimes ten minutes, sometimes four hours. It depends on the situation.

"Anyway, on this particular occasion, the Boss had trained both the crew members and their girlfriends to make this big play. The plan was to go into Caesars Palace with a group of young couples and simply have fun playing blackjack. The Boss was the brain, Dog and Muff were the arms, and the other couples stood behind the table to cheer on the arm and his girlfriend while they played $500 a hand.

"Skate," Spanky said, "was the runner."

I hadn't met Skate yet, but I didn't think it was worth interrupting Spanky to mention that.

"Anyway, they just looked like a group of young people out having a good time," he said, "and they were winning, and winning big. The black chips were stacking up in front of them, ten, twenty, thirty grand. They were drinking and laughing. It looked to be a really good setup.

"All of the sudden, the table was rocked by three men in suits who tackled the crew members. The suits took them to the floor right behind the table. I mean, they literally got pounced on. The Boss, the girls, and the arm were all tackled and pinned to the floor as well.

"Uniformed security had arrived and cuffed the crew as the suits began searching around on the floor for the gaff. They couldn't find it.

"Fortunately, before he was tackled at the table, the Boss was able to hand the gaff off to Skate, and he took off with it. But when it was all said and done, the casino had six people in custody, three girls and three guys. The Boss, Dog, and Skate were all detained."

"I thought Skate got away," I responded.

"Unfortunately," Spanky said, "Skate didn't get away. He was caught out in the parking lot, and he still had the gaff on him.

"You'll meet Dog and Skate in a few days, when we get

to Vegas—but you won't meet the girls. They're history.

"Like I said," he went on, "the three girls were detained as well, and the Metro Police and the gaming commission were called in, along with an outfit we called *Griffin.*"

"You mean griffon like the dog?" I asked, trying to keep up, while wondering if security used dogs like narcotic agents.

"No, it's a security firm. The Griffin Agency was there to identify Steve Kammeyer as the leader of the group."

The way Spanky told it, the two hours that the crew spent in the back room was terrifying for the entire group, including the Boss. The guards acted like they wanted to kill him. They kept beating their billy clubs into their hands, one strike after another, threatening to break their kneecaps.

The girls were threatened with their lives, and with rides into the desert, but they were told if they cooperated they could forgo that treatment. It turned out, the girls didn't fare so well under pressure, even though they'd been schooled by the Boss as to proper protocol in the back room.

"The girls ended up spilling their guts out. They told the authorities everything they knew. Of course, they didn't know much about the operation, so we still managed to keep the authorities guessing."

"The Boss, Dog, and Skate were threatened with the same things as the girls," Spanky said, "but they just kept repeating the same lines over and over: 'I don't want to make any statements and I want to consult an attorney.' The end result was, they were all arrested and taken downtown and booked into jail."

CHAPTER SIX

We sat for a few moments, waiting for the red light to change. I let the oppressive tone of the situation Spanky was describing sink in. Then he went on with his story.

"After they were booked, Steve got on the phone and called Johnny at the house. You'll meet Johnny in Vegas as well. Anyway, the casino cleaned the crew out of every cent they were carrying. Johnny had only five thousand with him, but they both knew the total bail would be from $18,000 to $24,000."

Spanky told me they hashed through a couple of ideas before deciding that Johnny should fly back to San Diego and get twenty-five grand out of his safe. The Boss was determined to get the crew out of jail as soon as possible. It was only a one-hour flight each way, and the paperwork at the jail wouldn't be processed for at least three hours. Johnny quickly grabbed a flight out.

The evening went to shit at 6:00 p.m., and it was almost eleven when Johnny touched down back in Nevada. With the money in his sock, he went straight to a phone and called the jail to see about posting bail. The paperwork had cleared, so he grabbed a cab and headed for *heat headquarters*. It occurred to him that by bailing the crew out, he was exposing himself as one of them, but there was nothing to be done about that.

Once downtown, Johnny went to the jail counter and politely said, "I'm here to bail out the group that was arrested over at Caesars Palace earlier tonight.'"

The officer at the desk never even looked up. He just asked, "What were their names?"

The question took Johnny by surprise. Even though they all had names, he wasn't sure about some of their real names, so he simply answered, "The Boss, Dog, Skate, Muff, Diane, and Kelly."

"Do you want to post bail for all of them?"

"Yup. How much?"

The officer at the desk worked his way through the charges, and he came up with $22,000.

"How would like to arrange bail?" the officer asked.

"Cash."

Everyone in the place stopped what they were doing and stared at Johnny as he said this, but he just stood there with his chin up and his gaze fixed forward.

"It will be a few minutes," the guard replied with an unconcerned manner.

Thirty minutes later, a heavy iron door groaned open and out walked the three men, with the Boss leading the way. He was walking tall, up on his toes, as they headed for the door.

"The girls were right behind them," Johnny told Spanky.

They all squeezed into a cab and drove around for a while. Steve wanted to make sure no one was following them. The Boss had the cabbie drop them off at a casino near the house.

"As soon as the first cab was out of sight, and no tail was detected, we hailed another cab and went to the pad," Johnny told Spanky.

Whatever Steve felt about the whole thing, they couldn't tell by looking at him. He didn't seem mad. He didn't seem sad. He just wanted to figure out what had gone wrong, like—*what the fuck just happened?*

The heat had been so well organized, no one saw it coming.

Steve had everyone dredge up any shred of information that might help, but he kept coming back to the same question—*how did security get organized so quickly without us seeing it?*

Finally, Johnny suggested, "They must have got on to us from the eye in the sky, someone watching from upstairs or through a camera. They must have organized it upstairs, so the pit boss wouldn't even know. That way, the pit boss couldn't do something to tip their hand."

The Boss concluded that he just had to train the crew better in the future. The casinos are tough opponents. In order to keep going, we would simply have to get better.

But the Boss knew, even in jail, that the girls had rolled over with some of the information. He'd overheard the phrase *They're singing like birds* coming from a couple of the guards.

"You girls didn't need to spill your guts," the Boss told them later. "We told you to ask for a lawyer."

It was no real surprise that the girls cracked. It isn't easy working on the Boss's crew, Spanky concluded to me.

"Steve took it easy on them. With one of the guys, a violation of the backroom rules meant immediate dismissal from the crew, along with a serious session with the Boss before you got the boot. But he simply saw the ordeal with the girls as an experiment gone bad."

When we arrived back at the house, I was tired and looking forward to getting some sleep.

CHAPTER SEVEN

Spanky wasn't finished yet, so we grabbed a beer and resumed our seats in the kitchen.

"The next order of business," he started in, referring to the aftermath of the Caesars bust, "was to find some way out of the situation that Steve and the crew found themselves in. Finally, the Boss decided to make arrangements to meet with his attorney, Frank Cremen.

"Frank is a prominent attorney in Las Vegas, expensive, but good. Every crew member who'd been charged with a felony attended the session. I went with them. Frank used the meeting to gather basic information, like past arrest records and past incidents in casino back rooms.

"Frank seemed surprised," Spanky said, "to discover that no prior arrests had actually turned up. They weren't criminals in the classical sense, they were simply outlaws with no previous arrests. Once he'd compiled his initial dossier—one file for each individual—he went to work on the charges and possible penalties that each of the players might be up against.

"Of course, cheating at blackjack with a mirror wasn't the kind of case that one would find a lot of case history on. Cheating with a mirror in Vegas was considered insane amongst other crossroaders and seldom ever even mentioned.

"But after digging through a stack of formal complaints, and a making a phone call or two, Frank confirmed that there were felony counts all around for the

Kammeyer bunch, and the worst was Skate's case. He'd been apprehended in possession of a cheating device—that being the mirror.

"Frank told us that Skate's case would be the toughest charge to beat. 'Simply cheating at gambling and conspiracy charges present a stiffer challenge for the D.A. to prove,' he said. 'There might be room to bargain down to lesser charges.'"

So, the reason that I've been offered this job was to help replace a bunch of other guys who'd recently been caught.

I'd been in a casino only once before tonight, and trying to form a mental image of how the bust went down at Caesars Palace only produced a blur for me. I was overwhelmed with what I'd just heard. It frightened me a bit, but then I had another thought—*I really have no place else to go.*

"After leaving Frank's office," Spanky continued, "the crew seemed buoyed by the feeling of progress that the attorney had left us with. But aside from starting the process of defending the crew, Frank gave them a direction from which to work—and that direction was anywhere north, south, east, or west of Nevada.

"The Boss and the crew were to stay out of the casinos over the next several months, at least until the preliminary hearings were completed. 'Stay completely out of the casinos,' he told us. 'Don't go in to use a bathroom, to play keno, nothing. In fact, staying out of Nevada entirely might be a good idea.'

"'That's going to be a tough deal to stick to, Frank,' the Boss told him.

"And the attorney didn't insist on a promise. He didn't say anything at all. He simply nodded his head and motioned us out.

"We all noticed that the Boss didn't say anything more in response to Frank's request for sanity. We also realized how unruffled the Boss was throughout all the doom and gloom. None of us sensed any despair or hopelessness on Steve's part. There simply wasn't any.

"The crew watched the Boss as he sifted through his options," Spanky continued. "The boss continued to tell us, 'Keep practicing.' I came away with the impression that Steve felt this incident would motivate the crew to work harder and sharper, primarily because we all knew that the casino system was on to us now.

"'We have to play this absolutely perfectly,' Steve told us. He seemed to think this incident would kick up the intensity a notch. It wouldn't be much different than before, except if we got caught again it would be double the trouble.

"The following week," Spanky said, "the Boss called Hiram, along with Wall, Johnny, and Footsie. He told them to get ready to play. The Boss had to make enough money to keep the machine fueled. *Damn the torpedoes and full speed ahead* was the battle cry.

"Two weeks after the bust, we loaded up the car and headed for the airport. My brother is one tough son of a bitch."

Spanky tipped back his beer and looked up at the clock—it was a quarter to two. I could tell by the relaxed way he sat, he was finally done talking.

I sat with a beer of my own, wondering if maybe I would have been better off if I had not known all of this, but I decided it's better to have all the information, no matter how bleak.

"Spanky," I asked, "how many guys does the Boss actually have?"

"He had twelve at one time, but most of them were arms—guys who only played the high roller, part time. He had six regular crew members before the Caesars bust, but he'll need more now."

He was silent for a moment. Then he went on. "The Boss wants to run two crews on New Year's Eve, so you and Bird will fill a couple of spots as screen and runner. Another new guy, a guy the Boss has dubbed 'the Kid,' will be there for the first time as well. He'll have to fill in for a screen or a runner as well."

"Well," I said, "at least I know where things stand."

Spanky nodded.

"I guess I'll go up to bed."

He nodded again.

When I walked back into the living room, everything was dark. The television was turned off and everyone had gone to bed. With the aid of the neighbor's security lights reflecting off the snow, I made my way up the stairs.

Just like the night before, I asked myself once again— *what the fuck have I gotten myself into?*

But there was something about the Boss that gave a guy a strong sense of self-worth and security. He ran a tight ship of hard-nosed, competitive people—and I would fit in just fine, with a background in collegiate athletics, having learned the discipline needed to be a dedicated team player. If the things Spanky just told me had happened to most of the people I know, the game would have been over. They'd never play another game of blackjack again.

Not the Boss, though. He was tenacious. It was the Boss that made everything work. It was the Boss that made the crew click. And in spite of all that had happened, and everything that I'd heard, I wanted to be a part of it.

CHAPTER EIGHT

When the 30th of December rolled around, the Boss wanted to be in Vegas and ready to go by noon. After the Caesars Palace bust had occurred, it'd been a while since some of the crew members had played.

The Boss's new airplane seated six. "It's bigger than my old plane," he told me. "It has twin engines and a lot more range."

Five of us were to fly down to Vegas with him. Wall hated flying, so he took refuge in the very back and went to sleep before we even got off the ground. It was the first time I'd ever flown in a small plane and the Boss had me sit up front. I was a little nervous about the whole scene, but Spanky assured me that the Boss was an excellent pilot.

It took only a few minutes to climb out of the Sierra Nevada Mountains. Then we sailed out over the dry high-desert of Nevada. Things on the ground appeared to get drier as we made our way south. And once we leveled out and got up to cruising speed, the Boss began to open up to me. He talked about his past. His father had left his family when he was seven years old.

"He never came back," the Boss said. "I don't remember much about him."

The Boss was raised by a single mother, and so were his two younger brothers, the youngest from a different father. It had been a real struggle growing up for him. He had nothing but his mother, his friend Wall, two little brothers, and a desire to make his life better than what he'd experienced as a child.

Parts of what the Boss said reminded me of my own childhood, though I didn't say anything to him about that at the time.

The Boss went on to explain that when he was sixteen he got a job bucking hay for a farmer who owned a place next to Wall. He worked all summer, helped his mother make ends meet, and was able to save $4,000. At the age of sixteen, he realized how important it was to look presentable. He took the money that he'd saved from working, went to an orthodontist, and had braces put on his teeth.

He worked whenever he could, after school and on weekends, to help his mother. As time went on, he ended up at the University of Idaho, where he played basketball. After college, with a business degree in hand, he moved to San Diego.

"I'd only been in San Diego for a couple of months," he said, "when I was listening to the radio one day and heard an announcer pose this challenge: 'If you can name the first three presidents of the United States,' the guy said, 'and be the first to answer correctly, you will win a one-week, all-expenses-paid trip to Las Vegas.'"

It turned out he was the first to answer. He won the trip, and he had one month to prepare. He bought a couple of books on the game of blackjack. Having a near-photographic memory, blackjack came easy for him.

After his return from Vegas, he had a bad taste in his mouth about the whole scene. He hated the idea of the casinos giving out free alcohol to people in order to draw them in to gamble.

"They kick out the winners and feed alcohol to all the

losers, Red," he told me with a frown on his face, while he was casually making an adjustment to the airplane's engine speed.

Having picked up the values of the little God-fearing town he'd come from, along with his austere experiences as a child, the mob-based, stoic-corporate Vegas moral code just didn't seem right to him—even though he didn't consume alcohol himself. He referred to the casinos as *toilets,* and as filthy houses of ill repute.

We were entering the final approach to the city. I was mesmerized by the view. It was nearly dark and the lights below were awesome. It literally looked like a Christmas tree. It was one of the most spectacular views that I had ever seen. Millions of bright, colorful lights everywhere. And then the Boss broke me out of my reverie with a very harsh pronouncement: "Get ready, Red," he said. "We are really going to ream those toilets."

The statement was delivered with enough conviction that I sat up in my seat and turned my attention to the stern and contemptuous expression that had suddenly taken control of his face. Those harsh words, along with the dark, grim facial features that accompanied them, combined to tell me more about the Boss than what he'd actually said.

It was all over in an instant, though, and by the time I took a quick peek out the window, everything was back to normal as he landed the plane.

He parked the airplane, grabbed our luggage, and hailed a cab that was parked along the curb.

We arrived at a house on the west side of town. It was a new location and everyone had been given the address. The entire team was expected to be there by the time the Boss arrived—and everyone except for Badger and Chopper had made it. Badger and Chopper, I was told, were college football players from my alma mater, Portland State. They'd come to know each other from school and were traveling together. Their flight had been delayed, but the rest of us assembled in the practice room—a room the Boss, Johnny, and Dog had set up with perfection to meet casino specifications. I quickly discovered that it was a room designed for training purposes.

The city of Las Vegas partied on a nightly basis, 365 days a year, but New Year's Eve cranked things up to a higher level—like a supercharger—and that's why this particular outing was so very important.

The crew was excited about the prospect of playing over the weekend, while everyone else in the city partied hard. The practice table was busy, and the Boss stepped back to watch the training. The brains were working with the gaff, while others watched and learned. No matter what a player's job was, that player could always polish his performance.

Each time the Boss's voice rose up over the clamor, everyone listened. There was no room in this game for undisciplined behavior. Once the Boss finished outlining his agenda, the crew resumed their practice.

I was soaking it all in as best I could. These people seemed to click together. They drilled hard and practiced with conviction. They were one extremely professional crew.

I was stunned by their dedication, but my nerves were beginning to bother me. The Kid and I were the new kids on the block, of course, so we hung together as we studied. We were both nervous; neither of us had any casino experience.

The Boss divided the group up into two crews. Johnny, Skate, Bird, the Kid, and Footsie composed one crew, while the Boss, Hiram, Dog, Wall, Chopper, and I would make up the other. I was told that Skate and Dog had to stay completely away from the pit, and the Boss did too. All three would be valuable in detecting any oncoming attack, however.

Badger was to stay behind, in order to come in later, when one of the crews needed a fresh face.

Johnny's crew would start an assault on the Strip, while the Boss would take his troops downtown.

I could feel the pressure building; it was being exuded by the veteran players. They all knew that their pictures were on display on the shift supervisor's podium at most casinos. But we all wished each other good luck—and told one another to stay out of jail. The Boss instructed both me and the Kid to stay away from the action on our first night.

"Watch and learn, you two," he said. "That's your job tonight."

We did just that—and wow, what a night.

CHAPTER NINE

Both crews played until early morning, and we all had breakfast before coming back to the house. Everyone got up pretty early, though, and they all went in to practice.

Later in the day, we were all bucking up our nerves, and as nightfall began to approach, as I was trying to squelch the butterflies in my stomach before going out to play, a loud bang hit the front door.

I immediately concluded that the authorities must have figured out that we were in town. I felt overcome with paranoia. But Wall reacted quickly. He ran to the front door and looked through the little peephole.

"It's Tidy," Wall shouted. He sounded surprised.

The Boss heard the commotion from his bedroom and stepped out into the living room. He was walking fast, up on his toes. He was aggressively making his way to the front door just as Wall stepped back and opened it.

At that point, Tidy stumbled into the house—though I had no idea in the world who he was at the time.

His eyes were blackened, and he was bleeding through the nose and mouth. His hands were bleeding and he held them cupped, one inside the other. Several fingers were visibly broken.

He seemed to be standing a little tipped over to one side, like he might have suffered some kind of injury to his rib cage, and it looked like he'd dropped something heavy— like an anvil, maybe—on his left foot. Blood was seeping out through the stitching in his shoe.

The Boss looked at Tidy with a shocked expression. Then a fierce look came across his face. "Tidy," he bellowed, "get the fuck out of here. You'd better not have brought us any heat. You made your choice, so get the fuck out and don't come back."

My breathing stopped. I could hear my heart beating in my ears. I hadn't actually seen this side of the Boss before—though I thought briefly of the outburst in the airplane. In this case, however, the spectacle was frightening.

But Tidy got the message. He turned around and started back out the door. Wall closed it. Then he locked the door behind Tidy.

The Boss simply turned around and continued on about his business, as if nothing out of the ordinary had happened. He paused to gaze over his rather large, awestruck crew, and said, "We'll leave in twenty minutes, you assholes. Be ready."

Skate and Wall went through the house, checking the perimeter of the building through the windows. I assumed that they were checking for heat, but they didn't seem to detect any. Then they calmly began to get dressed for the evening.

I was sharing a room with Wall and some of the other guys, and as I walked in to change my own clothes, he was there. I asked him, "Who the hell is Tidy?"

Wall paused for a moment, as though he wanted to choose his words carefully. "Tidy was an old friend of ours back in Potlatch," he said. "He was on the crew for a while. But after the Boss spent a bunch of time training him, the little worm told the Boss that he wanted to go out on his own.

"The Boss explained to Tidy, as he would have told

anyone in that situation, that if he left the crew, he could never be associated us again. The Boss also explained to him that he, the Boss, could not and would not help him if Tidy ever found himself in trouble."

I had to ask: "So they used to be friends?"

"Yeah, they used to be friends. But the Boss is a man of his word, Red. He told Tidy, 'If you quit, you're done,' and he meant it."

"Simple as that?" I questioned.

"Simple as that."

"I wonder what happened to him?" I asked, as we finished in the bedroom and moved to join the others.

"I don't really know," Wall responded, "so I shouldn't guess, but I'd say he probably got caught in the wrong place downtown."

"Caught with a gaff?" I asked in a loud whisper.

"I don't know, Red, but I'll ask around and let you know."

A few minutes later the Boss came into the living room and said, "Listen up."

A silence came over the entire house. We all stopped what we were doing. Then the Boss continued. "Some of you know who Tidy is, and obviously some of you don't. Tidy and I had an agreement and he broke it. That's all there is to it. I don't want to hear another word about Tidy, or about tonight's incident either, understood?"

"Yeah, Boss, understood," everyone said in unison.

I didn't have much time to think before we had to go to work, but what thoughts there were, running through my head, were numbing. I was scared because it was obvious that Tidy just had the shit beaten out of him. Probably because he'd been caught with a gaff in a casino downtown—and that's where we were on our way to play.

Oh shit. What have I gotten myself into?

CHAPTER TEN

Everyone was very careful to avoid mentioning anything about Tidy. I never heard one word about him after that. Then we silently left in different directions to go to work. The Boss actually decided to head back to the Strip—to the Riviera—instead of going downtown. I was glad to hear that.

Our crew began to search for a dealer at the Riviera—an interesting casino that looked to me like a huge silver cylinder rising up out of the desert floor. A gigantic Diet Coke can came to mind.

Dog took refuge in the slots, but he had to take a break for a quick trip to the restroom. On his way there, he caught me behind a slot machine drinking a beer.

"Don't let the Boss see you do that," he warned.

"I'm trying to calm my nerves," I told him. "I've never played blackjack in a casino, and this version of the game leaves a lot to absorb."

Frankly, I'd concluded that these guys were downright nuts. They battled the game, hand after hand, snagging the hole card with a mirror and working the pit bosses. They monitored and scrutinized every move the casino staff made. But they blended in so well, I couldn't tell that they were actually doing anything wrong. I was amazed.

On some occasions, the crew played with other high-dollar players mixed in. That helped to keep some of the heat off our high roller, the arm. But the arms drew some pretty good crowds on a regular basis too—two or three hands of $500 will do that. It commanded a certain respect from both sides of the table. If they only knew we were just some good ol' boys from the country having a little fun, with a certain twist in the game, they might have viewed things differently.

Both crews pushed it hard straight through midnight and into the morning. The crackling intensity of the big-casino scene kept pushing them along. They didn't back off until four o'clock the following morning, and by 8:00 a.m. they were out of bed and back in the casinos.

That second morning, I stood at my post watching Wall as he stood behind Hiram at the Hilton. The play was going well, and Wall was giving Hiram a running analysis of the security level through subtle verbal cues. I was close enough to hear him say the words, "Boy, it sure is cool in here."

The arm was stacking up a few chips, and attention on the table seemed normal, but I knew from what Spanky had told me that everything could snap in an instant. Then Wall caught sight of a group of security guards heading in the direction of the table.

"Suddenly, it's getting very warm in here," he said.

At that point, the pit boss seemed to acknowledge the guards. The Boss coughed from his position in the slot machines and gave Hiram the *heat* sign. At that instant, Wall stepped forward, nudged Hiram under the right armpit and said, "Give it to me."

Wall took the gaff with security now some ten feet from the table. It was an unnoticed handoff. I was watching and I didn't even see it—and I knew what was actually going on. Wall wandered away, cool as a cucumber, as the guards reached the table. It seemed to me like every step between the table and the exit would become a taxing chore for him. He was carrying the gaff, after all. He kept his cool and didn't panic.

I watched as Wall glanced at the glass doors and then turned to look at some shiny chrome slot machines—anything that would reflect enough light to let him see behind him. I expected him to break into a sprint at any second. He turned and searched slowly around to see if he was still unnoticed.

Then I saw a sudden flash of concern on his face. The pit boss had sent two security guards after him. Not knowing what else to do, I got between Wall and the security guards in an effort to slow them down a bit by just being in their way. They didn't know that I was part of the crew.

Wall maintained his cool and took three giant steps out the door. The guards were moving fast now, but Wall waited until he was out the door before he started running. He sprinted down the walkway toward the Hilton golf course. Then he slipped around the corner before the guards—now running too—even got out the door.

They knew which way he'd headed, but they couldn't see him anywhere. The walkway was empty, no tourists and no Wall. I couldn't see anything I could do to help, so I turned to go in the opposite direction of the heat.

Wall told me later, "I circled around the Hilton, flipped the gaff into the back of an old Ford pickup that was driving by, and found refuge in a dumpster. The guards seemed to be stumped. They didn't know if I'd jumped the ten-foot wall onto the golf course or if I'd kept on running. They searched around for half an hour and gave up."

I heard later that the other guards had grabbed Hiram—

they got him just seconds after the handoff. They had him standing up against the table. He had cuffs on his wrists, and then they began to usher him off to the back room.

Chopper, who was the arm for this play, just walked away when the ruckus began. The Boss stood back, a safe distance from the guards and the offending table, and he watched as Chopper casually walked out the door, undetected.

I'd left the area to follow Wall, and I tried to calm my nerves, but my knees felt weak and I turned the other way—I was a wreck.

For some reason, the authorities just didn't grab the high rollers. But, I reasoned, *the money player was the least of their worries.* They wanted the guy with the mirror. And this time they got him—at least, they thought they got him.

Hiram was ushered to the infamous back room, where he would be interrogated and searched by casino staff and the Griffin Agency. We were all hoping that Hiram would be okay. After all, Wall had gotten the evidence out of the casino. The rest of the crew met at the car and headed to the backup joint.

When Hiram finally showed up at the Peppermill, everyone was glad to see him. We didn't run up and hug him or anything like that, we were just glad to see him out of the casino. We still had to make sure he hadn't been followed, so we stayed apart and went through our routine. Once the crew was 100 percent sure they'd been cleared for any sign of heat, the Boss picked everyone up and headed back to the house.

On the way there Hiram said, "Once they had me in the back room, they demanded that I hand over the *shiner.*

"I told them, 'I don't know what you're talking about.'

"They searched every inch of my body," Hiram said. "They even stripped me down to my underwear—but they found no mirror.

"They went back upstairs and searched the floor of the casino, around the table where we were playing, and came up empty. They suspected that a mirror was there to be found, but they came up empty.

"A few minutes later, the guards who'd been chasing Wall walked into the security room empty-handed, and I let out a long, silent sigh of relief. The chief of security made an apology for detaining me without cause, but they still read me the official eighty-six notice and walked me off the property."

Wall said that he stayed in the dumpster until it was time to meet up with the crew, and he knew we were to rendezvous at the Peppermill.

CHAPTER ELEVEN

Back at the house, the Boss got us all together and systematically ran through the facts about the *Hilton Heat*. Everything checked out; all the bases were covered. Wall managed to grab the gaff on a good read and get it out of the casino—and by doing that, he saved everyone a lot of time and trouble.

The crew was tingling from the close encounter, but the Boss summed it up nicely. "That's the way it's supposed to work."

We'd cut it close. We were mere seconds from disaster, but that's how the system is supposed to work.

The Boss told everyone to shower up and get ready to go eat. "After a good meal, we'll get right back after it," he said.

With both crews pumping out hands by the hundreds, we'd chalked up a big New Year's Day haul. Then we came back and won a few thousand more without having to push it too hard on that afternoon and evening.

We topped it all off with a few early-morning hours on the day after, but by that time we were ready to take it home.

The Boss paid everyone. The two-crew system had run up a $36,000 weekend. Some of the guys got their cut and headed out to the airport to catch flights.

As the house emptied, the Kid and I sat off by ourselves. We were trying to make sense of the ups and downs of this business that we found ourselves in.

"These guys are fucking nuts," I told him, "packing mirrors to blackjack tables and running out of casinos. This is crazy."

The Boss had pushed the pace. He'd milked every playing-second he could out of the crew, and he'd seen it take its toll on new guys many times before. When he found the Kid and me alone, sitting there, doubting our existence, he approached us.

"Are you two guys going to cut it?"

He spoke with a little emotion, but there was a sternness behind his question.

The Kid and I looked at each other, and then back at the Boss. "Yeah, Boss," I said. "We'll stick it out until you kick us out."

"Good."

I stayed at the house in Vegas for the rest of the weekend and through the following week. I had nowhere else to go. The Boss left with most of the others, but Wall and Bird stayed at the house as well. Wall, Bird, and I hung around together all week and got better acquainted. They both knew I was struggling a little bit and they understood because they were also nervous. This system was not easy by any means. I know that Bird also struggled with this whole scene. He was a super nice guy and he had a heart of gold. I don't think he had a mean bone in his body. But he was a good ol' boy from Idaho and he was loyal to the Boss. That was all that mattered to him.

Everybody returned for the following weekend, and it passed without a glitch. Although there was an internal clash that surfaced within the crew. Early on Saturday morning, Johnny complained to the Boss, "This new guy, Red, doesn't know his basic strategy." Johnny was the

Boss's partner. He had made an agreement with the Boss for one year to be partners. He sported a Napoleon complex to go with his five-foot-seven frame. He was cocky and arrogant and a hard guy to like. He was actually the Kid's cousin. He played college football at Portland State University as a wide receiver. I did not know him from school.

The Boss had a conversation with Johnny and the Boss said to me, "Johnny says you don't know your basic strategy, Red. Is that so?"

"I know it, Boss," I replied, in a defiant tone.

The Boss sent me to the practice table, handed me the flash cards, and got out his stopwatch. Then he barked, "Go."

I had 290 flash cards to recognize in five minutes with less than three mistakes. The Boss had raised the standard the week before. Instead of the old seven-and-a-half-minute rule, I now only had five minutes to complete the task. A typical flash card was two-by-three inches and would have the dealer's upcard at the top of the card. There would be two numbers at the bottom of the card, representing the player's two cards. For example: If a ten and six were at the bottom of the card and a four at the top, there would be an "S" on the back of the card indicating that I was to stand on that hand. That response was based on a chart that I had studied several weeks prior. The rule in my mind was thirteen through sixteen, stand against a four, five, or six. Otherwise, hit. Since I had sixteen and the dealer had a four up, I would need to stand. I went through the cards, but I was having trouble from the start.

"Six twenty-five," the Boss said when he snapped off the stopwatch. "You don't know your cards, Red."

The Boss quickly turned his attention to the Kid. "Kid," he said. "If Red doesn't have his cards down to five minutes by Sunday night, you don't get paid."

The Kid wasn't sure how he'd gotten involved in this, but he heard what the Boss said. If he didn't push me to get my flash cards down by the end of the weekend, he would lose his pay.

The Kid's jaw dropped slightly as the Boss left the room.

"Fuck, Red, you've got to get your time down to five minutes by tomorrow night."

"I will, man," I told him.

I felt bad, putting the Kid's pay on the line. We'd known each other for only a week, but we were suddenly joined in a common cause—saving his paycheck.

This meant trying to find practice time during a weekend of rigorous live play. We squeezed out every second we could for practice. When Sunday night came, and it was time to break the bankroll, the Boss paid everyone but me and the Kid. Then the entire crew gathered around the practice table to see me tested—and to see if the Kid would get paid.

I grabbed the basic strategy cards and sat down. The Boss grabbed his stopwatch. "Go," he said.

I took off pretty smooth, but then I slowed for a rough spot—then another. The stopwatch clicked along—*tick, tick, tick...*

The crew sat forward in anticipation.

"One mistake," Johnny's voice rang out loud.

I pushed on. I hesitated on a card a few seconds later, and then I just guessed.

"Two mistakes," Johnny shouted out, and he was ready

to ring up another.

But at that point I hit my stride; I was nearing the end.

"Time... Just kidding." Johnny knew it was his last chance to throw me off.

I never missed a beat after that, right on down to the last card.

"Done," I yelled.

"Four fifty-five," the Boss reported.

I let out a huge sigh of relief.

"Yessss!" the Kid yelled. "Great job, Red."

The Kid rushed over, shook my hand, and gave me a hug. Everybody got paid, and the Kid and I had developed a new friendship.

CHAPTER TWELVE

I came to realize quite quickly that various crew members—some of them permanent, some not—would randomly come in on prescheduled weekends to play, and the third weekend after I moved in with Wall and Bird brought an encounter with the law. This time I got a close-up view of what *heat* really meant.

It was early evening. We were playing at the Frontier when the play ended abruptly and the crew scattered. Of course it didn't make sense to me, but I came to realize this was something a guy was going to have to get used to. What happened was, we had heat and I didn't know it. The rest of the crew, though, they did know it, and they just simply disappeared right in front of me.

At the time, I was up close to the table. I felt an adrenaline rush surge through my body, and then I headed out of the casino. I looked around to make sure I was clear of any pursuit or surveillance. After that, I worked my way carefully back over to the car, but I was the only one there. There was no activity at the car. I waited for a few minutes, and I got a little antsy, so I started back in the direction of the casino.

I didn't want to go back inside to locate the crew. The Boss had warned me not to go back into a casino after we got heat, but I wasn't sure whether we'd really drawn heat or not. I walked around to the front of the building and saw where Metro Police had Wall propped up against a patrol car.

I must have looked a little unsure of myself, because one of the officers singled me out of the crowd and asked, "Excuse me, can I ask you a few questions?"

"Sure," I replied.

"Do you know this guy over here?" He was pointing at Wall.

"No," I said, in a strained tone.

"He says he knows you. Well, if you don't know him, he's going directly to the jail," the cop said. Then he turned away.

"I think his name is Wall," I blurted out.

The cop spun around and said, "Up against the car, feet back, and spread 'em."

I suddenly knew I'd fucked up. The Metro squad marched us through the casino to the back rooms for further inquiry. They separated us into different rooms. Then the protocol that the Boss had taught us kicked in.

I was led into a small room with two chairs and a desk. A guard turned me around in front of one of the chairs and pushed me into it. I focused on the wall in front of me, remembering not to drop my chin below level with the floor. I was staring at the transition between the wall and the ceiling when the chief of security walked in.

The security chief was dressed in a suit and tie. He stood right in front of me as he gazed into my eyes from about a foot away just off to my left side. He opened the conversation with, "So, you're one of Steve Kammeyer's crew."

I turned my head slightly, looked him straight in the eye, and said, "I don't know what you're talking about, sir." Then I resumed my gaze at the ceiling-wall transition.

"Let me have him for a few minutes, boss," the guard

said, as he pounded his nightstick into the palm of his left hand. "I'll get it out of him."

Fear kicked in, but I put myself into a steady gear and held tough.

The chief seemed to ignore the guard, and said to me, as he leaned into my face a little closer, "You're telling me you don't know Steve Kammeyer?"

"No, sir," I said, and I maintained my gaze as before.

"Search him," the chief said to the guard.

"Stand up," the guard ordered.

I stood up and the guard began to search. He delivered a mild blow to my groin area and I flinched a bit, well aware that the guard would love to punish me.

"He's clean," the guard finally said.

"Bring him into the room with the other guy," the chief said, and I was ushered into the place where they were holding Wall.

After they searched us and found no evidence, all they could do legally was bar us from the casino and let us go. The guard read us an official *eighty-six* notice—barring us from the premises forever. Then we were free to go.

Wall looked over at me, smiled, and shook his head in disbelief. He couldn't believe that I was so dumb to get myself caught in that situation. After we were released, we cleaned ourselves up and the crew picked us up at the backup joint.

We had to report to the Boss, and the Boss was straightforward.

"You fucking idiot, Red. What did you do, try to go back in?"

I searched for an answer and said, "There wasn't anyone at the car, and..."

The Boss cut me off. "Don't ever go back into a casino after you get heat. Understood?"

"Yeah, Boss," I said in a demoralized tone.

The rest of the crew got a good laugh out of my stupid move. Wall laughed too, but he seemed to feel a little sorry for me.

"You were forced to make a tough decision under pressure," he said, "but you did what you thought would help your fellow crew member."

Like a lot of new guys, I was having trouble dealing with this new career. I wasn't *street-smart*. I wasn't savvy, and I'd been truly scared. I realized I had a lot more to learn.

The brush with the harsh reality of being nose-to-nose with a patrol car gave me some food for thought, and so did the Boss. It was a scary feeling to realize that my mistake had cost the crew unnecessary exposure to the authorities. I didn't want to be a weak link.

One thing I had going for me was my friendship with Bird and Wall. But I didn't mesh well with everyone. I clashed with Johnny and a couple others. At one point, I thought my career was over. The crew assembled in one of the rooms at the house and voted to boot me off the team. It all started with Johnny. "He's just not cuttin' it, Steve," Johnny said.

"Yeah, Boss, he's not going to make it," Dog added.

"He's going to bring us all heat and send us to jail, Boss," Skate said.

"Well, he's a loyal little shit, I'll tell ya that," Wall said in my defense. "But he is pretty green for this kinda work."

The Kid was in the room but didn't make any remarks.

"We need to get rid of him, Steve," Johnny demanded

"Yeah, Boss," Skate and Dog said at the same time.

"I don't know, I kinda like him," Wall said.

The Boss paced for a moment, thinking of how to respond to the crew's request.

"I appreciate all of your comments," the Boss said. "I like him and I think he'll work out once he learns the system. He's staying, and that's final." The Boss saved me with a veto. He decided to take me to San Diego with him. He figured he could teach me more of what I needed to know during the week.

I came to understand that these guys were extremely professional at what they did—and what they did was to cheat at blackjack, and they were really good at it. But I was just six months out of college and pretty naïve. To make things worse, I had very little *street knowledge*. It was obvious to me that the Boss was well aware of that. If I didn't get better soon, I would be useless to him.

CHAPTER THIRTEEN

Things were moving pretty fast by then. I moved into the Boss's condominium in San Diego.

The condo was a nice two-story, two-bedroom abode in Carlsbad, California, situated just north of San Diego. The Boss had expensive tastes in décor and furniture—the art on the walls was perfectly organized and well put together. His place was located just two blocks above the La Costa Golf Course, and the grounds were awesome—swimming pool, tennis courts, well-manicured lawns and flower beds. He also had good taste in clothing; in fact one afternoon I came back to the condo to find that the Boss had thrown away all of my clothes.

"Boss, where are my clothes?" I asked.

"Get in the car, let's go get you some new clothes, Red," was all he said. We headed to a local men's store and I was suited in an entire wardrobe to the Boss's liking. The bill was $1,800 for the three casual suits and shoes. The Boss covered the expense once again.

The San Diego area turned out to be a great place to live. The temperatures were mild and warm. There were beaches, golf courses, mountains, sporting events, and, of course, a very lively nightlife. Playing cards in Vegas on weekends was tough but living in Southern California during the week was relaxing. It diverted my attention from the anxieties encountered in Vegas. Life was just about as good as it gets.

Spanky was around during that time, working himself

into better and better shape for the upcoming baseball season. He was a senior at the University of Southern California and a starter on the pitching staff. And for Spanky, I turned out to be pretty handy to have around. The Boss provided me with a catcher's glove, mask, and a cup. Then he stuck me on the business end of Spanky's ninety-mile-an-hour fastball. I didn't mind, I loved the game of baseball. Spanky and I trained together, stretching, running, and talking pitching strategy. We both knew that he was heading for the pro ranks, and I was there to help in any way that I could.

When the Boss invested his time and effort into something, he'd really get after it. Before long, we had a video camera and a radar gun to analyze form and to chart arm strength. We went over every aspect of Spanky's preparation. Eventually Spanky headed back to school in L.A. The Boss and I attended several USC games that season to watch Spanky pitch. In June he was drafted by the California Angels and signed a minor league contract.

Over time, I got used to living with the Boss. During the week, I had nowhere pressing to go, so I cooked, cleaned, shopped, and kept things up as best I could. I came to take pride in the things I did. The Boss sticking up for me back in Vegas was a special gesture—I felt like I owed him, but he didn't seem to see it that way.

Another good thing was the Kid only lived about a mile up the road, and he was in constant contact. Every now and then, he'd come by and pick me up—giving me a break from the Boss, who could be hard to handle at times. He was so intense and precise that the Kid and I both felt like we always had to be on our toes.

I also got to see Wall, from time to time. He would stay

with the Kid when he was in San Diego. He'd often stay in San Diego for two weeks to two months at a time. And Wall would spend a lot of time with the Boss. They were longtime friends. The Boss relied on Wall to act as a go-between with the crew.

The crew related to Wall. When the Boss wanted the crew to do something, he'd often send the directive through Wall—like the captain of a ship, issuing orders through an executive officer or a first mate. The Boss was a bit of a rare bird. He was not only book smart, but he maintained a good measure of common sense as well. He was an avid reader, but he sometimes had trouble communicating with some of the crew members.

Wall, on the other hand, didn't read much, but he was extremely long on the common sense. He was also very observant, and he could pick things up in a hurry. He could relate to the Boss and interpret things for the crew.

The Kid and I were fortunate to have established a solid rapport with Wall, and we knew it. We paid attention to every piece of advice that came out of his mouth. Wall was an intelligent guy, and he'd developed a lot of street smarts, playing pool on the road in his younger years, and learning more during his time with the crew.

Wall taught us how to read people. "A guy can figure out what makes people tick," he would say. "During a play, you've got to look right into the pit boss's soul, read what's on his mind by his facial expression and body gestures. People are like a book, but sometimes you have to read between the lines."

To me and the Kid, Wall represented a guy who had managed to survive the Boss's weekend tours of Vegas for years. Knowing what we knew about the crew's history and the difficulty of the work, we were a bit surprised that we'd survived as long as we had. We were three and a half months in, and I had already been barred from a casino, but we were making $1,500 a week and it was hard to quit. We were getting better and we were going to stick with it until we got caught or run out by the Boss.

It came to a point, however, that we came to realize that Wall wasn't going to be around the casinos for a while; he had been recognized by casino staff too many times recently.

"It's time for me to cool off," he told us one day.

The Kid and I made quite a few trips to Nevada without him over the course of the next several months.

CHAPTER FOURTEEN

The crew continued to play hard, and we worked every weekend. We worked on through the end of the winter and on into spring. Johnny and Hiram did the braining during this period. I was handed the gaff several dozen times over the next six months, but I only had to actually run on a couple of occasions. We were getting the gaff out of the casino in a more-timely manner by then. If we were to become old pros at our various positions, we needed to stay in good physical shape and be on our toes at all times. We made a lot of money during this period too, though it came at considerable risk.

The Kid and I were being worked hard and we learned more each week. We were rapidly building up our confidence.

I had my ups and downs. Being barred from a casino was a real dose of reality. The more I became a part of the crew the more I learned about the entire game—the game that we were actually playing—and I began to become a real asset. Learning how to react by reading frustrated faces just before the shit hit the fan was a skill in itself, and one worth achieving.

The Kid's tour of duty had been a freebie up to this point, and he'd learned a lot as well. We both became part of the regular crew, and we both played as screens and runners for several months. We worked well together and he was fortunate to not have any harsh encounters with the law.

And the Kid's breezy beginning was not going unnoticed. Through the first six months of that year Dog and Cirk had become history. They'd been noticed by the law too many times. Plus, their faces had become familiar with too many pit bosses, not to mention several security-management types.

Dog moved to Vegas to live, but he wasn't involved with the crew, beyond an occasional fill-in appearance. Cirk made a go at braining, but he was uncomfortable in the hot seat, and he was caught twice in a matter of weeks—without the gaff, thankfully. He hastily made tracks back to Boise.

Dealing with the heat was just part of the business. Some members of the crew simply burned out, some exploded from jangled nerves, and others would freeze at the table. Sometimes a veteran arm would pick up his cards and appear to be looking at them, but then suddenly discover that he could not move.

The dealer would say, "It's your turn, sir," and the arm would just stare. When that happened, another crew member would have to tell him what to do verbally. Of course, we'd have to leave the casino at that point, to avoid the heat. Everyone knew that the arm was history, after such an episode. Nobody would ever recover from the *freeze*. When it happened, everyone knew it was over for him. Even the guys who froze knew.

For the most part, the Boss stayed out of sight, at least as far as playing the tables. But he continued to monitor the play from the slot machine area. And the veteran arms were burning out. Chopper was burned because he'd simply won too much money. Wart was in that same boat.

The Boss pushed his crews, week after week, but he had

to work extra hard during the down time to develop new players. Out of twenty prospects that were originally recruited to arm, only a few even earned a look at the practice table, and very few of them actually went on to bet the Boss's money in a real play.

CHAPTER FIFTEEN

With the crew losing players, the Boss called Wall back to work. It was great to see him again, and after a short reunion it was back to work. On the weekend following Wall's arrival, just after we'd finished an outing on the Strip, one of the new arms froze. We arrived back at the house and the Boss told the offending arm to pack his things.

After a short goodbye and an embarrassing moment for the arm, the Boss turned, looked directly at me, and said, "Red, you're going to arm. Get ready to go."

I headed to the room where my clothes were. I needed to change into something more fitting for an arm. But on the way to my room my mind was racing like never before. I'd been in on the training of some of the arms, but I'd never actually done it. I was downright scared and extremely nervous.

As soon as I was dressed the Boss said, "Let's go practice." We all headed for the practice table. We took up our positions with me in the arm seat. Johnny was at the brain seat, the Kid stood on third base, and Wall took up a position right behind Johnny as the runner.

Skate was there as well, but all he could do was observe the practice. The Boss dealt the cards and made corrections in my demeanor and posture as we played. We went through about fifteen hands. When we finished, the Boss tossed me a $10,000 packet of hundreds and said, "Don't lose it."

I let out a loud gulp, and hoped nobody else heard it.

"Let's go, you assholes," the Boss said.

"Where to, Boss?" Skate asked.

"The Stardust," the Boss said in a positive tone. So we got in the car and headed for the Stardust, with the Boss rambling instructions as we went. The entire crew listened to every word he said. We needed to make sure that we were all on the same page.

We entered through different doors of the casino and I went directly to the bar, as instructed. I ordered a Jack and Coke to calm my nerves. I wasn't there for three minutes before Skate was giving me the *come to the table* sign by rubbing his nose. I got up, grabbed my drink, and followed Skate to the table. The Kid was holding the seat. He knew I was on my way, and moved out just as I got there. I reached into my pocket, pulled out a wad of cash, and put $500 in the circle. The dealer started to grab the money to get change, but I waved my hand over the cash and said, "Just play it."

"Money plays five hundred," the dealer exclaimed, as she began to deal the cards. The pit boss came right over to introduce himself. "Hi, I'm Antonio Dioguardi," he said. He reached out to shake my hand.

I was really nervous and didn't know what to say. As I reached for his hand, I hit the top of my glass with my sleeve. Jack and Coke went all over the table. I thought some of the drink splashed up onto Antonio's tie.

Suddenly this strange voice came out of my mouth. It sounded like a dumb, young, high-pitched Midwestern accent. "I'm terribly sorry," the voice said. "Someone get me a towel," I turned to say, "and I'll clean that up."

Finally, I came to my senses and shook the man's hand.

"I'm Jerry Williams," I said. "I'm really sorry about the mess."

"Oh, don't worry about it," Antonio said. "It happens all the time."

A cocktail waitress started to wipe up the mess, and I continued my charade. A small crowd had gathered. I reached out and grabbed Antonio's tie to help the cocktail waitress clean it. Then I noticed the tie was silk.

I stated in the loud, high-pitched Midwestern voice, "Why, that there's real silk!" as I looked around, still holding his tie. The entire crowd began to giggle at my foolishness, so I continued the show.

As the mess was cleaned up, and the tie issue came to a close, I continued to play five hundred a hand. The small crowd grew larger. I was making quite a scene and my chatter continued on in my newly found accent.

I looked over at Antonio. He had a funny smirk on his face, as I said in an overly loud tone, so everyone could hear, "Yep, my daddy give me $10,000 to come out here to gamble. Then I'm heading to California to see the ocean. I ain't never seen the ocean before." Again, the crowd giggled and so did Antonio.

We were able to play for forty-five minutes with me carrying on like an innocent young farm kid. After all, I was just twenty-two years old, and I did spend two summers in Iowa playing baseball with some fellas from the Midwest.

The play was called off when the dealer went on break. I headed to the cashier cage to cash the chips I'd won. I actually cashed out for five thousand and I was in for nothing.

I headed out the side door of the casino to grab a cab to the backup joint when two hookers came up to me, one on each side.

"Do you need a date?" one of the hookers asked

"No, I don't have time. Leave me alone," I said.

But just as I said that, one of the hookers reached over and unzipped my pants. I was protecting the five grand in cash with my left hand on my pocket. When I reached to zip my pants up, though, the other hooker said, "Fine, we're leaving."

But when I reached back to continue to protect the five grand in my pocket, it was gone. I panicked and took off after the hookers. I hit the two girls from behind like a linebacker in a football game. I grabbed them both by their long hair and drug them to the ground.

"Give me that fucking money," I screamed, as I pinned their faces into the sidewalk with my arms and my 220-pound body.

One of the hookers took a handful of hundreds out of her small purse and threw it up in the air. The wind typically blows in Las Vegas, and this particular evening was no exception. Within seconds, $100 bills were blowing everywhere.

I let go of the hookers and tried to track down the blowing money. I ran around and grabbed as many as I could find, but when it was over, I'd come up with only thirty-eight hundred bucks. I suspected that the girl who threw the money in the air kept a few of them for her troubles.

I gathered myself and headed for a cab. I was mad— mad at the hookers, mad at the circumstance, but most of all I was mad at myself. Now I had to go hook up with the crew and tell them what had happened. I was not looking forward to that.

I arrived at the MGM and went directly to the bar. Skate was leaning against the wall. I sat down for a moment and casually looked around the lobby, not wanting to see Skate's signal to head to the car—but as soon as I looked back, he was doing just that.

When we arrived at the car and got inside, I blurted out, "I just got ripped off by two hookers."

"What happened?" the Boss asked in surprise.

I told them the story, and as I looked around, the guys were all staring at the floorboards—smiling and shaking their heads.

"You'll have to pay that money back, Red," the Boss said.

"Yeah, I know, Boss."

Later that evening, Wall came up to me and said, "Red, you gotta get a little more street smart. If you don't, you're gonna end up broke."

He began to give me some pointers, one scenario after another, and he told me how to respond to each of them. "Red, if someone approaches you on the street, take an aggressive step toward them and say 'Get the fuck away from me.'" Okay, I replied. "If you had done that earlier, you would still have the money," Wall continued. "When you got the Boss's money on you, be aware of everyone and everything around you. Look for trouble brewing and react," he barked in a friendly tone.

"Got it, Gator," I said, remembering that Spanky called him Wally Gator.

Wall helped me a lot about learning the streets, but at that point in time, I still had a long way to go.

CHAPTER SIXTEEN

Several months went by, and some of that ever-building internal pressure surfaced during the first week of May. That's when things between Johnny and me flared up again. I knew I stood to come up on the short end of the situation. Johnny and the Boss had a one-year verbal agreement as partners in the bankroll, and it's not a good idea to piss off a guy who banked with the Boss.

But I'd had a bad feeling about Johnny from the start. One Saturday afternoon at the house, I got up to grab something to drink. Trying to push my buttons, Johnny took my chair. When I returned from the kitchen, I went over to Johnny, grabbed him out of the chair, and picked him up over my head.

"Put me down!" Johnny screamed.

I threw him toward the ground, but before he landed, I turned my arms around underneath and caught him.

The entire crew was there to see it happen. Johnny was embarrassed, so he disappeared for an hour. When he returned, he jumped all over me with a tongue-lashing of verbal abuse. He had some rank behind him, so I had to show a little respect. I didn't want to have a real confrontation with him. I decided that I had better get out of there before something bad happened. I left Las Vegas on a Saturday night and headed back to San Diego.

When I got to the Boss's house, I realized I had left my keys in the Boss's airplane and I couldn't get in. I found the hidden key at the Kid's place, went in, and waited for him and Wall to return the following day with news of my fate. I figured I probably wouldn't be around much longer.

The Kid and Wall arrived on Sunday evening. They sadly told me that I was off the crew. It was hard to take. I'd become one of the boys, but it was a reality I knew I had to deal with. I actually felt like I'd showed some promise. I had run the gaff out for Hiram and Johnny on several occasions and was praised by the Boss and the crew. I had done everything that the Boss had asked of me and I had learned a lot from Wall about getting along on the streets. I just couldn't take any more of Johnny's smart mouth.

I stayed Sunday night with my friends, and we enjoyed some downtime together. I didn't go over to the Boss's until Monday evening to pick up my stuff.

It turned out, the Boss had been thinking long and hard about what to do. He must have seen some good in me—I was strong, smart, fast, and mentally tough, plus I'd learned a shitload. It was a really rough moment for me, and for the Boss too. I'd developed a sense of loyalty towards the crew, and he knew it. It was hard to simply walk away.

When I walked in, the strain of it all showed on the Boss's face. "What are you going to do, Red?" he asked.

"I don't know, Boss," I said, staring right at his chest, as he'd taught me.

I gathered up my things, and there were tears pushing to the surface for both of us when I stepped back into the living room. The Boss was pacing back and forth between the front door and the walkway to the kitchen. I could tell he had something more he wanted to say.

There was a nineteenth-century wingback chair with an ottoman that sat in the corner of the Boss's living room.

A large Tiffany floor lamp stood behind it. That individual chair always seemed strange to me. It was upholstered in supple cream-colored leather, and it violently clashed with the postmodern furniture that adorned the rest of the house. It was as if the chair didn't belong here—like it had been transmitted through some kind of a time warp from Queen Victoria's sitting room to challenge the very concept of modernity.

The chair seemed like an outcast to me—and feeling like an outcast myself, I took a seat in that chair. As I sat there with my worldly belongings scattered around my feet, the Boss went on with what he wanted to say.

"What do you want out of this life, Red?" he asked.

I looked up at him and replied, "I wanted to be a baseball player, Boss. But after training with Spanky, I came to realize that I wasn't quite good enough. I suppose I just wanted to be a part of something interesting."

The Boss continued to pace, but he didn't make any effort to say anything.

Finally, the silence got to me, so I went on. "What do you want out of life, Boss?"

He thought for a moment and started to speak, but then he seemed to think better of it and continued to pace. Finally he confided, "I would like $10,000 to be delivered to my doorstep every month so that I could just sit on a warm beach someplace and read all day. That," he said, "would be real living to me."

"Huh," I said. It was the only thing I could think of to say. Then, in a state of mild bewilderment, I gathered up my meager possessions and started for the door.

But the Boss stepped over beside me, and he spoke just as I opened the door. "Red," he said, "you can stay on the crew, under five conditions."

I stopped and turned, interested in what he had to say.

"First," he continued, "you have to move out of my house. Second, you take no pay for this last weekend. Third, you can't work with Johnny anymore. Fourth, you have to train arms for the next six months. And fifth, you have to make a formal apology to the crew for leaving in the middle of the weekend. If you can live up to all of these stipulations, you can keep a spot on the crew."

I didn't hesitate. "Thanks, Boss, I'll do it," I said, as I reached out to shake his hand. "And I won't let you down again, Boss," I promised, and I looked him right in the eye when I said it.

I immediately hustled back over to the Kid's place, but before I got there I slowed my pace and thought about what the Boss had said. And suddenly that old Victorian chair made a whole lot of sense to me. I guess the Boss liked outcasts, like me.

When I got back to the Kid's place, I burst through the door and announced, "I'm back on the crew." I yelled it out in a loud, happy tone.

"How did you do that?" the Kid asked, more than a little surprised.

Before he could answer, Wall popped up with, "That's unreal, Red. Nobody gets back on the crew."

"I'm back," I assured them.

We all felt like we'd all been given a break, and we were excited about continuing to practice and play together. Another playing weekend was four days away, and knowing we had the next day off it seemed like a good time to celebrate my return.

We jumped into the Kid's car and headed for the Belly-

Up Tavern to shoot some pool and have a few beers. We smoked a little reefer on the way.

The Boss wasn't around—it was time to party.

When it came to partying, Wall seemed to fare a little better than the Kid and I. He was a better pool player and a little better at chasing girls. But we all managed to catch our share, and that night was no exception.

CHAPTER SEVENTEEN

It took almost two months for me to complete all of the duties I'd obligated myself to do for the honor of being given a second chance to play with the Boss's crew again—though I still had to complete the additional training—and I'd come to understand that training new arms would be a permanent job for me from now on.

My first weekend back proved to be a difficult time, too. Some of the guys really wanted me off of the crew. They seemed to think the Boss had gone soft in the head for letting me come back. Of course, not everyone treated me that way, but I knew I had to win over the doubters. I knuckled down and concentrated on doing my job. I remained polite and humble. I was determined to prove to the entire bunch that I had what it took.

We went to a casino called the Hacienda. We'd never played there and the Boss wanted to give it a try. It was a casino on the Strip but it was removed from the main drag—like it was waiting for the rest of Las Vegas to build on out to it. The place featured a giant marquee out front that displayed a giant palomino horse with a rambunctious rider. I was reminded of Teddy Roosevelt on a horse.

I discovered later that the Hacienda had once been owned by one Allen Glick—a San Diego real estate investor. It turned out Nevada state officials believed that Glick was really a front man for an organization of Midwestern crime families. They further suspected that the casino's real owners were engaged in a huge skimming operation that included other Nevada casinos they were tied into. And to add to their suspicion, Glick's purchase was financed through a loan from the Teamsters' Central States Pension Fund.

In any event, when the heat finally came down on Glick, he denied any wrongdoing and was never charged with a crime. He did become a cooperating witness, however, and that immunized him from prosecution, unlike some fifteen other individuals who had connections to the Milwaukee crime family and the Kansas City crime family as well.

Unfortunately, I didn't know anything about the history of the place at that time. We had only one objective: making our way towards the bright lights and the *ding ding ding* of the slot machines.

We entered the casino through separate doors and met up at the blackjack pit, where we began to scout for dealers—hoping to set up a play. Twenty minutes later, Wall saw a pit boss snap on the Boss. The Boss had gotten too close to the action and the pit boss recognized him as the leader of our infamous gang. Things around the pit started to stir, so Wall gave us the all-around *heat* sign.

We hurriedly picked up our chips and headed out the door, arriving outside without incident. Once we were all safely ensconced in the car, I noticed that the Boss was in one of those moods where he wanted to show the crew that he was, without any doubt, *the Boss.* He ordered me to go back into the casino to cash in everyone's chips—chips the crew still had in their pockets, left over from trying to set up a play.

"Boss," I said, with a little alarm in my voice, "we shouldn't go back there after just gettin' heat." But I knew the minute I said it that I should not have tried to question the Boss.

"Do what the fuck you're told, Red," he barked.

I gathered everyone's chips and made my way back into the casino.

I went in through the front door and headed over to cash out. As I approached the cashiers' cage, a pair of security guards walked over to meet me.

"Excuse me, sir, could we ask you a couple of questions?" one asked.

I sort of expected that there'd be trouble, going back in after arousing the heat. I looked directly at the two guards and said, "Nope." Then I sprinted for the front door.

I hit the exit at full speed, and the guards chased me out into the parking lot.

The Boss and the crew were waiting for me to return, but when they saw me running out the door, heading for the main part of the Strip—which in this case was over three hundred yards away—the Boss drove off in an effort to protect himself and rest of the crew.

Out of the corner of my eye I saw another guard in a three-wheeled Cushman security cart. He saw me running and took up the chase. I was scared to death, but I was committed to getting away. I was outrunning the foot pursuit, and the Cushman was blocked by the curbs. I thought I might make it.

I had a two-hundred-yard lead, and I was pulling away, when two Metro police cars arrived on the scene. The police saw me running, and then one of the cruisers jumped the curb in front of me to block my path.

I turned, at that point, and headed out into the desert.

Then four cops jumped out of the two cars and drew their pistols. I could hear the actions slide back on the guns, as each man chambered a round. Then one officer yelled, "Yeah, just keep on running, pal!"

I wisely stopped and threw both hands in the air. Then one of the cops tackled me to the ground. The other three officers reefed my arms around to my back and slapped a pair of handcuffs on. By that time, the Cushman and the two guards who were chasing me on foot finally caught up.

I hadn't really done anything illegal. Metro police had no choice but to turn me over to the security guards. All four of the cops picked me up and tossed me into the back of the Cushman. With no use of my hands to protect my sudden stop, my face smashed into the wall of the trunk, but I hardly noticed from the adrenaline.

I had it made until Metro showed up, but I was caught now and on my way to the back room. As the Cushman pulled up under the canopy of the main entrance, I could see myself in the mirrors above, all curled up in the cart. It was an awful feeling.

The three guards grabbed me, dragged me out of the cart, and ushered me down one flight of stairs and into a small room. We were in the security section of the casino.

They unlocked one cuff and wove it through the back of the chair. Then they reattached it to my wrist. Now I was handcuffed to the chair, and one of the guards was standing there, again with a billy club pounding into his hand.

"What are you, some kind of track star or something?" the other guard asked, as the chief of security came into the room. By that time, the guard had gone through an entire box of Kleenex from his sprint after me. He was still wiping sweat from his forehead when the chief began to question me.

"Do you have any ID?"

"Yes, sir, my license is in my back pocket," I replied.

He instructed the guard to retrieve my wallet. The guard then handed it to the chief, who extracted my driver's license and looked at the name.

"So, Mr. Red, why were you running?"

I stared straight ahead at the wall and the ceiling. Then I turned my gaze on the chief, looked him in the eye, and politely said, "I don't wish to make any statements sir, and I would like to have an attorney present."

The guard laughed as he resumed the pounding of the billy club. He said, "Attorney, huh. Just let me have him for a few minutes, boss. I'll get it out of him."

I thought to myself—*that's what the last guy said.*

"No," the chief said, as he motioned the guard out of the room.

Then he turned to me and said, "I'll be right back."

I could hear muffled voices in the room next to me. Then I heard the chief say, "He's not talking."

Another voice said, "He's one of Steve Kammeyer's group. You probably won't get anything out of him." I assumed that voice was coming out of the mouth of a Griffin agent.

The door opened once again, and the guard and the chief both came back into the room. "Search him," the chief said.

The guard unlocked my handcuffs, stood me up, and began the search.

I didn't have a gaff and he didn't find anything else incriminating, so the guard said, "He's clean, boss."

"Read him the official eighty-six notice and walk him off of the property."

As the guard read the notice, the chief started to leave

the room, but he stopped at the threshold and said, "I don't ever want to see you in here again, understand?"

"Yes, sir," I replied.

The guard finished reading the notice, which said something like I was officially barred from the property and could never return in the future. Then I had to sign the notice. The notice was not dated, but it stated unequivocally that I had not been harmed in any way shape or form by the casino staff. It further acknowledged their right to engage in more intense interrogation if I were ever to be caught on the casino's premises in the future.

At that point, we were joined by the other guard and the two of them walked me back upstairs and out the main doors to the sidewalk.

The second guard said, "Go ahead, come back and see what happens."

I hurried down the sidewalk, crossed the street, and disappeared into the Aladdin Casino. Then I went out the side door and flagged a cab to the Peppermill, where I called the Boss to come get me.

The Boss and crew picked me up.

The Boss never said anything about the incident at the Hacienda after that—no apology, no nothing. I just took it to be one more tough experience, designed to make me better at the career in which I had found myself—or maybe, more able to deal with the downsides.

CHAPTER EIGHTEEN

The Boss began to pour his energy into the development of new arms. The arm was a unique position. To fill it, the Boss needed to find a person with a gift of gab, and an individual who was quick-witted and reasonably intelligent—and, most importantly, a person who was out of a job and broke. A desperate man with bills to pay will do desperate things. Hiring somebody to help the crew cheat at blackjack was not the ordinary, everyday job. A man who was down on his luck was more likely to succeed at the arm position. After all, that's how I came to the crew.

In short, the Boss needed some very special people, so he put an ad in the *San Diego Tribune* that simply read, *Las Vegas assistant, $1,000 a week.* It included a phone number to call if interested. The Kid and I were manning the phones. We would screen applicants for interviews and it turned into quite a task. Six hundred people responded.

About a third of the respondents showed enough interest and intelligence to be granted an interview. One hundred and sixty people showed up for their appointments. Of those, the Boss hired three.

If a woman called, she was told the job had been filled— a policy that didn't exactly fit with the anti-discrimination laws, but the Caesars Palace bust had soured the Boss on women operatives. Plus, the Boss didn't like the crew getting too close to women crew members on a personal level. Arrangements like that could provide opportunities for outside authorities to infiltrate the operation.

I had the task of training the arm candidates, as prescribed by my agreement. The training sessions took place at the Kid's apartment—which was now also my apartment. It turned out that the Boss had us training these new arms for an additional reason. It made us better blackjack players for one thing, and the Boss would need fresh brains in the future. He saw this as a good opportunity for us to learn.

He had refined the training regimen, and it was clicking along perfectly. This teaching and rebuilding process was an important function.

As it turned out, at one point, the Boss needed to go to Philadelphia over a weekend, but this didn't mean the crew got the weekend off. We were headed for Vegas as usual. Johnny and I had put our differences behind us by this time. We decided that, being on the same side, we should act like professionals. We'd both grown enough to show some respect for each other.

On this trip Johnny would run the crew. He would stay back in the slots and keep an eye on the overall picture. Wall, the Kid, Hiram, and I would make up the nucleus of the crew. Toosh was to be the arm. He was one of the new arms that the Kid and I were training. Johnny would arm as well, to give Toosh an occasional break. Hiram would do the braining all weekend, and Skate was on deck to be field marshal. Wall and the Kid and I would trade off as screens and runners.

By this time, I'd found a place for myself in Hiram's heart. He liked the idea of having a six-foot-tall, 220-pound protector—one who would run through the fires of hell for him. It was my job to protect Hiram, allowing Hiram to devote his entire attention to the cards.

With the Boss gone for the weekend, we were determined to have a good showing, and by four o'clock Saturday morning we were up sixty-four hundred. At that point, though, Hiram was beat, so we cashed in and followed procedure back to the house.

Toosh had been given a comp room at the Riviera, and he was taking them up on their hospitality.

Hiram, Johnny, the Kid, and Skate were all tired and went right to bed, but not Wall. Wall wanted to go down to the Crazy Horse strip joint and see his Vegas girlfriend. He didn't want to go alone, so I went with him. We always had fun at the Crazy Horse. Wall was a regular, and the girls all knew him.

The minute we walked in the door, the girls began to take good care of us. April, Wall's girlfriend, escorted him to a room in the back. Two other girls, Nikki and Amber, took me to another back room for a double table dance. We didn't stay long. It was the middle of the work weekend for us, so we headed back to the house.

The crew had been entrusted with a large sum of money for this trip. The bankroll was twenty thousand. On top of that, Wall and I were responsible for an additional forty thousand of the Boss's money, extra money that he'd sent to cover expenses and bail—if necessary—while he was out of town.

Johnny, Skate, and the Kid divided up the bankroll after the win. They would each keep their portion and they were accountable for that money. Wall and I were responsible for the other forty grand.

Usually we would carry the money around in our socks, but forty grand was a little much for our socks. The gas company hadn't turned on the gas in the new house yet, so on this particular weekend we stashed the money in with the pilot light on the gas stove. *No one would look in a stove for money*, we thought, *especially at the bottom, underneath the splash pan*. Also, there was a safe in the house, a floor safe in the master bedroom, but it was rusty and the tumblers wouldn't turn. The stove seemed like a pretty good alternative.

By the time Wall and I returned from the Crazy Horse, the rest of the crew was already in bed. We'd only been gone for forty-five minutes when we returned in the predawn quiet, and we parked in the street out front. The solitude and quiet was striking, in this city of constant and frantic turmoil. It was a peaceful scene, but it erupted in a flash that nearly cost Wall and me our lives.

A man stepped out of the bushes. He had a Halloween mask covering his face, and he was holding a twelve-gauge shotgun in his hands.

Wall and I looked at each other. We smiled for a split second, thinking it might be a prank by one of the crew, but our faces turned to horror when we realized—*no one on the crew had a shotgun*.

The shotgun man didn't say anything, but he motioned with the barrel of the gun to make us stop and back down the walkway, halfway to the street.

Another bandit came out from behind a retaining wall. He brandished an automatic pistol with a silencer.

Wall spoke up. "I don't know who you're looking for, man, but we're nobody."

"Shut up," Shotgun said, in a baritone voice. "We know you're the card players."

The guy with the pistol slipped around the corner to talk to a third party. The guy stranding back around the corner spoke with conviction. In the distance we heard him confirm, "Yeah, this is the right house."

The handgun looked like a .25 automatic—a baby Browning, maybe, with a silencer. The silencer was as long as the gun. I got a real good look at it just before it was planted up against my skull.

At that point, Shotgun told Wall to get down on his knees. Wall paused for a moment, as if he was contemplating some heroic move.

"I'll blow your fuckin' knee off," Shotgun warned.

We both got down.

The pistol packer pushed the silencer up against the back of my neck, right under my ear lobe. My heart was tripping along at 150 beats a minute.

I felt a tremor from the gun, like the trigger was being squeezed. I was preparing myself for the end—it was a numbing anticipation.

Wall, on the other hand, was fairly calm through the ordeal. I knew how he thought about things. He was keeping his cool, waiting to see how professional these guys were. He didn't seem impressed.

Personally, I didn't give a shit if they were professional or not. The little twerp with the baby Browning was flat fuckin' dangerous, whether he knew what he was doing or not.

The intruders tied our hands behind our backs with large zip ties. They searched our socks for money and took the money out of our pockets. Then they cinched our ankles together with a couple rounds of duct tape and put a strip of tape across our mouths, telling us to keep quiet.

At that point, Shotgun headed up the walkway to the front door and slipped inside. Baby Browning tapped us on the head with his silencer, and said, "Shhhh."

Then he went up the walkway and followed the lead man into the house.

Once they were both inside, Wall tried to talk to me, even though his mouth was taped.

We were on the ground, face to face. Wall whispered, "I think I can get out of these cuffs."

Then Baby Browning ran out of the house, bent over the top of us, and smacked us both in the head. The metal bit into my scalp.

"Shut up," he hissed. He hurried back inside.

Wall struggled to get his hands free, but I was forty to fifty pounds heavier than Wall, and a little stronger.

I thought, *If Wall can get out of his cuffs, surely I can get out of mine.*

I sucked in a deep breath and tensed every muscle in my body. I focused on one physical push of my arms—"Uh." This forced the riot cuffs to unzip.

My hands were free.

I stood up in a panic and started to tear the tape from around my legs.

I tried to ignore the unseen, ever-present threat of that Browning ringing out from a dark window.

I was working to help Wall get free, but he whispered, "Run, Red. Run."

CHAPTER NINETEEN

I hesitated for a brief moment, concerned about leaving Wall behind, but I knew somebody had to get away. I sprinted quickly out of firing range. Ten short seconds from the time I'd freed myself, I heard shouting from the house. Thinking my escape had been detected I dove for cover under a thick row of bushes.

I crouched and waited, my senses tuned as sharp as a needle. I tried to pick up some indication of pursuit, but all I could hear was my own breathing. I took a deep breath and held it. I could hear the snap of shoes clapping against the sidewalk—*tap, tap, tap, tap*. But the sound was constant and rhythmic, and it didn't seem to be coming any closer. At that point I realized I was hearing an outdoor faucet on the other side of the street. It was dripping onto a concrete splash pan that magnified and altered the sound.

I decided to run on down to a small convenience store on the corner, where I stepped into a phone booth and deposited the only quarter I had into the phone. Then I called the only person I could think of who might help, a name I'd heard only a couple of times, the Boss's attorney, Frank Cremen.

I told Frank what had gone down.

"Call the police," he told me.

I explained to him that I didn't have any more change, and asked if he would call.

He said, "Sure. Give me the address of the place."

I gave it to him. Then I headed cautiously back up to the

house. By the time I got close, a Metro Police wagon was already coming up the street with its lights off.

I stood in the middle of the street with my hands out to the side, wide open so they could see that my hands were empty. An officer hopped out of the wagon with a pump-action assault shotgun. He approached me with authority.

Shotguns must be a popular choice of weapon in Vegas, I thought. *At least they seem to be tonight.*

I threw my hands in the air and said, "I'm the one who called." But the officer was taking no chances. He forced me up against the patrol rig and patted me down for weapons.

They let me go, but they told me to stay put. Still, I felt like I had to inch a little bit closer. As I did, I could see another group of officers deployed in front of the driveway. They began to disappear around the front corner of the house in a single-file line, like a column of ants. It was the Metro SWAT team.

A moment later, another group crashed through the front door and yelled, "Freeze, Metropolitan Police Department."

The crew was caught totally off guard. They reacted as if a play had gone bad. When the door burst open, the yelling returned, and the crew must have thought that the robbers had come back.

Every door in the house was employed to produce our patented escape plan—but not all of the players got away.

I was out front when I saw Hiram being escorted out. "He's one of ours," I called out. Johnny was next. "Him too," I said.

Skate, Wall, and the Kid had managed to get away, and to further complicate things, the three holdup men had vacated the premises after my escape. They were never seen again. I discovered, too, that Wall had gotten free right after I did. He was the one who'd been shouting, trying to wake the others.

The police secured the area, and brought Hiram, Johnny, and me back inside. When we entered the house, the detectives found something of serious interest—the practice table and the casino record sheets.

They began to question us as if we were the criminals in this incident.

"What do you do for a living?" one of the detectives asked Hiram.

"I'm a carpenter," he replied.

He grabbed Hiram's hands and twisted his palms over. He was checking for calluses, but he found smooth card player's hands.

"Sure you are," the cop muttered.

Then the questions shifted to me. "What do you do?"

"I'm a mill worker in Oregon, but there's a timber shortage right now. I haven't worked in several months."

"What if we don't believe you either?"

I didn't know how to answer that. I didn't try.

Johnny had been taken to another room for special questioning. He told us about it later.

Hiram and I just sat there and looked at each other. We knew not to say anything, either to the cops or to each other.

When the officer who'd been interrogating Johnny came back into the living room, the police decided they'd done all they could for the moment. But because of what they found in the house, they appeared to think this had been a productive stop for them.

The cops didn't seem to doubt that the gunmen had

been there, and now that they knew where we were staying, they thought they could keep an eye on us as well.

When the officers finally left, Johnny said, "Dog's still in Vegas. Let's go see if anyone has checked in with him."

Even though Dog had burned out as a Kammeyer team player about four months earlier, he still lived here with his fiancée. Dog had played with Johnny and the Boss for about a year before he was forced to retire. He and Skate were college buddies and they both came to the crew at the same time. For some reason, Johnny thought that might be a place to meet.

"Get the money out from under the stove, Red," Johnny said. "Let's get the hell out of here."

I got down on my hands and knees, dug out the $40,000, and gave it to Johnny.

Then we grabbed our bags and headed out the door.

Once we were in the car and moving, we began to hash out the details of the entire episode. Even without everyone present, we went right in to what we knew to be facts. Then Johnny began to tell us what had gone on in the back bedroom with the detective.

"The cop had the sheet in his hand," Johnny started in. The sheet was the record we kept on every play of every weekend that we were in town. It consisted of where we played, how much we'd won or lost, and the rating of the dealer. We rated every dealer to remind us how many cards any particular brain could catch out of ten cards. Mostly we played a ten-dealer, which meant that the brain caught ten out of ten cards, but sometimes we would play a nine.

"He was asking questions like a speed-wired auctioneer," Johnny continued. "He was going over the sheet, one item at a time. The sheet had a handful of detailed plays on it, with dollar amounts next to each of the plays that we'd been in the night before. But when everything was totaled up at the bottom, it looked like the crew was up only $640."

We got a chuckle out of that. When we totaled up the proceeds of our winnings, we always dropped a zero on the sheets, just in case something like what we'd just gone through might happen.

Johnny went on. "'Only up $640?' the detective asked suspiciously." Johnny made his voice high and squeaky. He sounded a lot like that Metro detective.

"'We just do this for fun,' I told him. 'We get together once or twice a year and try to pay for our trip by counting cards.'

"But the cop was not deterred. 'That's not much to split between six of you.'

"I just kept my mouth shut after that," Johnny said. "Finally, the cop laughed and left the room. He went out to talk with two other suits."

"I wonder what happened to the bandits," I mused, not expecting either Johnny or Hiram to know.

"The guy who was questioning me," Johnny said, "indicated they were going to continue to pursue it. He told me they have robberies in Vegas every minute of every day, but when the robbers use guns, it puts the whole thing into a different category."

CHAPTER TWENTY

The sun was up and bright by the time we got out to the main drag. Johnny turned south and continued on to Dog's house. It was about eight miles outside the city limits, a modest ranch-style home with typical desert landscaping

I took a moment to reflect on all that had happened—both recently and in the past—as we turned onto Dog's little cul-de-sac street. There were bushels of colorful flowers in the yard that made his fiancée very proud. We were in a small development that depended entirely on the Hoover Dam for its existence—water from Lake Mead and power from the dam's giant turbines. Without the dam, Dog's place would be sitting in a desolate and uninhabitable desert.

Of course, that was true in spades for the city of Las Vegas itself. It was a town made possible by the unlikely alliance of President Franklin Roosevelt—building a giant dam in a desperate attempt to pull the country out of the Great Depression—and a little-known Jewish gangster from New York City named Bugsy Siegel, who was simply looking for a cheap way to make a quick buck.

It was like a family reunion when we pulled into the driveway. Wall, Skate, and the Kid were already there, and we all let out a sigh of relief. It was really strange to see them there. No one had ever talked about Dog's place as being the *backup*. For some reason, it just seemed natural for them to come here—which said a lot about Dog, and the way the crew felt about him. It certainly wasn't my idea:

three of these guys, including Dog, had tried to vote me off the crew six months ago. But I knew that they were old friends and I was just glad to be alive. And now they had some great stories to share with their old crew member.

Skate said something about feeling a little "woozy."

Dog knew that we'd been exposed to some kind of a heavy scene. We were buzzing with excitement, and when we all came together in the same room, we nearly brought the walls down.

Skate's eyes appeared to be plastered open with a look of surprise, a look that seemed to be glued on his face. As a remedy, he went on the hunt for some industrial-strength Pepto-Bismol. Things might have really gone to hell that weekend with the Boss out of town, but we'd pulled through in an admirable fashion, considering.

"What a rush," I said when the nervous chatter subsided.

"No shit," was all Dog could add.

Then, as if on cue, we shifted gears and began to assess what information we had—just like the Boss would have done.

The first order of business was to figure out who had put together the armed robbery. There were several possibilities: some loser trying to get his money back, one of the casinos, a former associate of the crew with inside information about the house and our operation, or maybe someone who had simply followed one of us home.

But the one name that kept coming up was our former arm, Chopper. Chopper had invested a large sum of money with Johnny eight months earlier. The investment had been paying 25 percent interest on principal per month. But after two months, the money stopped coming in and the principal simply drained away.

Chopper and his associate lost over $200,000 in what turned out to be a counterfeiting scheme. Johnny had been involved in the scheme on his own—totally detached from the crew. Personally, I thought it had been a selfish move on Johnny's part, to bring that kind of heat down on the crew. It was greedy.

Wall, Skate, the Kid, and I all came to the conclusion that Chopper must have been behind it. The deciding factor being that the bandits checked for money in our socks first. Only someone from the crew would have known to do that.

But the Boss had taught us to analyze every situation by breaking down each and every detail, so we discussed every minute that passed, from the time the assault started until the cops finally left. Eventually, we thought we had all the facts. After the pieces to the puzzle were assembled, they painted a pretty clear picture that Chopper was our man.

In any event, quick action by Wall and I saved the bankroll from a total wipeout. In this business the name of the game is keeping a tight hold on the money—this time it was *no harm, no foul*. But after this, Chopper had to be considered dangerous and not to be trusted.

We decided to get out of town without further delay. Hiram and Skate made some quick calls for airline reservations to San Diego and San Francisco, while Johnny, Wall, the Kid, and I all flew in Johnny's plane to San Diego.

On the flight back, I sat in the rear seats with Wall. I was curious about what had taken place at the house after I left.

"I got loose from my cuffs," Wall said, "right after I told you to run. Then I ran out into the street and started yelling. After that, I scooped up some little pebbles from the gutter and started throwing rocks at the windows. I was hoping to break the glass, to shake up the intruders and wake up the crew.

"I never actually saw the robbers run off, but the lights in the house came on, and then Johnny stepped outside.

"I ran up and met him. Then we headed back inside to tell Skate, the Kid, and Hiram what was going on. We all wondered where in the hell you had gone."

I told him about my sprint down to the convenience store, and my call to Frank Cremen. "I got Frank to call the police," I said. "Of course, it was his idea."

"I wondered where all the cops came from," Wall said. "When I heard them coming up the street, I thought it was the robbers coming back with help. That's when I ran off to find Skate and the Kid.

"After that, we were just running through the night, waiting for gunshots to ring out behind us."

"That's exactly what I was doing twenty minutes earlier," I laughed.

"For a while we took refuge in somebody's storage shed," Wall went on. "We laid low there for about an hour. Skate threw up several times. The heat from the robbery attempt was a little more than his stomach could handle. We just stayed quiet and waited for some sounds of danger from the night.

"Finally, we got back on our feet and made our way out to civilization. Then we caught a cab and came out to Dog's."

As far as I was concerned, that pretty much pieced things together. But even if Chopper had been the mysterious guy around the corner of the block wall, we still had no idea who his two accomplices were. And, if it was Chopper, it would have been a one-time heist, so there wasn't much chance the police would find them—and as long as the money had been saved, there was no reason for the Boss to pursue it either.

I sat back in my seat and let my thoughts return to the phenomenon of Las Vegas and Hoover Dam. I must have looked like I'd drifted off into space, because after a few minutes Wall asked, "What are you thinking about, Red?"

"Hoover Dam," I told him. "Originally they called it Boulder Dam, but they changed the name to Hoover sometime after World War II."

"Yeah, I think that's right," Wall said. "They named it after President Hoover."

"Think of the expense," I told him. "They would have had to change all of those signs; encyclopedias in libraries would become obsolete all across the nation, overnight. History books in public schools would have to be updated. And it all could have all been avoided."

"Yeah," Wall asked, "how's that?"

"Back then," I said, "Herbert Hoover could probably have changed his name to Boulder for a couple hundred bucks."

CHAPTER TWENTY-ONE

The Boss returned a few days later. He talked with Johnny first about what had happened. After that, he came to me. After I gave him the scoop on the robbery, the cops, and the aftermath, all he said was, "Good job, Red."

Then he went right into the money that Wall and I were responsible for. "What happened to the sixty grand, Red?" the Boss asked.

"Well, Boss," I told him, "Johnny had it all."

"Uh-huh," the Boss said, with a short tone. After that, he stormed out of the house in a big hurry.

The next weekend, when the crew got together, Johnny wasn't there. We were at the Desert Rose Hotel on the Strip. It was a shabby single-story row of rooms, kind of a drab place, but it was perfect for our now-mobile operation.

The Boss sat the crew down and explained the latest developments. Johnny had stolen $30,000 from him. He would no longer be associated with the crew.

"Johnny used the money to pay a second mortgage on his house," the Boss told us. "He'd been living way beyond his means for some time.

"So, here's the deal," the Boss continued, "Nobody is to associate with Johnny in any way. Understood?"

"Yeah, Boss," the crew said in unison.

"Johnny and I have come to a verbal arrangement. It will last the rest of the year. From now on, I will keep his cut of the play until all of the money is made right. If Johnny asks you to play with him, and you do it, you will never play with my crew again. There will be absolutely no exceptions to this ultimatum."

The Boss glanced around the room and glowered at us. Then he asked, "Understood?"

"Yeah, Boss." And, of course, I had no problem at all with that.

The Boss had been very calm and businesslike during his delivery. It must have hurt to have to expose his friend that way, but he didn't show it. He came right to the point and gave the reason for his decision.

"My relationship with Johnny is over," he said.

They had known each other for over twenty years, and they'd been good friends. When it ended, the cut was made with surgical precision—clean and precise.

The Boss appeared hardened by this breakdown of trust. He'd done what he had to do, and it was obvious that he didn't like doing it.

As for Johnny, his problems had just begun. The house he bought was costing him a fortune. He also owed Chopper money, and he was in debt to other people as well.

Johnny went downhill fast after that, but the crew did the only thing we could do in the wake of the split. We carried on with business as usual.

It wasn't long before we got wind of a rumor that Johnny had formed his own crew and was playing in Vegas. Not long after he formed the new crew, he got caught and was run out of town.

The Boss decided that, after the holdup fiasco, we would stay in a different hotel each week. We would have to move the base of operation each time.

The Kid would begin braining, along with Hiram—we'd

suffered a few casualties and needed to reload. The Boss had the skeleton crew of Hiram, Wall, Skate, the Kid, myself, and four or five arms.

The gaming commission was still trying to put a stop to our operation. The Griffin Agency was keeping the authorities informed—they'd spotted us at different locations on several separate occasions. They were beginning to piece together our mode of operation, and they'd assembled a pretty good file on the *McCloud Gang*, which is the handle by which we'd taken to call ourselves.

Then too, the Metropolitan Police Department had its own *Metro anti-cheat squad,* and they had experienced a number of encounters with what they still called the *Kammeyer Group*.

With all of these agencies working together to stop us, we were quickly becoming a Vegas headline act. A growing number of law enforcement officials would like to be able to claim the arrest of the Kammeyer Group as their own personal trophy, so there was an element of competition between them.

The authorities had been close in the past, but the key to the whole thing was to catch the crew in place, at the table, with the gaff in the brain's hand. If they couldn't get all of the evidence at one time, they simply didn't have much of a case. And in order to get a conspiracy conviction, they would also need some film, or maybe some still shots from the cameras above—pictures that would demonstrate a definite connection between the brain and the arm.

If they couldn't catch Steve Kammeyer and put him out of commission, they would never be able to stop the mirror team. And as their pursuit continued, we were extremely resilient, with continued training and new faces on the crew each time we were spotted in a casino.

We continued to work nearly every weekend, traveling all over Nevada. And we'd taken to disguising ourselves, to gain a little playing time and to stay ahead of the heat. Wall and the Kid dyed their hair. Skate and I chose different types and shapes of glasses, along with different styles of dress. The Boss actually purchased a goatee and a mustache. A fake hairpiece of any kind, though, was extremely noticeable up close, so he would never play at a table with his disguise on.

One morning, the crew was ready to set up a play in the Hilton. As we went through our routine around the tables, something seemed a little out of place. Of course, Skate noticed it right away. He signaled two of us over to the slot machines.

"Look at Bob Griffin," he chuckled. "He's curled and dyed his hair."

We pulled on both collars of our shirts, and gave the cash-out sign to the Kid, the Boss, and Toosh. Pulling on both collars at the same time was a new sign we'd developed. It meant that Griffin agents were in the casino.

After that, all Mr. Griffin could do was to stand and watch the crew disappear out through the door.

Actually, there had been several Griffin agents that Skate had pointed out to me over the course of the last several months. We didn't really know any of their names, so we just referred to them all as *Griffin*. They were mostly retired or off-duty cops, hired through the agency by the casinos. Bob Griffin was a six-foot-tall, slender, dark-haired guy, and he seemed to be the leader. Then there was Mike—six-two, curly, sandy hair. Mike appeared to be their number two. The other two that I had names for were Phil and Rick, both of them a little over average height and stocky. They were easiest to recognize—they looked like cops.

Skate was doing his job well. He paid close attention to every detail in the casino, and the Kid was coming into his own as a brain.

Once a brain had logged his solo hours, he advanced to the stage of working for the crew in live play. But there was another milestone a new brain had to reach. A brain in training didn't begin to make their 25 percent cut until they'd won at least $50,000 for the crew. It took the Kid just over a month to hit fifty grand.

The Boss appeared to be pleased with the Kid's progress, and it seemed like Hiram was beginning to fade. From the very start, Hiram had to push himself to get past his original fear. Winning money seemed to sustain him for a while, but eye-to-eye confrontations with the law had taken a toll.

Hiram seemed to feel like he'd made enough money, and that the risk was no longer worth it. There was no big ceremony when the Kid took the lead in the hot seat—and Hiram appeared ready to give it up.

Hiram was a good man to have around, and the crew would truly miss him, but he simply left one weekend and never came back.

CHAPTER TWENTY-TWO

The Kid and I had both been training to be brains, but the Kid progressed much faster. The Boss was interested in developing me as well. He needed a backup brain in case the Kid got caught, so I trained intensively.

I found it difficult to position the mirror on the table correctly. My arms were short and I had a stocky build, all of which made it hard for me to get comfortable at the table. To give me a feel for the pressure a brain had to encounter, the Boss told me carry a gaff everywhere I went. I would practice slipping it in and out of my coat and shirt pockets in restaurants, bars, and airports, and I tried to develop a better posture at the table. Good brains had to handle the gaff very deftly.

It was nearly a year and a half since the Kid and I had started, and as Mother's Day weekend approached the Boss had gathered up a crew for a trip to Vegas. We rented a car at the airport and I drove to the hotel. I'd taken to driving the Boss around San Diego, and weekend wheel duty had become part of my job. We headed straight to the hotel and made our plans for the evening. Then we got back in the car and left for Vegas World.

I parked the car and put the keys under the seat—as the Boss had always instructed. The fact of the matter was we never knew for sure who was going to make it out of a casino. We had to leave the keys so anyone who did get out could use the car.

The Vegas World Casino was something of an anomaly

for Las Vegas. It was a plain building, by Vegas standards, and it sat on one corner of a city block—a mediocre-sized, rectangular building, unattached to anything else around it.

The crew entered the nondescript building and went to work on setting up a play, but we couldn't find a playable dealer.

Giving it up, Skate gave the cash-out sign and we headed to the car. But just as the Kid and Skate were approaching the parking lot, they saw our car backing out of its space with a black woman at the wheel—a black hooker, and she was obviously trying to steal the car.

The Kid was quick to act. He yelled at the top of his lungs and jumped at the driver's-side door. Then he managed to open it.

Skate was yelling as well, and the hooker was so surprised she simply slammed on the brakes, jumped out, and started running.

The Kid and Skate were still outside of the car, so they had to physically grab it and hold on to keep it from rolling.

There was no reason to chase the hooker. That would just develop into a hassle we didn't need, but losing the car would have been a costly delay—just one of those things that happen in Las Vegas.

We went on about our business after that. The Boss had some good people in place, probably the best crew he had ever assembled, and he guided us to a serious winning streak. In fact, things were going so well for us that it provided an opportunity for me to log my solo hours as a brain.

Over the course of the last few months, as I'd been training and breaking in new arms, I'd also been practicing five to six hours a day with the mirror. So, not wanting to miss any playing time with the crew, I left right from Vegas one weekend to go on to the next step in the process. I intended to get this stage of the training over and done with in time to play on the following weekend.

I arrived at the Boss's house in South Lake Tahoe, just as I had a little over a year and a half earlier, but this time I was the only one there. I was on a solo mission, and it was turning out to be really scary. I was nervous even sitting around at the house, thinking about all the things that could go wrong. But around midmorning on Monday, I went to Harvey's, a place we seldom played, and I began to look for a dealer.

The only reason I could muster the courage to put the gaff on the table was because I'd practiced over and over. I could have done it my sleep. Besides, I had no high roller present to draw attention by betting the big bucks. As I sat readying myself to get the mirror on the table, I felt pretty naked. There was no field marshal here to cover my backside. But this is how the Boss had to progress in the beginning, so he made the rule that every brain had to go through this initial first step. He wanted every new brain to feel the fear, the intensity, and the apprehension.

I put the gaff on the table and simply sat there for several hands, playing my cards without even looking for the dealer's hole card—I couldn't bring myself to look in the mirror. I played for another ten minutes, and then I took the mirror off the table, put it back in my coat pocket, and left the table. I walked about fifty feet, turned around to look back at the table that I'd just left, and everything seemed perfectly normal. But I didn't feel normal when I was sitting there.

At that point, I began to talk to myself—*Red, you dumb motherfucker. You've got to take the next step and get that hole card. So, suck it up, you piece of shit.*

I took a deep breath and let it out again as I cinched up my belt a notch before returning to the table. The Kid and I would often stop, take a deep breath, and cinch our belts up before the first play of every weekend. It helped to ready ourselves and calm our nerves before heading into battle.

I took the gaff out, set it on the table next to a glass of tomato juice—just like practice—and I was able to pick up my first hole card.

Wow!

I looked around, and since everything was normal, I continued on for forty-five minutes until the dealer went on break.

I left the table just as the break dealer came on duty. Then I did the same thing as before—went fifty feet towards the exit, stopped, turned to see if all was normal, and discovered that there was absolutely no reason to doubt myself. That gave me all the confidence in the world, but I knew not to let my guard down.

I went back to the house for lunch. Then I filled out my log sheet—I'd managed to put in seven-tenths of an hour at the blackjack table. I needed four and three-tenths hours to complete the five hours required for solo training.

I continued on.

I went through my routine at a number of different places over the course of the following three days, and I encountered only one incident. I was at a different table at Harvey's, when a dealer asked, "Sir, what is that in your hand?"

I looked at the lady and said, "There is nothing in my

hand." Then I got up and left the table. I immediately headed out the door. But that was a wake-up call—*a brain could never let his mind wander, not for a minute.*

By the end of my time in Tahoe, I'd managed to log in a total of five hours on the sheet. Then I flew back to San Diego. Proud of my accomplishment, I wondered if Wall and the Kid would want to hit the town.

CHAPTER TWENTY-THREE

The team's success at its peak was overwhelming for me. The crew was working hard and living well. It would take us the better part of three days to fully unwind from a weekend play—just in time to crank it all back up again.

When we had time off, we would socialize together, traveling, partying, and having a good time. For a bunch of young men, most of us not yet twenty-five, we were living very well indeed.

We had to deal with the job's stress, to be sure. Still, it was an exciting time to be alive for guys like Wall, Skate, and the Kid and me. The combination of youth, money, and travel offered a freedom few could imagine, much less live. Especially in Southern California during our free time, hanging out down by the beach.

It is written in the great beyond of gambling, however, that in the game of blackjack, hot streaks do not last forever. The same went for the game of life. We couldn't get lax, or let our guard down. We stayed sharp and kept winning without stirring up much trouble. We were operating at peak levels, knowing we had to watch ourselves very carefully. We didn't want to get overconfident. We were playing so sharp and tight, we almost felt unstoppable.

The problem was, winning was a sure way to draw attention in the casinos. The crew's good fortune was beginning to set the stage for a swing in the momentum.

A few months before the summer of 1982, winning was

coming so regularly that playing time was reduced to just minutes before the casinos would get sick and tired of getting whipped at *twenty-one*. They just glared at the arm when he would place his bet—and the sheet began to have a lot of *point-ones* on it. By way of explanation, in the terminology of the sheet a full hour of playing time was sixty hands, or 1.0, on the sheet. That was one hour. If the crew managed to log one hand per minute, it would take six minutes to post a 0.1, or six hands.

Many of the plays were reduced to a fraction of the time we'd been used to. The bets were up, and the playing time quick. We were becoming so well-known that it was hard to play for more than five minutes.

More and more, the outside agencies were trying to stop the *Kammeyer Group*. They would work with the casinos to gather information and to identify patterns of operation. Johnny's new crew created a lot of the heat when he tried to hire and train his own crew. Johnny's bunch failed miserably, and fortunately they were so bad, a good crew could still pull it off. Although Johnny's crew got the town stirred up a bit, and the Boss was not happy about that. The casinos were all looking for the mirror.

For all the information, pictures, and encounters our opponents had in their possession, their best piece of workable information was a pattern they'd discovered about the guy with the mirror. Of course, at that time, we didn't know it.

For instance, it seems they'd come to realize that the guy with the mirror always left a glass of tomato juice behind.

Once they identified this trait, they communicated it to casino staffs around town. Of course, the glass of tomato juice was what the brain would use to hide the gaff. That made it normal for the brain to have his hand on the table, holding his juice. The procedure couldn't be carried off unless the brain had something to hold onto.

So tomato juice became the problem. It was like waving a big red flag under a pit boss's nose. It got to the point that, as soon as a pit boss saw tomato juice at the second-to-last seat at the table, he was on the phone.

One morning, we were at the Stardust, the Kid sat down at a table and a pit boss went right to the phone. There was no arm at the table yet—no nothing. And the call went right to the Metro anti-cheat squad. Skate gave the heat and cash-out sign, so the Boss, Wall, the Kid, Toosh, and I all left the casino.

CHAPTER TWENTY-FOUR

When we were safely back in the car, we headed for the Marina Hotel Casino at the end of the strip. But just as we arrived, Wall saw a Griffin agent park and get out of his pickup. I recognized the man as Phil. He seemed to be headed across the street to the Tropicana Hotel.

And the Boss, always on his toes, seized the moment. "Red," he said. "Go see if his Griffin books are in that truck."

He wanted me to walk by the truck and look in the window for the casebooks that were used by the agents—pictures of suspected cheaters and case histories. These books often show all the known gaming violators in the state, along with their associates. We called them *the Griffin Books.*

I walked nonchalantly past the truck and back to the car. I noticed too that the Boss had moved into the driver's seat.

"They're in there, Boss," I said. "Three of them."

"We need to get 'em, Red."

The Boss positioned the car down the street and waited for the Griffin man to move on. Twenty minutes later, the guy came out of the Tropicana, fired up his truck, and headed down the Strip.

The Boss started the car and followed. He kept his distance. The truck turned in at the parking lot of the Silverbird, where the agent parked and walked the fifty yards into the casino. He appeared to be making his rounds.

Skate made his way quickly over to the corner of the casino. From there he could see both the front door of the building and the truck in the parking lot.

Once Skate was in place, I bolted over to the truck to get the Griffin Books. The door was locked, but the window was down a couple of inches or so. But I couldn't get my arm through the window to unlock the door. I motioned for Wall to come and help.

Wall hurried out of the car, watching Skate all the way, for it was an intense moment for us. When he got to the truck, I pointed to the window and said, "Reach in and unlock it."

I pulled down on the edge of the glass as hard as I could, with my feet actually leaving the ground while Wall slid his arm through. As soon as he unlocked the door, he left to help Skate field marshal. I opened the door and leaned inside. I couldn't help but think that the Griffin agent would coming out at any moment. I identified the three mug-books, tucked them inside my windbreaker, stood up, closed the door, and headed back to the car.

Skate gave me the *cool* sign, telling me—*No sign of the agent.*

Wall and Skate and I all arrived back at the car at the same time. The Boss was standing outside with the doors opened.

But just as we were getting in, he asked, "Red, is everything 100 percent clean?"

"No, Boss," I replied, thinking about it. "My fingerprints are all over that window," I said in a panic.

"Go back and clean it up Red," the Boss ordered

We kept a spray bottle of Windex and some paper towels in the car at all times, items we needed to keep the gaffs clean. I tore the top off of the Windex bottle and emptied it into the wad of towels. This time, with no field marshal to watch for heat, I ran over to the truck and wiped down the outside window and the door.

Then I opened the door and did the same to the inside, with my hand wrapped in the damp towels. I couldn't help but think the agent would be coming any moment. I hurried to wipe down everything I could think of that I might have touched. Then I rolled up the window, locked the door, checked the casino entrance, and sprinted back to the car.

As we drove off, the Boss asked, "100 percent clean, Red?"

"Yeah, Boss, 100 percent clean."

CHAPTER TWENTY-FIVE

Once we were back in our hotel room, we were excited about our recent escapade. At the same time, we were very much aware of how enraged the authorities would be if they were to catch the perpetrators who'd stolen the books out of the agent's pickup—and I was the headliner for this one, personally. I didn't consider myself as a thief, I was just doing what I was told by my boss. Besides, I was worried about myself being caught later.

Skate and Wall repeated over and over how much *balls* I'd shown in following the Boss's order to go back and wipe the fingerprints off the truck. *"Without even flinching, Red,"* they kept saying. And though it was quite the caper for the crew, it would greatly escalate the warfare with the agencies if we were ever linked to the incident.

The Boss took the books and went alone into his room. It was a good ninety minutes before he came out and called us together.

"These books were never intended to be seen by anyone's eyes outside of the authorities'," he started in. "We are not supposed to have them."

The Boss was speaking in a very serious tone. "I want all of you to look at them. All of our pictures are in there, side by side, on the same page. They have been working very hard at stopping us. But before you look at this, I want every one of you to swear you will never breathe a word about this to anyone, and I mean it." He said that last part with a very serious look and tone.

The Boss caught the eye of each and every crew member—we all nodded in agreement. A slight nod of the head by each man was as good as his spoken word to the Boss.

After that, we pored over our individual sections of the book. We were at it for over an hour. We looked long and hard at our own images on the pages. Only a few of our most recent members had been left out.

There was a caption under each mug shot. It stated the person's real name, any aliases he used, and these phrases: *Obtains dealer's hole card with a mirror* and *Associated with Steve Kammeyer.*

I found it curious to discover that the Kid and Hiram, from the main crew, were not pictured. They did have pictures of some of the arms, though, crew members who were never caught doing anything. These were mostly photos that had been taken from back in the slot machines, with a telephoto lens.

The books shined a bright light on how close the crew lived to danger in the pits. This material demonstrated the extent and veracity, and the very serious effort that had been mounted against us. We could see that their efforts were becoming more organized as well.

When the weekend ended, the Boss took the books back to San Diego, and they were never seen or mentioned again.

A few days after the Griffin Books caper, the Boss paid Wall and I an extra $500 each. We looked at him curiously, but he just winked and put his index finger to his lips, as if to say "Shhh." Obviously it was for last week's escapade.

We understood. We were never to speak another word about this incident, ever again. Not even to another member of the crew.

CHAPTER TWENTY-SIX

Not long after the Griffin Books incident, I found myself at a table as a brain. It wasn't by design. A search for a dealer had ended at the Holiday Casino on the Strip. The Boss told the crew to go to the Barbary Coast.

But the Kid had gone to the restroom, and he didn't get the word to go to the B.C., so everyone else went over to the B.C. to check things out. Once inside, the Boss found a dealer who was aching to be played, but I was his only available brain.

"Got a piece on you, Red?" he asked.

"Yeah, I got it," I replied.

The Boss turned and walked away at that point.

I watched him, anxiously, for about ten steps. Then he reached around and scratched the back of his leg—it was the *follow me* sign.

I was being called into a play to brain for the first time.

As I followed the Boss toward the table, I felt my heart rate quicken and my breath shorten up. I could feel myself breaking out in a cold sweat. My skin was tingling as I worked to maintain my composure.

Months before, the Kid had seized the opportunity to move up in the operation. Once a brain had logged his solo hours, he had the respect of all the other brains who had faced this moment, all four of them. As much as I'd told myself in the past that I'd be ready for the challenge, I had no idea how it would actually feel until I found myself carrying the weight of the gaff as I approached the table.

I had butterflies in my stomach. A term we used on our high school football team, just before the game started—the last feeling before battle.

One thing in my favor was that it had been the Boss who had found this *ten-dealer*—and he was standing right there, touching his nose to signify which table was to be played.

A *ten-dealer* was a dealer with whom a decent brain could catch ten out of ten hole cards, and I wasn't about to show any weakness now. Whatever I felt inside, the Boss was only going to see composure and eagerness on the outside. I drew a lot of strength from the boss's training at that moment.

As I approached the table, there was absolutely nothing on my mind. All of the practice and standing behind the brain for a solid year made my every movement routine. I neared the table and looked in both directions in a nonchalant manner. My nerves were calm, but I was ready to run at any second. I'd been trained to always have a consistent, calm facial expression. *Icy calm*, the Boss called it. And at that point, the training seemed to take over. It was as though I was somewhere else in the room, watching myself from a distance, like in a dream:

I sit down in the brain seat and set my chips and a beer on the table—I'd ordered an English porter; it was dark and opaque like tomato juice.

Anyway, my concentration and attention go right to the dealer. I study exactly how she will pull the card off the deck. I get the gaff ready for the table; I look at my field marshal. He sees what I'm doing and gives me a brush across his forehead, letting me know—things are cool.

He knows I received the signal and goes back to watching for heat. I know he'll give me a signal and get me out before they can react. It's an intense moment. I put a chip in the circle so the dealer knows I'm now in this game. I stack my chips in two stacks on the table right next to my left hand, and leave a gap directly in line with the exact spot where the dealer will show the hole card. When the dealer shoves the card underneath the upcard, I need a perfect angle to see that card.

I look at my field marshal again; he gives me the cool sign. After taking the gaff from my pocket, I hold it under the table to adjust the paper clip. Then I look both directions and bring the gaff onto the table, while making a move to grab my beer. I softly set the mirror on the table, using the chips for a screen and the bottle to hold on to. This all takes place in less than a few seconds. The dealer throws me my first card. I stop it and hold it as I glance at the field marshal. I then pick up the first card—and at that exact moment, I lift my left hand off the table, just slightly, and expose the mirror. My second card comes. I stop it with the little finger on my right hand, while holding the single blocking card—the card is used as a screen as it blocks the gaff from the dealer, and from the pit boss as well. He's standing right next to her. I stare into the mirror and wait for a flash. I try to appear as though I'm looking at the card in my hand and not the gaff.

Then I see the hole card flash underneath the upcard, but the gaff needs to be adjusted ever so slightly. So, I scratch my arm, which signals the crew to get the arm seat—in order to secure the seat— while I adjust the gaff. The dealer pays the winners and takes the chips of the losers. Then she starts another round of cards. I stop the first card and wait for the perfect time to pick it up. This will expose the gaff for just a brief instant. Then I see my second card and a flash. I can see the hole card perfectly—so I signal the field marshal to go get the arm.

Another minute goes by, and I play my hand while waiting for the big money to come to the table. I count the rack for black chips, so I know how many there are.

Toosh hits the table and throws down $500 in cash and says "Play it." Now the entire crew is in place. Wall is about two steps behind me, Skate is positioned across the pit, the Boss is in the slots, as usual—and Toosh is playing $500 a hand.

Everything is cool.

The pit boss comes over to meet Toosh while I catch the hole card and give Toosh the "stiff" sign. I do this by resting my fist on the table—that means the dealer's hand totals from twelve to sixteen—so the dealer has to hit. One card will very likely bust her hand.

Toosh has a pair of tens, so I roll my hand over to let him know to split the tens. He looks up at the pit boss and asks, "Should I split these?"

The pit boss shrugs and offers no advice. Toosh splits the tens and takes a hit on the first hand. He gets a six and stands. He motions for a hit on the next hand and gets a seven. He stands on that.

I rub my thumb and forefinger together and glance at the field marshal at the same time, signaling Toosh to up the bet on the next deal to two $500 hands, and again I check for any sign of heat with Skate.

Then the dealer works her way over to me and I stand. She turns the hole card over to reveal a total of fifteen and hits it with an eight, busting her hand.

The dealer pays the winners and starts to deal another hand.

As it turned out, Toosh won the first six hands in a row. And while he was in the process of doing that, my fear began to dissipate. By that time, I was really tuned. My competitive nature had kicked in.

But just fifteen minutes into the play, the Boss cruised up behind the table and told me, "This is your last hand."

At that point, we were about to play three hands at five hundred again.

The dealer had a six up. I saw a ten slide underneath. Then Toosh flashed me a pair of threes on his first hand. He split the treys and was dealt another three. He split that three and drew a fourth three. Then he proceeded to draw four tens (or face cards) on the four threes. He stayed on four thirteens. Then he doubled down on the last two hands. He had $4,000 on the table.

The dealer worked through me and the other players, but the other players were all mostly finished at that point. Then the dealer turned over the ten. She ended up with a busted hand again.

I was gone before Toosh was paid off for the big win.

I saw the Boss giving Toosh the cash-out sign, and then he followed me out the door.

I couldn't wait to get out. My adrenaline was pumping like never before. I was so pumped up, I felt like I was going to explode.

By the time we arrived at the car, we were as clean as could be, and the Boss started giving me high fives.

The Kid was back at the car by then, and he climbed out to see what all of the commotion was about.

JERRY REEDY

The Boss was giggling like a little boy. "Red crushed 'em for ten," he declared proudly.

The Kid was in shock. "He won ten? Where?"

"Yeah, ten grand at the B.C.," the Boss said.

"Nobody told me to go to the B.C," the Kid said.

The Kid was upset for a brief moment. He had totally missed an opportunity and let me slip in. A slight crinkle of the forehead told me that he was a little ticked off, not at me but at the situation. Also, he wasn't there, so he wouldn't get paid on the big win. He should have been the one braining, not me.

But his initial reaction quickly passed. It was replaced by a sense of happiness for his friend.

"You put the gaff on the table at the B.C., Red?" the Kid asked, surprised.

"Yeah" was all I could say with a big smile on my face. After all, we had learned how to use the gaff together.

It was my first play for the crew, and I'd managed to get it done somehow. Although it had taken every ounce of energy I had to do it.

We met Toosh at the Sands, after he'd been cleaned up, and he jumped into the car.

"You're one lucky son of a bitch, Red," Toosh's Philadelphia accent rang out.

I was grinning from ear to ear.

"How much, Toosh?" I had the honor of asking. It was a great feeling.

"Well, let's see. I was in for, uh... nothing. And I cashed out for, uh... I cashed out for eleven-six."

"Yeah!" I yelled out. In ten minutes I had won $11,600.

The Boss, as usual, knew how to cap the moment off perfectly. "Let's break it," he declared.

CHAPTER TWENTY-SEVEN

We headed for the hotel to get paid—to break the bankroll—which is what we called it when we got paid. The Kid was up $12,600, and I was right behind him at $11,600: $24,200 racked up by the two young brains. It was an electrifying moment for the well-paid crew. We packed our stuff and headed for the Boss's plane.

Later that night, back in San Diego, a bunch of us headed out for a night on the town. We intended to celebrate the big win all through the night and well into the next morning. But the Boss planned to celebrate in his own way. He said he was going to read a good book and get a good night's sleep out of the deal. He was carrying one of the thickest paperback books I'd ever seen.

"*Atlas Shrugged*," he told me, holding the book up in his left hand, "by Ayn Rand—over a thousand pages."

A couple of days later, I met the Boss for a cup of coffee, and he expounded on the book. "I can't even pronounce her real name," he said, speaking of Ayn Rand. "One of those great big, overly long Russian names, but rumor has it that she was looking for an American pen name, looked up, and simply took the name she found right in front of her—*Rand*, off her Ingersoll Rand typewriter.

"She came from a prosperous family of merchants in Russia, but the Bolsheviks confiscated all of their holdings during the 1917 revolution, so they came to America. That being the case, it's no surprise that *Atlas Shrugged* is an exposé of the advantages of capitalism over the collective.

"Frankly, her analysis seems a little simplistic to me," he went on. "I don't see how you can privatize absolutely everything.

"The lady just recently died, Red, but she would have been extremely proud of us. We just cleared over twenty-four thousand bucks, and our initial investment was one little thirty-nine-cent mirror."

"Yeah, Boss," I laughed and said. "Only in America."

We finished our coffee and our conversation as we headed off in different directions to carry on our beautiful day in San Diego.

From that point on, the Kid and I split the braining duties. The Kid worked 60 percent of the time, and I snapped up every play I could get.

But things were beginning to deteriorate, especially in Las Vegas. It seemed like things had always been deteriorating, since day one. It was no surprise to any of us, especially the Boss.

The authorities knew who individual members of the crew were. Photos were compiled and distributed. We were getting harsher looks from the pit bosses. Dealers were constantly schooled about our group—the group with the mirror—and most of them had seen our pictures. It was hard to turn a buck under those conditions, so the Boss developed a counterattack to offset these cumbersome obstacles. He decided to take the show on the road. He wanted to find other places to play, places outside of Vegas.

I was starting to crumble, too. My nerves were getting to me, and the Boss seemed to know it. He gave me a couple hundred dollars one day and told me, "Red, go get yourself a sexy blond hooker, on me."

Maybe the Boss was onto something. "All right," I said,

"I'll be back in a day or two."

"Relax," he told me, "and get some rest."

"I'll do that, Boss."

Although sometimes we did have relationships and flings, it was hard to keep a woman around for very long. We couldn't tell them what we did for a living, we were gone almost every weekend, without explanation, and if it was someone we cared about, we didn't want to lie to them. All of that left too many questions for a poor girl with a strong sense of nesting, and she would eventually simply fade away from lack of trust. I didn't blame the girls. It was one of the sacrifices we chose to make during this time of our lives

Later that same week, I discovered that the Boss had been flying his plane all over Nevada, and his reconnaissance mission had paid off. He decided to make a run on Laughlin, Nevada.

In 1982, Laughlin was a small gambling town with three casinos: the Riverside, the Colorado Belle, and the Pioneer Club, and the parking lots always seemed to be loaded with motor homes. And there was a buffer zone of sorts, another little town in a different state right across the Colorado River—Bullhead City, Arizona.

The Boss decided to land on the Bullhead City side, at the Municipal Airport, but before we did, we got a real panoramic view of Laughlin, Nevada, from the air. It was a tiny gambling town, sporting a nice layout by the river. It was kind of exciting to be at a new place, and we all sat back and smiled as the Boss repeated his favorite mantra: "More toilets to clean up, boys."

Once on the ground, the word *desolate* entered my mind. It was the word that best described the local surroundings. In the midst of the sunbaked desert, the Colorado River rushed by, providing a watery border between the two states. But crossing into Nevada, from any state, never failed to pump up the crew, and once we'd worked our magic, leaving always brought a strong sense of relief.

We got rooms in a hotel on the Bullhead City side, away from the casinos and out of Nevada. We'd be safe from prosecution on the Arizona side—but in this business, of course, we were never really safe from extermination.

The first thing we noticed was there was no place to hide if any heat started up. A little town in the desert left no room for running. There was no scenery to blend into. There weren't thousands of tourists; there weren't multitudes of flashing lights, and there were very few street corners to disappear around. It was all open, one street and five buildings—and one of those buildings was the police station.

As good as we were, it would be hard to cope with this landscape.

I called a cab for the crew and we rolled away from the hotel. The river, only a quarter mile away, was flanked by a large parking lot. It all belonged to Don Laughlin, the owner of the Riverside Casino. From the Arizona side, the Riverside Hotel looked like a huge tombstone with hermetically sealed windows. It was narrow and flat, and seemed as though it could blow over in a strong wind. The casino itself was in a more conventional building, adjacent to the hotel.

A little further on, we discovered the other two casinos, and they also had parking lots on the Arizona side. We wondered about that, but then the Boss spotted some shuttle boats crossing the river. The boats were loaded with tourists and casino employees—both coming and going. These shuttle boats were simply a convenient way to travel back and forth, saving gamblers and employees fifteen minutes of driving time each way.

The Boss instructed the cabbie to drive through Bullhead City, so we could get a firsthand view of the layout there. After that, the cab took us over to the casinos, and we went the extra fifteen minutes across Davis Dam to get there.

We kept ourselves tight-lipped in the presence of locals, especially cabbies, and we carried on distracting conversation as if we were simply there to have fun. When we arrived at the Riverside Casino, the cabbie was told to wait for half an hour, and we went in to scout things out.

There were a number of variables to deal with. This was a unique setup. The Boss's first order of business was to lay out a plan of attack. He realized that special backup plans and contingencies would have to be worked out. We couldn't just simply rush in and drop the gaff down on a table. We'd have to test the waters for this new money pool before diving in. The crew hit the streets and cased out the area around the casinos. We had to know the streets as well as we knew the twists and turns of Las Vegas.

It wasn't such a tough chore for our seasoned crew. We would always check out the entrances and escape routes before we'd play. We had to scope out each security team and observe the way they worked their rounds. We had to know how dealers dealt the cards, how their break system worked, and we needed to become familiar with the overall operation of each casino. We also had to know the various table limits, and of course, we had to look for playable dealers.

The Boss made one thing clear—our photographs had probably been circulated here, too, so we needed to be on our toes at all times.

When the crew completed our recon, we regrouped, hashed out all of our outside escape routes, and headed back to Bullhead City. We walked over to the hotel restaurant to grab a bite to eat, and while we ate, the Boss went over what input he had. He told us that we were going to wait until after dark to play here for the first time. "If we need to find a place to hide," he said, "darkness would give us better cover."

We figured we'd be heading back later that night, and that eventuality was made official before lunch was over. The Boss's strategy depended on getting the brain out at any cost, and just knowing that would give the brain a better chance to perform. The Boss told us that the shield of darkness would be the key to everything. So later that evening we boarded the shuttle boats in shifts. Wall and I went over first, in order to distance ourselves from the rest of the crew.

I couldn't help but wonder what the Colorado might have looked like in this area before the dams and cities and agricultural interests began to draw water from her. I recalled reading about the Colorado pikeminnow—a fish found nowhere else in the world, now endangered. It could reach a length of five feet and weigh up to eighty pounds. I puzzled over why they called it a minnow, as I watched Wall study the people.

Wall, serious as always, soaked it all in. With eyes narrowed to slits, under a thatch of curly light-brown hair, he studied the folks as they filed into the boats. He picked up on the dealers and pit bosses immediately, as they shared boats for the ride over. The tourists were chatty and festive, but the casino staff didn't display the same revelry. Wall could pick out the staff as if they were wearing flags.

CHAPTER TWENTY-EIGHT

The Boss had rented a car and drove it over to the Laughlin side, with the Kid, and Fats. He wanted to have the car handy for a fast escape. Fats was a fairly new arm who had trained with the crew at the same time Toosh did. He was a jolly, heavyset fellow in his early forties. His smile was infectious, and he used his hands to mold his words when he talked. He was smart, out of a job, and well-liked by the crew and his peers. More importantly, most of the pit bosses quickly took a liking to him.

The three of them convened in the pits to set up a friendly game of blackjack. We were all still engaged in reconnaissance work.

Wall and I took a leisurely route to the Riverside, and we spotted a helipad in front of the casino. We quickly realized that if they had a helicopter in their security arsenal, any escape through the desert on foot was out. We ignored it then, yet it made us all a little nervous.

We met up with the others while I was double-checking exit routes, making sure there were no dead ends. The Kid was doing the same on the opposite side of the building. The Boss stood and dropped quarters into a slot machine, while he worked out the chain of command in the pits. He quickly identified the pit boss, and a few seconds later the shift boss came through for an uneventful chat, so we had him pegged too.

I watched as the Boss scanned for other players, big shots who might be running the show. Then a fellow walked into the pit area—six feet tall, gray hair, thin, and smartly dressed in a suit and tie. I recognized him from some promotional material I'd leafed through earlier. It was Don Laughlin, the owner himself. He was the founder of this little paradise on the river. In this part of Nevada, Laughlin was *the man*.

The casinos were roomy and packed with tourists, a perfect atmosphere for the crew to play. When the casinos were crowded, we could blend in better. The downside to that, of course, was that it was hard to get the right seats at the tables.

My understanding was that, up until recently, the difference between the Nevada side of the river and the Arizona side was striking—gambling on one side and welfare and poverty on the other. But this was a case where the Ayn Rand theory of economic prosperity proved to ring true—due to the affluence of the gambling houses on the Nevada side of the river, Bullhead City was booming with new construction, too.

After we went through our procedures, we met up at the blackjack pit and began to scout. I caught a dealer with potential and sat down, instantly losing the qualms and tensions that had surfaced earlier. I called Fats in after a couple of hands. While we played, Wall, the Kid, and the Boss scanned the scene for heat.

I came in wondering how the pit would react to $500 hands. Surprisingly, we didn't draw too much attention, and I was able to play the dealer out to his break.

We had a good run.

When I called for the *cash-out*, the crew instantly kicked into cleanup mode. This was a new angle, and we'd managed to work it well. Like any weekend, the first play was tough, but it helped when I managed to jump on a dealer and get on the scoreboard early. The prospects for this virgin territory suddenly seemed very promising.

We casually made our way out of the casino, looking for signs of trouble as we went. I headed straight for the shuttle boats, while the rest of the crew kept an eye out. Things appeared to be cool, so the others headed for the docks as well. We crossed over, got our gear together, and headed for the airport.

We loaded up and were off the ground thirty minutes later. Once airborne, the consensus was the Laughlin operation had been a success. We'd needed a boost. There'd been talk of calling it quits lately, due to lack of places to play.

But the Boss knew this wasn't a long-term solution to the heat problems. We would wear out our welcome in a real big hurry in a town as small as Laughlin. Las Vegas, however, had become a full-alert zone; it was a complete burnout. The Boss needed a broader base of operations. He would need to develop fresh faces and fresh places—so he hit the phone on Wednesday to organize a crew for the following weekend.

He called Wart in Spokane. Wart was the athletic director and a math teacher at a local high school there. A weekend with the crew would make a nice break from the kids. Wart got his nickname from the Boss, as we all did. The two of them had grown up in the same small town in Idaho. Wart was a large man, forty years old, six-feet-two and 240 pounds. He was raised on a farm to be as tough as nails, and he had a solid work ethic, plus he was used to long hours.

Wart had run with the crew, off and on, for a couple of

years. The Boss was anxious to get him involved again. Wart also had a brother named Mole who'd worked a few stints with the crew. He ran the gaff out of the Riviera once, and saved the Kid's ass. In every instance, Mole had performed well, but eventually he had to turn in his track shoes. He couldn't afford to blow his career, which is what a felony conviction would do. He'd been moonlighting in the casinos to supplement his income as a Navy helicopter pilot, but after a recent promotion, he had too much to lose from the service.

Wart, on the other hand, was willing to come to Las Vegas.

We picked him up and took him to the hotel. The Boss brought Toosh along as an extra arm. We also had Wall, Skate, and the Kid lined up for the play. Originally, the Boss had brought Skate aboard as a runner—tall, slender, and alert, he'd been a track star at Rutgers University when he was in college.

We had a solid crew, to say the least, probably the best expanded crew the Boss had ever assembled. This weekend's twist featured a two-crew attack. The Boss intended to work two brains in the same casino at times, but there were only a few places left where he felt confident about doubling up that way.

So out we went on the following Friday night. We headed right back into the hostile Las Vegas storm. Wart was to play on a crew with the Kid at the Imperial Palace. It was a place we seldom played, though. This was only our second visit ever.

The first play was designed to be a single crew, an experiment to feel things out.

The Imperial Palace consisted of a short, squat building

with an Asian motif. It had a series of pagoda roof structures over the entrance. The front of the building was bathed in a soft blue light that left me with a nagging *blue* feeling of foreboding as we entered.

Wall and Skate both worked as field marshals, and I planted myself right behind the Kid. The Kid liked the feel of having a friend close by, a friend who could take the gaff and run like hell. I was kind of proud of the fact that I was a pretty good screen-runner. This added a sense of security that helped the Kid direct his attention to the cards. As usual, the Boss sat off in the slots with a newspaper, hoping to appear disinterested in the entire casino scene. Toosh stayed over at the bar.

Then Wart got the call and headed to the table.

I had a handle on the vibes around the scene. It seemed like everything was okay, so I casually leaned over to a tourist next to the Kid and said, "It sure is cool in here." That simple statement meant *Ream 'em, Kid. It's all clear.*

Once the Kid had Wart in place, the $500 hands were on the table—$500 to $1,000 being the standard opening wager these days.

But after a while, the Kid started to sweat. The play had reached the twenty-minute range and we were up forty-three hundred.

Suddenly, Wall picked up on something. Skate was on it as well. A pit boss had made a quick move to the phone. Wall reacted instantly. He gave the cash-out sign to the Kid, just as I whispered, "Give it to me." The Kid and I performed a perfect handoff.

We left in opposite directions.

When the pit boss turned around, phone in hand, the Kid was gone. I looked back to survey the situation. The pit boss looked like he'd been stabbed in the ass with a cattle prod, and he acted accordingly. He scrambled about and turned a couple of circles, with an expression on his face that reminded me of Little Bo-Peep after losing her sheep. He looked everywhere, but the suspects were gone.

That is, except for Wart. Wart still stood at the table with his bet down, now reduced to $100 a hand. He was going about his business like nothing unusual had happened.

But there was something at the table the pit boss didn't like. Maybe it had something to do with some educational bulletins that he'd received. He acted like he wanted to stop Wart. Of course, now he seemed unsure of himself, so he couldn't take it any further.

The Kid, Wall, and I got back to the car without incident. We scrunched inside and waited for Skate. Skate stayed to watch Wart cash out.

Skate's simple crosscheck ensured that the arm had gotten out okay. It saved hours of searching for him later. Skate was at the car moments later.

"They hated him, Boss," he said. "They were all over him. They watched every step he took, all the way out to the cab."

"Let's go clean him up," the Boss said with confidence, and he drove off unruffled. We went down the Strip toward the MGM, took a left on Flamingo Road, and parked across the street by a side door. The Boss sent two field marshals in to perform the cleanup job—extra caution was needed on this one.

"He definitely has heat," the Boss stated flatly. Of course, we all knew that.

We all kicked into cleanup mode. We knew casino

security would follow Wart back to the crew. Then they'd try to take us all down.

CHAPTER TWENTY-NINE

Wart told us about his ordeal. He'd showed good sense and directed his first cabbie to a casino about ten blocks from the backup. He was an experienced arm who operated with patience and composure. He swaggered into the Frontier like a guy who'd just had a good run at the table. Then he powered down a couple of drinks. Anyone watching would think Wart to be a waste of time as a suspect, but IP security thought they had a real prize in front of them. When he pinched a cocktail waitress on the butt, and caused a small scene, most tails would have given up on the guy.

Thinking that he might be under surveillance, Wart wandered down to a roulette table, dropped $250 on one play, and left. He caught a cab after that and headed for the MGM Grand, feeling pretty good about the heat situation. But he was an arm, and arms were taught to never look over their shoulder so they wouldn't appear to be guilty.

Once he was inside the MGM, Wart noticed Wall standing thirty yards off to the right. Seconds later, he saw Skate up near the bar. Both field marshals began to pore over the scene, observing everyone in sight. Wart made his way to the bar. At that point, Wall and Skate both detected heat simultaneously.

A houseman from the Imperial Palace was still on Wart's tail.

The IP guy was trying to be casual, but the crew was onto him the moment he came through the door. Skate cleared his throat to let Wart know there was heat. Wart wasn't surprised. He played it cool. He confirmed the signal and went on about his business.

The house dick made his way over to the front desk to place a phone call. He kept his eyes on Wart the entire time. As the house man milled around, keeping Wart in view, he appeared as if were waiting for someone else. A moment later, a detective from another agency came through the door—a man in very nice suit—either a Metro anti-cheat squad or a Gaming Control agent.

The field marshals didn't know the man in the suit, but they knew he was trouble. The house man motioned the other fellow over. They obviously knew each other. The two of them moved off to the side, and the house man began to point in Wart's direction.

After a brief moment, the new agent moseyed over to the bar, and turned to study Wart from another angle— probably trying to recognize him from pictures he might have seen in some mug books—but as far as we knew, Wart had never been pictured.

Then the agent in the nice suit began to look all around the casino, to see if he recognized any other patrons in the casino. He was a suspicious cop, probably one of the top dogs in his agency.

Skate and Wall were aware of the agent's agenda and hid behind the slot machines so the nice suit couldn't see them. They knew their pictures would be familiar to him. They needed to stay out of sight. But the heat couldn't place Wart with anyone, even though two of his comrades were close at hand.

The two field marshals drifted back and kept an eye on the cat-and-mouse game. The entire crew was under surveillance most of the time, but there was little danger. We could cover the heat better than they could keep track of us. The two agents had no cause to detain or arrest Wart. They were simply there to shadow Wart until he met up with the rest of the cheaters—and that was not going to happen.

It was pretty much basic police strategy—stick to one you know, and let him lead you back to the rest. But we were a step ahead of them with our 100 percent cleanup policy. The two men's pursuit had been thorough, but their lead wasn't adding up to much. After no one got in contact with Wart within thirty minutes, the two cops had had enough. The agent in the nice suit shrugged his shoulders, in a gesture that indicated he didn't know the man in question. Wart's routine was purposely set up to decoy casino security. It appeared as though it was working— again.

But things were moving too slowly out in the car, so the Boss sent me in for an update. Wall saw me as I came through the side door. He made eye contact and flashed the *follow me* sign. We disappeared into a maze of slot machines.

"The Boss sent me in to see what's up," I told him.

"Wart has big heat," Wall said, "a house dick from IP and a Metro detective. But it looks like they're about to give up. Wart's handling it well."

I nodded.

"Hey! There they go," Wall said. "The two guys by the front door. They're history."

Wall was right on the money. The heat departed less than fifty yards from where we stood.

"Skate and I will clean it up from here," Wall said, as he

left to go to work on Wart.

I headed back to the car to update the Boss, while the other three went through procedure. Wall gave Wart the signal to go to the car, and Wart acknowledged. He got up from his seat and headed down the long hallway to the side door.

We watched from the car as Wart came out the side door and headed down the sidewalk. Skate stayed back to make sure that Wart wasn't followed. A minute later he came out the door behind Wart.

Wall was the last to exit. He gave us the *cool* sign, letting us know it was okay to pick them up.

The pickup was executed and the crew headed to the hotel.

Everyone was stretched a little thin by the extended cleanup of the arm that night. It took a little longer than most, but we had to stay with it until the arm was clean. If we didn't follow procedure, the cops could easily catch us.

The Boss let us sleep in before a Saturday morning sortie to the Stardust Casino—one hour of bonus rest; quite a gesture. But the sands were constantly slipping through the hourglass on these weekend missions—and time was a key element in the formula.

CHAPTER THIRTY

The wake-up call came at seven in the morning, but the memory of the heat from the night before stayed with us. The Boss, though, was right on top of the situation. He understood the physiological variables that came with the human element of the crew. Sometimes it was hard to get us started after a tough night, and lately, every working night was tough.

So, the Boss adjusted. He began to take the crew out to breakfast most every morning. A little food and a couple of cups of coffee helped warm us up. It cost him a few minutes of playing time, but it improved the productivity. Modifying the crew's routine produced positive results, so the Boss made it standard policy—and on this day, after breakfast, we made our way to the Stardust.

We'd been to the Stardust several times before, but it was during my first few months with the crew and I had so much to learn at the time, I wasn't able to take note of the unique characteristics of the individual casinos. But after I became better acquainted with things, I started to look into the origins and histories of the various gambling halls.

The Stardust was an older casino. It was built in a two-story configuration with security, accounting, and management on the second floor.

Construction of the Stardust was originally started by Tony Cornero—also known as Tony the Hat—a Prohibition-era Southern California bootlegger. But Tony died at a craps table, under mysterious circumstances, just as the project was being completed. After that, the casino was taken over by another gangster, one John Factor—a.k.a. Jake the Barber. He was the half brother of the famous cosmetic tycoon Max Factor.

At the time of Tony the Hat's untimely demise, John Factor was looking for something to do. He'd just completed a ten-year sentence for mail fraud a few years earlier, and he was sort of between jobs.

But Jake the Barber was a little smarter than the average crook. He was wanted in England, after having been convicted in absentia on a stock swindling charge, and the pressure was on from the Brits to have him extradited. He even had himself kidnapped at one time in order to avoid the British authorities. But as it turned out, John Factor had been the largest single individual donor to John F. Kennedy's 1960 presidential campaign. As a result, just before he was scheduled to be deported back to England, Attorney General Robert F. Kennedy was authorized by his brother to grant Jake the Barber a presidential pardon.

I came away from my research more than a little disillusioned after reading that.

In addition to everything else, the Stardust—one of the mob-owned casinos famous for questionable dealings at the time—had come under investigation by both federal and local authorities. There was suspicion of money laundering. But these were the folks we were dealing with—and we knew it—as we all filed out of the car and warily crossed the street to the casino. We knew that we definitely did not want to get caught here.

We descended into the pit from our respective angles and then clicked into scouting mode. The Kid never let the crew forget that he was their lead man. He was working hard to find a play, knowing I was waiting in the wings to play myself, and he found a dealer quickly. He looked at two hands, and then called in the arm.

When a brain worked that efficiently and confidently, it didn't give a new brain much of a chance. If I wanted to brain in the future, I'd have to earn it. Most everyone on the crew had tried to become a brain, at one time or another, but only a small handful ever managed to do it.

The Kid had Wart on the way in minutes. The field marshals were keyed up and on the lookout—both of them remembering the heat from the night before. And it wouldn't be long before they were put to work.

Wart stepped up to the table, threw down a $500 bet, and a pit boss went for the phone before the first hand was even dealt. As he dialed an eight-digit number, Skate got close enough to catch the brief and direct communiqué.

"I think they're here," was all the pit boss said.

In seconds the phone was in and out of the pit boss's hands. But before the receiver was back in its cradle, Skate coughed out loud and gave the *all-around heat* sign by grabbing both tabs of the collar of his shirt.

The crew dissipated into the busy casino before the pit boss had a chance to move. We got out quick and clean. We met up at the car—all of us, except for Wart. He caught a cab, knowing he had to make a preliminary stop before working his way to the backup joint.

The Boss fired up the car and headed for a viewpoint of the front door of the Stardust. He wanted to see who was responding to the call from the pit. The heat was coming down fast these days, and the Boss wanted to know who was involved in this interagency effort. We sat in silence as the Boss watched the front door. Then, right on cue, two unmarked police cars rolled up to the curb. Two men got out of each rig.

We didn't really know what agency the cars came from, but we suspected the Metro anti-cheat squad. We watched the occupants fly out and run inside. A minute later, they sprinted back out, jumped in their vehicles, and left in different directions. The Boss whipped the car out of the parking lot and decided to tail one of the cars. He was seeking more information. He wanted to know where the cheat squad thought the crew might be heading next. Since the two cars left in different directions, they obviously had a couple of joints in mind.

But in less than a minute, the Boss's counterintelligence operation backfired. The Metro agents were a hundred yards ahead of us. Then they suddenly hit the brakes, left a puff of smoke, and whipped their car around and came back toward us in the opposite lane. Once they were by us, they hit the brakes again, caused a cloud of smoke, and whipped around again so they were right behind us. They started to follow the Boss's car.

The crew was stunned for the most part.

I snidely retorted, "Pretty smart cop, huh, Boss?"

CHAPTER THIRTY-ONE

The Boss seemed too preoccupied to render a response. He made a couple of attempts to lose the pursuit, but the traffic was too tight. No need to risk exposure with a law-breaking car chase. Besides, they weren't chasing us to arrest us. They were simply showing the Boss how smart they were.

Still, the Boss kept up a pretty good pace. He tried to distance himself from the heat behind us so he could think. Then he began to drop crew members off at different casinos along the strip.

The Kid went first. We let him off at a small casino, one frequented by local folks on fixed incomes. The Kid was inside the joint in seconds, and the Boss and his four remaining passengers continued on.

Metro continued to follow.

We knew the Kid wouldn't stay in the casino more than a few minutes. He'd catch a cab back to the hotel, grab his stuff, and beat it to the airport. He'd be on his way to San Diego within an hour.

Toosh was next out of the car. He got out at a place that looked more like a diner with a few slots and an ongoing Keno game. His procedure mirrored the Kid's. The same for the next three stops. I was last to get out of the car. I kept my face hidden from the pursuit so they couldn't recognize me from any photos as I hurried through the front door of the Flamingo. At that point, the Boss was alone in the car with the tail still in place.

The crew, however, didn't just smooth through this whole process. We were shaken up. Paranoia had set in and we felt as though our every move was being watched. We managed to stick to procedure, though, until we had vacated the area. Wall and I flew home via Los Angeles, while Skate headed for his new place in San Francisco.

That left the Boss alone, to shake himself loose. He told us later that he pulled up to the valet parking at the Sands, threw the keys to the rental car to the valet parking attendant, and then ran inside. After that, he moved quickly down the corridor and on out a side door. He then made a quick check all around, crossed the street, and entered the Frontier Club.

He went straight through the Frontier Club and exited through another door, caught a cab to the hotel, got his stuff together, and cabbed it out to the airplane. He went through his preflight inspection, which now included a bomb check—*there had been threats.* After submitting a flight plan, he fired up the engines and was in the air within minutes.

Knowing his airborne progress could easily be charted, he flew to a small airport in L.A. County. He stayed there for a few hours, before cruising into Palomar Airport later that night.

We all knew it was hard for the Boss to be patient. We also knew he'd be anxious to find out how the rest of the crew had fared. But he didn't have to worry. He was in command of some extremely skilled troops by this time.

When the Boss arrived at his house, he got on the phone. He found me, the Kid, and Wall all together on his first call. Then he dialed Toosh—he was okay, and Skate was well. Having confirmed all of this, he had one more call to make—a call back to Las Vegas.

Wart had been laboring through a long five hours at the backup casino. When he finally got the call, he wasn't surprised to hear the Boss tell him to leave town. Things were too hot.

Wart checked in again later that night. He thought he'd been followed to the airport, but he was able to board his flight without incident, and he made it back to Spokane.

It wasn't quite the red-carpet treatment for the crew this time around in Vegas—it had been hot before, but now it was boiling. The inside joke was, *our crew was the hottest act in town, Wayne Newton included.*

A break from the heat in the Vegas night might be a good move right about now, and that desolate patch of desert-turned-casino out along the Colorado River looked more attractive than ever.

CHAPTER THIRTY-TWO

The following weekend, a commercial flight that we were calling the *Bullhead Express* loaded up with the Kid, Wall, Skate, Fats, and I. Footsie accompanied the Boss. We flew in to Vegas, rented some wheels, and drove the ninety miles to Laughlin. The Boss had set up shop at a hotel on the Bullhead City side of the river. Once again, we went over all contingency plans and went to work.

The Boss maintained his usual low-profile post in the slots at the Riverside. The crew was working so well, there wasn't much for him to do anyway. He paid a certain amount of respect to us by staying back and letting us work. He seemed to sense our frustration, but as playing time in Las Vegas diminished, we were eager to give the casinos here another go.

By staying in Bullhead City, we were able to operate pretty much unnoticed in Laughlin, and we worked hard straight through Friday night.

The Boss woke the crew around seven the next morning, and coaxed us out for some breakfast. We sat dutifully in the restaurant, awaiting orders, not knowing that the Boss was about to shatter the early-morning calm. He returned from one of his daily trips to a newspaper stand with an April 3, 1982, copy of the *Las Vegas Sun*. We sensed something was up by the way he approached the table. He looked like he'd seen a ghost.

He slapped the heavy paper down on the table in front of Wall and the Kid and me. The front-page headline read

"California '21' Cheaters Sought." The caption below read "They did it with mirrors." This was a better morning jump-start than a strong cup of coffee ever could be. We jerked up to full alert and began reading the story. This was a new level of heat—front-page heat.

We maintained a cool front for the restaurant crowd as we pored over the article. It was written by one Scott A. Zamost of the *Las Vegas Sun* staff, and read as follows:

Metro police have been alerted to a sophisticated blackjack scam in which a team of gamblers use tiny mirrors to detect a dealer's hole cards, police and gaming sources said Friday. The cheaters may have gotten away with as much as $10,000 per day. Metro's anti-cheat squad followed the group of eight men, all from Southern California, to at least four major casinos two weeks ago. A source said Metro officers could not arrest them because they were not spotted attempting the scam. "We are familiar with the people" a Metro source said. "We are just waiting for them to come back." Members of the group were videotaped at one casino allegedly using the mirror but the scam was not apparent on the tape.

Intelligence Comdr. Kent Clifford confirmed there was such an alleged scam, but could not immediately provide details. "We never did see the mirror," a Metro source said. "We had information that they played prior to us getting to them. All we could do was just follow them. They are pretty sophisticated for what they do. It's big money and unique," the source said.

The alleged scam, as described by the sources familiar with the case, involved the use of a mirror slightly less than 2 inches long and wide. A team member who sits in the fifth position on a blackjack table positions the mirror on the table, using a small paper clip as a stand. The mirror is hidden by the gambler cupping it inside his hand. When the dealer looks at his "hole card," the card is picked up by the mirror. The gambler then signals to another person betting at the table. By knowing the hole card, a player may obtain a healthy advantage over the casino by knowing when to "hit" or "stand" and adjusting the basic blackjack strategy.

The group uses several "blockers" who stand around the table attempting to obscure the mirror, the source said. Group members usually wait until they find a dealer who is sloppy and might accidentally show the hole card. Gaming sources said the group typically "goes in and out fast," and may average $10,000 a day for the team.

On their latest visit to Las Vegas, the group stayed only three days, supposedly because they knew Metro was watching them, the Metro source said. While none of the alleged cheaters has been arrested, the source said, two men connected with the group were charged with cheating crimes within the past two years involving use of a mirror.

"They are big time," the source said. "But you have to show the mirror was used. We didn't see them take a 'run' at anyplace." Metro has been aware of the group for several years, the source said, and February's trip was the first time they were in town in six or seven months. There was no evidence the group used any "insiders" at casinos to help them cheat. Local experts familiar with gambling crimes said the use of a mirror to cheat at blackjack was not common in Las Vegas. They said mirrors are more frequently used in poker games.

The Boss had already absorbed the article. He waited for us to read it, in anticipation of the conversation to follow. One thing stood out—the knowledge the authorities had about how we functioned was extensive, almost a mirror image of how we'd studied the opposition and learned the jobs of casino staffs and authorities. The article was fairly accurate, but there were a couple of glitches. The first mistake was, *the hole card was* not *picked up when the dealer checked his hand.* It was actually picked up when the hole card was loaded under the upcard. The second misinterpreted item was this: *"February's trip was the first time they were in town in six or seven months."* Actually, we'd been in town and working, cautiously, a couple of weekends a month.

Before that, we'd taken December off to prepare for New Year's Eve, but in the previous eleven months we'd been to Vegas at least every other weekend. Evidently, we'd been able to get in and out a number of times without detection. There were many occasions when we went into a casino and the system worked perfectly. We'd often set up a play, were detected by the casino staff, and we were able to hand off the mirror without incident. The casino would detain the arm, but they'd find no evidence, which left doubt in their minds about the use of a mirror at all. It was obvious to us, however, that we'd been studied very carefully.

The greatest advantage the Boss had with his crew was the element of surprise. The authorities who were trying to catch us never knew when, or where, we would show up. And we were careful to never develop a pattern of consistency that would allow the casinos, or the cops, to anticipate our next move. We planned our attacks accordingly, for that exact reason.

Our mode of operation was never the same twice in a

row—ingenuity and surprise were our best friends. The authorities were actually looking for us twenty-four/seven and they were wearing themselves down. When they did actually see us, they were so surprised that the field marshals could read it on them before they could react to catch us.

There was one time when we entered the Hilton one Sunday morning and found three Griffin agents there waiting for us. They had coordinated with the Hilton house dicks in an effort to catch us in the act. Apparently, they'd studied the eye-in-the-sky film, and they'd figured that we had, indeed, been playing there for quite some time.

They must have waited for weeks, or maybe months, until we came back that morning. But Skate spotted all three men, even though they were all wearing disguises. To their credit, they did spot me as I came into the casino. But Skate was awesome at his job. He instantly coughed and signaled *heat all around,* so we headed for the exits, without incident.

The one lead agent, however, the one we all called Bob Griffin, was giving us our own heat sign back. He was grabbing both collar tabs of his shirt as we walked out the door. He knew Skate, so when he saw Skate initiate the *heat* sign he mimicked the signal with a sarcastic expression on his face.

The Griffin agents' body language changed from inflated to deflated in a matter of minutes. They really looked disappointed.

But getting back to the issue at hand—the issue involving the newspaper article in Laughlin—the Boss immediately went to work on a game plan to offset this challenge. I could tell he was working on it while we finished breakfast.

With the morning meal out of the way, the Boss hurried us out the door—he was obviously ready to take action. We drove all over Bullhead City and took every copy of the *Las Vegas Sun* out of every newspaper kiosk we could find— convenience stores, casino gift shops, restaurants, and hotel lobbies. The Boss would drop in thirty-five cents and then take every copy in the canister. We did the same across the river in Laughlin. It wasn't long before the rental car trunk was overflowing with hundreds of copies of the paper.

But the *Sun* had both a morning and evening edition. There was no way we were going to stop the distribution of a major Las Vegas paper completely. Taking the morning paper was just to slow the flow of information in the Bullhead area, and once the Boss was satisfied with the great paper theft, he moved on to the next phase of his plan. He told us to get ready to play, though it didn't look like he was sure how we would react to that order. He seemed pleased to see we were ready—not one man flinched or had a negative comment.

It made sense to play before the news spread any further—*head 'em up, move 'em out* was the unsung motto, and we all knew it.

We started at the Pioneer Club. Wall found a dealer that kept the hole card low and close to the table. I'd begun to specialize in the low, fast dealers. I'd developed a knack for catching the tough cards. The Kid preferred the card higher off the deck.

I sat down to play and called in the arm. It just happened to be Footsie, even though he had burned out in

Vegas for winning too much money. Because the crew was playing a new town, he'd been offered another chance to arm.

Footsie was a college roommate of Skate's. He came with a heavy New Jersey accent and the demeanor of a cocky East Coast, Ivy League prep boy. He stepped up to the table and began to bet the big hands. The pit boss cordially said hello and watched the play for a few minutes.

Just as the crew was easing into the game, the dealer jolted us to full alert by casually commenting, "Did you read in the paper about those blackjack players that use mirrors on the table?"

"They'll never get away with it here," the pit boss shot back, with a cocky tone to his voice.

Footsie had a little trouble digesting that exchange, and he emitted a slight choking noise that was picked up by the dealer. The dealer looked over at Footsie with a smile and said, "You must be one of them."

"Oh, yeah," Footsie replied, as he rolled his eyes in obvious denial.

This came off in a joking manner, but I was sitting there with a piece on the table. It wasn't funny to me. This job was tough enough without bringing up that disastrous newspaper article.

I played on for another ten hands. Then, without warning, I got up and left the table. I was a pretty tough, well-seasoned veteran by then, but my nerves were shaken. Wall, Skate, and the rest of the crew headed for the car. It turned out that they were all surprised I'd stuck it out as long as I did.

CHAPTER THIRTY-THREE

We regrouped at the car. The Kid expressed the same concern that I had. It didn't take long to realize we had to call the weekend off. There was little to be gained by pushing it, in light of our newfound fame. The Boss understood and flew us out of Bullhead City. He didn't say a word the entire flight home. Footsie, Skate, and Fats returned the rental car to Vegas.

We arrived in San Diego County feeling a little beaten down. Our severely depressed Boss unloaded his luggage and headed off to regroup. Wall, the Kid, and I went back to the apartment I shared with the Kid. On the way, we discussed our future—a future that seemed very bleak indeed.

"Looks like we're history, boys," Wall said.

"Yeah, for good this time," the Kid agreed.

"The casinos will have our pictures everywhere," I chimed in, with a longing sigh, in order to let everyone know I still wanted to play.

We didn't know what the Boss was thinking, but we could read the handwriting on the wall. And if that wasn't enough, all we had to do was pick up a copy of the *Las Vegas Sun*.

He proved relentless though, the Boss did. He had us back in the air a few days later, headed to Tahoe to feel things out there. He was going to run us through Harrah's first. That would give us a pretty good idea of how hot things were up in the mountains. We'd enjoyed some success there in the past, with little heat around the gaff. But we'd been featured on the front page now. Before, we came and went unnoticed.

One thing that drew the Boss to Harrah's was the big table limit, two thousand bucks a hand. The Boss realized that the way things were, he had to kick the bets up in order for the formula to work. Playable hands of blackjack would be hard to come by now.

But surprisingly, the trip paid off. We played Friday night and Saturday before drawing any heat at all. The Kid and I both played twice before the casino became suspicious.

Core members of the crew felt we had handled the pressure pretty well up to this point. We'd come a long way, but casino sprints, court dates, and interrogation sessions had all become part of a day's work. We couldn't expect things to get much better, either. In the past, the stress of our jobs seemed overwhelming, but it all paled in comparison to the present conditions.

Our secret was being splashed across the front pages of the biggest papers in the region. The one article that stated, in big bold print, "California '21' Cheaters Sought" sported two other headline stories on that same day. They were in smaller print than ours and stated "Killer Storm Roars Across the Sierras" and "Argentine Troops Invade Falklands."

Our small band of raw country boys had upstaged some quality news stories. Our cover had been blown. We'd been successful for some time because we were well schooled and well organized. After looking at the Griffin Books—the books I cabbaged out of that agent's pickup a while back—and gaining front-page attention in the papers, the full scope of the authorities' efforts against the crew had come to light.

Top experienced career men from a combination of agencies all across the state were going balls-out to stop us. After reading the challenging comments in the papers, we'd become aware that the battle lines had been sharply drawn. Play from this point forward would be in the face of much tougher odds. It had been hard enough to work the gaff in the first place. With our pictures distributed, along with this front-page stardom, the odds swayed back in the favor of the casinos.

The Boss ordered us to keep up with our weekly workouts, and to run a few extra miles to keep in tip-top shape. "Stay sharp, you assholes," he barked.

And when we got the call to play the following weekend, we had to confront all of that additional pressure. It bordered on insanity to go up against the defensive effort that the authorities had put together. Still, we had to pay the bills, and more than that, we didn't want to let the Boss down. Quitting at this point was not an option. Sticking together and seeing it through had its own rewards. Now it was more than the money. We'd never know just how good we were if we backed away at this point. The integrity of our grade was related to the difficulty of the test.

We knew we'd have to either back the bets down to two hundred a hand to keep the heat off or bet a lot higher so that the few hands we could play would actually pay off. These circumstances demanded both patience and adjustments.

When Friday came, a tentative crew assembled at the airport. But as the Boss approached his airplane, he noticed something out of place. A red tag and some plastic-coated chains had been wrapped around the propellers. There were padlocks holding them in place.

"What the fuck is this?" the Boss howled. Wall and the Kid and I shook our heads in disbelief.

"Come on, you guys; let's go see what the fuck is going on around here." We headed for the building that housed the airport authorities.

The Boss walked into the main office and found three men standing by the windows that overlooked the runways. They seemed to be expecting him.

"Excuse me, gentleman. Why are there chains and a red flag on my aircraft?"

A small, slim-looking man with glasses stepped forward with a folder in his hand. "My name is Ron Hughes," he said. "I'm from the Internal Revenue Service. According to our records, you owe $14,860 in federal taxes on that airplane. It can't be moved until that money is paid."

The agent spoke with a smirk on his face, shaking his head from side to side, but the Boss reached into his sock, pulled out three five-grand packets of $100 bills, and threw them at the agent.

As the money bounced off the agent's chest, the Boss said, "Now, get your fucking chains off of my airplane. And hurry the fuck up."

The agent's face went blank. He stumbled when he stooped to pick up the money. He seemed to be in total shock—along with the rest of the men in the room, including us, who had witnessed the ordeal. The agent gathered himself quickly and headed toward the aircraft. He counted the money as he went.

He unlocked the chains and we were on our way.

CHAPTER THIRTY-FOUR

We flew into Reno, rented a car, and checked into a hotel. Instead of pushing right into a play, though, the Boss traipsed around Reno and tried to get a feel for The Biggest Little City in the World. It gave us a few extra moments to calm ourselves before strapping on some balls and taking a shot at little Goliath.

When the Boss finally turned us loose, we were ready to go. We opened with a successful blitz through the massive Reno Hilton. The Kid went in and got right after it. The Peppermill was next, with the same results. We were on the lookout for heat from the moment we approached a casino—any casino—until we were out of it. But once we were up and going, our skills kicked in, and that gave us that slight advantage of the element of surprise.

After the Peppermill, it was out to Sparks to play the Nugget. At that point, we were up $12,000, which meant we were still able to turn a buck under some very tough conditions. Once we left the Nugget, we turned in and got a good night's rest.

Right after breakfast on Saturday morning, though, a wrench fell into the works. The first place we hit was Harold's Club—a casino that really took a guy back to the Old West. But the minute a play started to come together, a pit boss caught a face he recognized. He went right to the phone, and Wall picked up on four dangerous words: "I think they're here."

The heat sign was flashed and we faded away without

incident. The deceptive sense of calm from the night before was gone in an instant. No chance for a play to even begin. But this was part of the job—get knocked down, get back on your feet, and take another swing.

As time went along, another fearful axiom began to develop—*as we got better, we made more money, and the more money we made, the more the authorities would be willing to spend to catch us*. And, of course, they had a lot more resources than we did. It was like the local militia taking on the Chinese army. They could just keep coming in waves until we were finally worn down.

These were dangerous times, and we all knew the Boss had a lot to think about. *At what point was he crossing the line? Was he putting his crew in jeopardy for personal or selfish reasons?* He wasn't the type to just walk away from confrontation. Life had confronted him with some brutal shots in the past and found him to be a man who stood out in a crowd.

The crew members knew it had been the Boss who'd put it all together. We also knew he felt the frustration and desperation that came with this shift of momentum. So did we—although he felt it deeper than the rest of us. The walls were closing in on one of the best scams of all time.

As time went on it seemed to me as though the Boss was starting to get a little reckless. As the pressure built up in the larger casinos, he began to work the crew in every hole-in-the-wall he could dig up. We started to bet less money and made less money, and we were still running for our lives. It seemed as though the Boss's decisions were based more on his obsession with the game than on well-thought-out plans and formulas. The one thing we didn't change, though, was our 100 percent clean routine.

Meanwhile, Wall and the Kid and I had become close friends. We talked amongst ourselves about the Boss's stability. We didn't mean to be disrespectful, but the Boss himself had trained us to read signs and recognize when things were out of sync. It was a little scary to be reading those signs in him.

Wall had always been the liaison between the Boss and the crew, but attempts to bring our concerns to his longtime friend's attention fell on deaf ears. The Boss was locked into the game with all his energy. Any suggestion that he might be pushing things too hard was brushed aside. He'd been up against hard challenges since he was a kid. For him, there was no such thing as pushing too hard— if you let up just a little bit, life would kick you in the teeth.

The crew endured, but Wall had duties at home to take care of. He didn't want to leave me and the Kid in the midst of all the trouble, but he was drawing a little too much attention lately. His face had been recognized in a whole lot of places, and he didn't want to bring more heat down on the crew than necessary. It wasn't just Wall either; a number of the crew members had become too hot to work—Wart, Footsie, and Chopper had all returned to normal lives. Before his departure, Wall warned us not to be pushed too hard.

The Kid and I had the pleasure of braining through this stress-filled stretch. For us, even to put the gaff on the table was a tribute to how mentally tough and skilled we'd become. It took a lot of confidence to get in this deep. We approached the gaming world with all of our senses firing at peak levels. We understood that staying out of the wrong hands was the extreme top priority. We pushed to play, but we chose wisely where we played. The Kid and I were friends, but we were also competitors for playing time. Whichever of us found a dealer and set up first got the play. And we both still needed the money, so it was very competitive.

This was a luxury of sorts for the Boss. He had two top brains to work for the crew and to push each other at the same time. It was one of those little angles the Boss uncovered and exploited nicely. The Kid was extremely skilled by this point. He didn't make mistakes. He led the crew through some pretty tough times. My development was more a tribute to tenacity and relentless drive. Some of the crew never saw much brain potential in me, and that was one of the motivating factors for my success, to prove them wrong.

The Boss helped us develop a professional rivalry. We became more focused and more efficient than any brains the crew ever had, mostly because we each had a talented rival to push against. The Boss might have wondered if we would try to push him a little, or maybe break away and start our own operation.

Of course, this kind of pressure could blow things apart at the seams, even the seams of a well-stitched crew. As concerned as the Boss might be about someone breaking off, or walking away, he was equally impressed that the Kid and I were sticking with it, still leading the team. He might have wondered what drove us. We were all loyal and dedicated to the Boss, and to the game.

Of course, it had been the money at first, but no brain could ascend to the heights we'd reached just for money. The two of us liked the rewards that came from playing the *Kammeyer brand of twenty-one with a mirror*. We'd formed the kind of frontline troops that the General Patton of blackjack would be proud to command.

The next few weeks dragged along, but the Boss showed no signs of retreat. He would stay as far away from the action as possible during plays. He couldn't risk being seen—a stinging setback for a guy who loved the thrill of the game. He'd put together a great scam, but he wasn't able to taste the action.

So, the Boss stayed back in the slots with his standard newspaper, trying to keep an eye on any casino security movement, trying to detect any slight bit of heat. When someone came by that he wasn't sure about, he'd watch their every move from behind his paper. A game of hide-and-seek that was a lot less exciting than the play the Kid and I were rolling through, but nevertheless an important role.

The Boss kept the details sorted out too, even in his reduced role. He would often wear a baseball cap and hide his eyes beneath the brim. His best effort was at Bullhead, where he and the crew and the tourists all wore cowboy hats. There he wore a simple mesh hat with a brim he could see through. He would pull the brim down over half of his face, and then peek through the holes to keep an eye on things.

He looked ridiculous to us, but it was part of the thrill. No one else saw the Boss the same way we did—effective and ingenious—a guy who had his own airplane and six houses, a guy who grew up in a broken home without a father to raise him, so he did it himself. He had pushed the casino version of blackjack in a way no one ever had before. No card counters, no spooks, no team from MIT.

The Boss scratched and scraped and took his lumps. Then he applied what he'd learned. He had gotten so good at it, he'd become too famous to play.

And now the same thing was happening to his crew.

CHAPTER THIRTY-FIVE

Members of the main crew gradually developed the habit of watching the Boss. He'd always been unpredictable, but now he'd become more analytical. We'd catch sight of him, from time to time, as he'd sit and contemplate his options—which were our options as well. His mind seemed to pore over things so fast, it was dizzying. His concentration was so intense, it seemed as though it would be hard for him to draw his next breath sometimes.

The Boss seemed to know, in one sense, that he was stoking the fire of an engine about to run off the tracks, but he couldn't convince himself to stop shoveling coal. Signs of disaster were flashing all around, but he was determined to forge ahead. He was a man with a full head of pent-up steam, and he had his hand on the throttle.

One morning he told us about a dream he had. In the dream, he went to Las Vegas with the crew, and the first casino we walked into, the management had changed every table in the place to a dealing *shoe*—a mechanical mechanism used to deal cards. It holds multiple decks for the purpose of cutting down on card counting. It also dealt cards in a manner that would make it impossible to pick up the hole card with a mirror.

In the Boss's dream, he took the crew to every casino on the Strip, and he found the exact same thing. Dealers were using shoes everywhere we went. He said he woke up with a fright, sweating, at three o'clock in the morning, and the fear of the dream stayed with him.

Of course, the casinos could change all of their hand-held decks to a shoe overnight. The Boss had always known that there were two ways the casinos could stop our game. One way was for the dealer to deal the first card down and the second card up, the second way was for the casinos to change every game to a shoe. Both would make it impossible to see the hole card. And really, those simple changes wouldn't affect the game of *twenty-one* much at all. But we didn't want the casinos to know that.

During this period of transition and soul-searching, I was scheduled to go back home for a friend's wedding over the course of one weekend. The crew decided to return to Reno while I was gone. When I arrived back in San Diego the following week, the Kid filled me in on what had taken place in my absence.

It all centered around Skate. A long, hard struggle had come to an end for Skate. His mother had finally passed away after an extended, one-sided bout with cancer. Her funeral was scheduled for the following Tuesday, but Skate decided to stay on and play over that weekend.

The Boss felt he was professional enough to handle it, as did the rest of the crew. We all shared Skate's pain, of course, and strangely the added camaraderie seemed to help the crew hold up under the pressure. Each of us drew strength from one another, and we shared each other's burdens.

On this particular weekend, Skate was scheduled to field marshal, the Kid would brain, and Toosh was to arm. And the Boss would support as he could.

It was unusual for core players to miss a weekend of work, but this was one of those rare exceptions for me. Not such a bad deal when you had two solid brains, but with Skate at something less than 100 percent, and with me gone, the crew went in feeling a little vulnerable.

The biggest adjustment they had to make would be that Skate would field marshal from right behind the Kid, instead of across the pit, where he preferred to work. But this was a crew that lived on its ability to adjust on the fly and maintain its flexibility.

When they got going in Reno, they were able to put together three solid plays and a couple of smaller wins right out of the chute—four or five grand each, a good start. But the Boss didn't want to push it, so he decided to load up and take the show over to Sparks, to John Ascuaga's Nugget—the only hotel-casino around with a freeway built over the top of it.

The crew walked in through separate doors, but it was hard for them to deal with the nagging feeling of operating at less than full strength. Each man needed to do a little extra. Toosh was watching from the bar. He was positioned where he could see the pit, and he noticed the Kid was ready for him. He saw the play coming together, but he was anxious.

Toosh started for the table, observing the ambiance of the casino as he went, and Skate was also on the ball. He grabbed the arm seat before Toosh had taken three steps. The Kid caught a few cards as the arm made his way over—and he got set up to fire a few live rounds.

Toosh kicked Skate's chair and Skate lazily stepped out, drifting over by third base to watch the action. He had been running on high octane all night, which was standard for an arm. The arms couldn't help but believe they were big shots, big-money players—able to play in front of the wide-eyed tourists, and then walk away with thousands of dollars. It was impressive. It was the only glamour role on the crew.

Toosh laid down his first two hands of five hundred, and the closest pit boss was on his way in an instant. He came over to the table in an unhurried fashion with a smile on his face. Then he stepped over to Toosh, stuck out his hand, and announced, "Hi, I'm Tony D'Amato. Welcome."

Toosh reached for his hand and shocked his crew members with his reply: "Hello, my name is Gaffney Mirrorstein. My friends call me the Count."

The pit boss was shaking Toosh's hand as he heard this. His face had been pleasant up to that point, but when he digested the obvious alias, his face turned red. He took a few involuntary steps back, glanced at the rest of the table, turned, and went directly to the phone.

Skate tried to make his way over to catch the conversation, but working from a different position he arrived at the phone too late. He'd paused a bit as the pit boss moved for the phone—just for a second. The pit boss said a few quick words and hung up, but Skate came away with no information, so he gave the Kid the cash-out sign.

The Kid had been at the table for only a few minutes, so it was hard to tell if it was just a reaction to Toosh's smart-ass alias or what. So he too hesitated, for just a split second.

Skate then glanced over at the Boss. They gave each other the cash-out sign, but too late. That's when the heat showed up, alive and kicking, and the shit hit the fan.

CHAPTER THIRTY-SIX

I was back in our apartment in San Diego, where the Kid and I were comfortably sitting on our outside balcony, relaxing in a pair of stout wicker chairs with a couple of beers. The late-afternoon sun was just making its way to the eastern coast of Japan. It had become a dull orange glow in the western sky, and the Kid was filling me in on just what had taken place when the heat came down during that fateful trip to Reno.

"Just after Skate gave me the cash-out sign, he coughed loud and hard," the Kid said. "He was giving me the *run* signal at the same time. I could tell by the expression on his face, he thought we were looking at some pretty serious shit.

"But when I jumped out of my chair, the first thought that came to me was, *I wish I had one of our really good runners right now*—like you, Red. Or Wall."

I nodded to accept the compliment, and took a sip of beer. A brain never took a good runner for granted. A runner was an invaluable part of the crew.

"I hit second gear as I headed out the door," the Kid went on. "My lead over my pursuers, once we were out on the sidewalk, was about five seconds. I turned my head enough to see that two of the guards had slammed through the doors right behind me.

"That feeling of running from the law was something I just never got used to, Red," he said. "I've always hated that feeling, but it did give me an extra boost—adrenaline, I suppose. I've never run so fast in my life.

"The other thing that had me scared half to death was

that goddamn gaff. The gaff is a real friend at the table, but it's a guy's worst enemy if he has it on him when things boil down to a footrace.

"It was hard to think clearly at that point," he said. "I wanted, in the very worst way, to get rid of that mirror, but I couldn't afford to lose one step while I was being chased by the guards."

At that point, the Kid smiled, and his face assumed a kind of childhood calm. "You ever skip flat rocks across a river or a lake, Red?" he asked.

I nodded, as my mind slipped back into the innocence of childhood. I could remember spending many long summer hours searching for flat rocks along the banks of the Rogue River, just to skip them off across the calm, summertime waters, always trying to get my rock to outdistance the rocks of my friends.

"Anyway," the kid went on, "that's what I did."

He took a slug of beer.

"Just like the old days, skipping rocks," he said. "I got around a few cars to where security couldn't see me, and let that mirror fly with a sidearm sling. Even with traffic buzzing by, and the sound of my footsteps pounding in my ears, I could hear the shattering of the glass.

"Looking ahead, I could see that I was coming to the corner of a building. We seemed to be in kind of a business/residential area. Anyway, I turned the corner with a pretty good lead. Security was nowhere in sight. Then I turned another corner and came into an alley."

Hearing him tell his story kind of got my nerves up. I pictured myself in that same situation, scared to death. I knew the Kid had battled asthma as a child. Any sprint that went much further than a half mile was going beyond his maximum range.

"I was pretty much spent by then, running as far as I did. My body had given everything it had." The Kid paused for a moment. "But then I spied a dumpster halfway down this dead-end alley. It was half filled with cardboard boxes—there were boxes around it, and flaps of cardboard sticking out under the lid."

He put his head down and then he looked back up at me.

"So, I hopped inside and wallowed down into the cardboard," he said. "Then I covered myself with the cardboard strips that were stowed in there, along with the boxes. I was so glad the garbage hadn't been picked up that day."

I took a long pull on my beer. The sun was all but gone now.

"Still," the Kid went on, "I felt a kind of sinking feeling. I wasn't sure I was making the right move—waiting for the heat to show up was a new concept for me. Though, looking back, I can't think of anything else I could have done."

Our crew had been conditioned to avoid heat by fleeing. *Keep moving and get away*, the Boss always told us.

A dumpster was a confined environment. It could very well be a mistake. The Kid hoped he'd made the right decision, but he also realized he was a sitting duck.

"Anyway," he continued, "all I could do was wait it out. I know I wouldn't have gotten much farther running. So, I lay perfectly still under the cardboard, trying to catch my breath as the agonizing seconds ticked by. I could hear sounds from the street, but nothing that sounded like pursuit coming my way."

I nodded, encouraging him to go on with his story.

"Then I heard footsteps coming up the alley," he said. "They stood out against the other noises that I'd been monitoring from the street. They were clearly coming closer; they rang out like alarm bells.

"As the steps closed in, I began to pick up muffled bits of conversation. The thoughts in my head seemed to become mixed up with the sound of the approaching footsteps—*I regretted not running farther; was I covered well enough by the cardboard?*

"By the time the steps drew to a halt outside the dumpster, I'd heard enough of the conversation to know this was the last-gasp effort by the agents.

"I braced myself for my uncovering," he said. "The heavy metal lid groaned open and light poured into the once dark and safe hideaway. I was buried pretty deep, and I could feel a hand push away the top layer of cardboard, but there didn't seem to be much conviction to the effort.

"One detective mumbled that this was a waste of time. I had a glimmer of hope. The lid was actually creaking back down. But then it stopped. The goddamn lid didn't slam shut with the happy ending I was hoping for.

"It paused, and then it started to creak back open. Light streamed in again, signaling that something had warranted a second look.

"'Look at the dust pattern on these boxes,' I heard one of the detectives say. 'They're different in the middle than around the edges.'

"This time the hand came through the cardboard and smashed into my hip. More panicked thoughts ran through my head—*high-speed chase, cat and mouse, ditch the mirror, hide in the cardboard, almost pulled off the incredible...*

"For some reason, the voices of the agents trumpeting their discovery suddenly sounded far away," the Kid told me. "I thought I was in real trouble, Red. All I could think of was I was about to get the shit beat out of me, or worse.

"With their weapons drawn, they said, 'Come on out—hands first.'

"So, I moved, slowly and submissively. It took all the energy I had just to get to my feet. For some reason, I felt detached from it all. I could hear their voices, but they sounded far away and faint, as they wrenched the handcuffs onto my wrists.

"I guess my thoughts were simply focused inwardly. I was trying to handle the shock and despair of capture."

CHAPTER THIRTY-SEVEN

It was still warm and pleasant out on the balcony, but the gnats and mosquitoes drove us into the kitchen. The Kid was whipping up a super-hot concoction he liked to call *Bitterroot chili.* The bitter root, in this case, was a generous portion of chopped habanero chili peppers.

"Just so you'll know," I told him, as I watched him peel an onion—he was holding it at arm's length, over the sink—"a habanero chili isn't really a root."

"That isn't the point," he replied. "Root or not, the recipe was developed in the Bitterroot country of Idaho—that's where I come from, you know."

And while he began to chop the onion—with his head turned and eyes watering—he got back to telling me what happened after the guards found him in the dumpster.

"The guards shook me back to reality," he said. "They weren't really all that rough, but they let me know I was in custody and they were determined to see that I stayed that way.

"They were talking amongst themselves, and it was hard to understand them, but the word 'mirror' was mentioned several times. I heard that plain enough.

"We were all standing there. I kept expecting them to do something, take me in, or..." He shrugged his shoulders. "But they seemed to be waiting for somebody. Then this younger guy, a detective with thick glasses and short, curly blond hair, rounded the corner and started up the alley. He was carrying a little baggie of something. I felt my diaphragm muscles tighten. It was hard to breathe. I thought these guys were going to try to frame me for some kind of a drug possession thing, or even a dealing charge.

"The young guy handed the baggie to an older detective with white hair—short fellow, looked kind of like Spencer Tracy. Then the young guy said, 'I got all the pieces I could find.'

"At that point, I took a closer look at the baggie. All I could see was it contained little pieces of broken glass, and it dawned on me—*the gaff.* That dizzy idiot had been out in the street picking up the remnants of the gaff. He even found the paper clip.

"If you don't mind me bragging a bit," the Kid went on, "what I was thinking at the time was this—*whether these casino goons know it or not, they just bagged the number-one player of the number-one blackjack scam in the country.*"

In other words, the Boss's brain was in the wrong hands—a brain had been caught with the gaff—a staggering blow to the Boss and the crew.

"Anyway, they had me by both arms as the guards ushered me back towards the casino."

The Kid started to fry some ground-round steak in a cast-iron skillet—*no cheap hamburger for this guy.* I went to the refrigerator and helped myself to another beer.

"Of course," the Kid went on, "by that time I'd started to wonder about what might have happened to the rest of the crew. I found out later that the Boss and Skate made it to the car. After that, they headed away from the casino as fast as possible. And it turned out that Skate saw Toosh headed for a cab, so they figured he was out clean.

"And that left me to worry about. The Boss had seen the

security guards chasing me, and he suspected that I might have gotten caught. So, he decided to go back and look around. He knew which direction I'd gone, so it didn't take long.

"When they got within a block of the Nugget, they saw the two security guards with me in custody. I was cuffed and on my way back to the Nugget.

"You know how it is when you feel like you're being watched, Red?"

I did know, and I nodded, as I watched the Kid begin to chop up celery.

"Anyway, we were just crossing the street and I had that feeling, so I turned my head and I saw the Boss creeping up behind us in the car. As he rolled by, he flashed an improvised signal to me—one last glimmer of hope.

"The deal was," the Kid went on, "the crew was going to try to pick me up on a drive-by."

He was now mincing bell peppers with a large kitchen knife, an activity that demonstrated his ability to stick with tedious tasks. The funny thing to me was he appeared to like it.

"So, I went along with the guards," he said, "like I had submitted to being in custody and had no intention of stirring up any trouble. But just as the Boss's car got up next to us, the rear door flew open and I shook my arms free from the guards. Then I took two giant steps out into the street.

"The Boss jumped on the binders—it almost caused the door to slam shut, but a foot shot out and propped it open. Skate must have been lying down in the back seat. Anyway, I almost made it, but...

"I'm here to tell you, Red," he said, deviating from his

story, "getting into a car without the use of your hands isn't as easy as a guy might think.

"But what happened was, I almost made it into the car, but at the very last instant one of the guards dove for my feet. He managed to trip me up just as I was climbing in. The Boss didn't have any choice. He had to speed away without me.

"It was a bad turn of events, but it sure tells you what the Boss will go through to save one of his brains. Of course, if he hadn't taken off, the guards could have reported the incident to the police, and they were already out there looking for him and Skate."

At that point, the Kid uncovered a large saucepan full of kidney beans that must have been soaking from the day before. He drained the water out through a colander. Then he poured the beans back in the pan, added fresh water, the chopped celery, and the minced bell peppers, and put the pan back on the stove over medium heat.

"I could see the Boss's eyes in the rearview mirror," the Kid went on, "and as I was lying there in the street, all I could do was watch the Boss drive off. My captors, though, they seemed to have lost some of their professionalism. They started shoving me around for trying the escape attempt.

"I knew that was going to be an issue when I was finally marched into the casino's eerie back room. I also knew that the security folks from the casino would have gotten a pretty good look at the Boss, and maybe even Skate, as they went by in the car."

"Wow," I added, with a sense of amazement. "The Boss went against his own rule about never going back to a casino after getting heat."

The Kid nodded. "Yeah, I was pretty impressed with that. The Boss made a very valiant effort to save me.

"Anyway," he said, as he drained the grease from the well-cooked ground round and dumped it in the garbage, "Skate filled me in, as far as what happened after that. He said the Boss couldn't think of anything more he could do for me, so they went to pick up Toosh and headed back to headquarters to wait to hear from me."

He added the ground round to the now-boiling beans and stirred the concoction. The aroma was intoxicating. Then he added the remaining ingredients, except for the tomatoes. The large tomatoes still needed to be cut up into quarters. He stopped talking and began slicing.

After the tomatoes went into the mix, he added some other spices, the names of which he refused to disclose. Then he put the lid on and turned the heat down to simmer.

"When I got to the back room of the casino," the Kid resumed his story, "they handcuffed me to a chair. The chief of security came in with two Reno cops. One of the cops stepped forward and placed me under arrest for cheating at gambling."

I sat and shook my head with a heartfelt pain. I really felt bad for the Kid; he was like my brother to me.

"Right then, Red, I knew I was fucked. The chief of security was pissed off and wanted to hurt me, but the Reno cops calmed him down. They ushered me to jail in downtown Reno, and I called the Boss."

I knew the Boss was very distraught about the whole thing. "He was really concerned about you," I said to the Kid.

When I talked to Skate he told me that the Boss asked the rhetorical question "I wonder if they got him with the gaff?"

Skate said they sat in silence until the phone finally rang. It tore through the murky silence like fire through a dry forest.

"Skate thought the phone ringing was good news," the Kid went on. "He figured it probably meant I was still alive. But he knew the call was most likely coming from a jail someplace, and that was the bad news.

"He said the Boss reached out and grabbed the receiver—he was on it before the first ring passed. But then he held the phone out away from his ear so they could all hear what was said.

"The Boss simply said, 'Hello.'

"He said they heard my voice, with a little nervous shake in it, when I said, 'Hey, Boss, this is the Kid.'"

CHAPTER THIRTY-EIGHT

While the Kid dished up the chili, I went over to peek in the refrigerator. I wanted to make sure we had enough milk to put the fire out later on.

The Kid howled in outrage as I crunched up Saltine crackers and stirred them into my dish of chili, but I tried to ignore him. Then he went on with his story.

"Like I said, Skate told me the Boss was holding the phone away from his ear so the others could hear. I didn't know how long I had to get my message across, so I wanted to get it out in a hurry.

"'I'm in the slam, Boss. I don't know what the bail is yet.'

"Then the Boss got to the tough question: 'Did they get the piece?'

"'Yeah, Boss.'

"'Fuck,' the Boss said.

"'They got it, and I'm in jail.'

"'I'm really sorry, Kid. We'll be down to get you out as soon as they set bail.'

"Skate told me the Boss put the phone down and said, 'Son of a bitch.' Then he headed to his room. Skate and Toosh could hear him pacing back and forth for the next hour."

By this time, I'd eaten a few spoonfuls of Bitterroot chili, and I could feel multiple beads of perspiration breaking out on my forehead. I poured myself a large glass of milk, and quickly took a gulp.

"It's a good thing you've come into your own as a brain, Red, because without a brain there couldn't be any crew."

Of course, I never wanted it to happen this way, but it was beginning to look like my turn at the plate had come. It was a tough time to continue on. The crew was catching more heat now than ever.

And while I felt ready to pick up the slack, I didn't cherish the thought that I was the last brain standing. I'd been with the crew for two years by this time, and I'd been braining, off and on, for most of the last year. If the boss wanted to go on with this program, he didn't have any other choice. I was it.

I looked over at the Kid. He seemed to be plowing through his Bitterroot chili with no signs of discomfort. In fact, while I was going after my second big gulp of milk, he got up to fix himself another bowl.

"Anyway," the Kid continued, as he dug into his fresh bowl of chili, "the Boss posted my bail, and the crew did what they could to pick up my spirits. I'll tell you, Red, I was damn glad to be back with them again.

"The Boss and I had a long conversation after that, in the privacy of his hotel room. Of course, it was a sad deal for me because I would have to leave the crew. The Boss told me how much he appreciated my loyalty. He also said I was always welcome back once my court hearings had been completed.

"He asked me what I was going to do. And actually, the question kind of took me by surprise—I had no idea what I was going to do. I'd never really thought about it."

The Kid was looking intently into my eyes as he said this, and I could tell it was some kind of a warning. The very same thing that had just happened to him could happen to me in a heartbeat. We sat there silently for a moment, and then he went back to his chili.

"Anyway," he said, "after the Boss and I had our little talk, the crew was anxious to get the fuck out of town."

A lot of things happened over the course of the following few days. The crew split up. The Kid was out of action for a while, and he would need time to sort out his life—and there was plenty to sort out, aside from his unknown trouble with the law. A few years on the crew would do that to a guy—any guy. It was a good time for the Kid to dig deep for a reality check. All of the stress and other psychological baggage that went along with his tour of duty on the crew would be with him for years to come, probably for the rest of his life.

Then, about a week later, on a Wednesday in early fall, the Boss gathered the small crew together at his house in Tahoe, where he announced that the crew would continue playing. Of course, that was no surprise to me.

It was then that we discovered that, along with the Kid's troubles, Skate had reached a breaking point too. The tragic loss of his mother had brought him back into contact with his family. And though he never said anything, I couldn't help but suspect that he thought his personal distractions might have contributed to the Kid's downfall.

In any event, after that weekend Skate chose to leave the crew.

The boss knew Skate had been going through some tough times, but he hated to lose him. Skate had signed on a long time back, and he'd been along during some of the crew's wildest twists and turns. But this was not an enterprise designed for a lifetime of service. Nobody ever got a gold watch or a fat pension out of our business. It was *grab what you could get your hands on at the time and thank your lucky stars that you made it out alive.*

Skate's parting was sad yet understandable. It was the best move for him at this point. He shook hands with the Boss and me.

"I'll never forget ya, Boss. Thanks for everything," Skate said. And I wondered if I'd ever see him again. *Probably not,* I thought. It was a solemn, very sad feeling.

But there wasn't time for the rest of the crew to dwell on it—and the rest of the crew, at that point in time, consisted of only me and the Boss.

CHAPTER THIRTY-NINE

After Skate left, the Boss stood in the doorway of his splendid, large Tahoe house and stared out into a small grove of Jeffrey pines that adorned the property across the street. He stood like that for several long minutes, while I tried to guess at what might be taking shape in his deep, overstimulated brain. Then he closed the door and began to wander around the house. He went out onto the patio, briefly. Then he walked back through the living room and into the kitchen.

I was waiting for some kind of direction.

Finally, the Boss came back in and simply said, "Let's go, Red." And at that point, I knew he was up to something—something that certainly would not be boring, but something that could end up being very hazardous to my health.

It wasn't a tough decision for me, though. Going back to Oregon to work in a lumber mill could wait. No matter what kind of trouble might lay ahead, it held more potential for the future than mill work.

And while I didn't know what the Boss had in mind, it obviously wasn't going to be the two-brain, three-arm, three-screen division that he'd put together just a few months earlier. Things were down to the bare bones now. This new operation—whatever it was—the one I thought I saw taking shape in the Boss's head, wouldn't, and couldn't, look like much on the surface, but he must have seen some potential in it.

"Where to, Boss?" I asked.

"Downtown, Red. We're going to find a play."

Just me and the Boss against the casino world—I was scared, but I got a big lift out of the confidence he was showing in me. And a lift was what I needed in order to face the action that was waiting. The money was good and I'd become extremely competitive. So, we loaded the entire crew into the car and headed for town—just me and the Boss.

The Boss talked all the way into town. He brought up the Kid's capture, and mentioned how he could see a different pattern developing in the casino world. "As corporate America continues to own and run more of the casinos," he said, "the mob-owned places seem to be turning into corporations themselves. Because of that, they see themselves more as legitimate enterprises, and they handle card counters and card cheats differently."

A Brink's truck slowed down in front of us as it began to turn into a casino for a pickup. I tapped the brakes, checked my mirror, and pulled out around it. When we were back up to speed, the Boss started in again.

"Instead of backroom beatings and rides out to the desert, the casinos are using the due process of the law—catching and arresting the violators, instead of the old standard practices of the past. Of course, there are still a few of the die-hard mob-owned casinos left, and they'll continue to use their old tried-and-true tactics, but they are the tactics of the past. Those threats are still very real, though, and they will be for some time to come."

As a result of the Boss's revelation, we decided to play the corporate casinos, and to leave the syndicate-run places alone. Hopefully we could keep from acquiring any broken bones that way.

Then the Boss made one additional observation. "Even the places we've come to think of as mob-owned," he said, "are changing their *modus operandi*. They might be run and managed by the same folks who ran them in the past, but in order to raise capital they've acquired boards of directors. The directors are there to protect the casino's gaming license, which is the single most important item for them to stay in business. The old bosses are advised not to revert back to their old ways—or there will be consequences.

"It's funny," he said, "how effective it is for a guy to threaten *consequences,* without actually mentioning what those consequences are."

I recalled some of the ghastly stories I'd heard in the past about guys who'd been taken for rides into the desert— some of whom never returned. I thought briefly about Tidy.

I concluded that the Boss was absolutely right—as he had been right so often, about so many things. The casinos in Nevada were definitely changing, and new casinos were being built all over the state. They were imploding some of the older casinos and building new ones in their place. The Boss figured all of that growth and change would result in new employees and new dealers coming on board, which meant some weak spots in the casinos' armor would come with the growth.

We arrived at Harvey's, got out, and went inside. It didn't take many doors to accommodate the entry procedure now. Two would do nicely.

We began to scout for a dealer, but before I had time to think, I was called to the play. The Boss had found a dealer. I went through the standard brain procedure, and the Boss took the arm seat. He began to bet $25 a hand—a far cry from the $500 bets of just a month earlier.

I was snagging hole cards and feeding information to the Boss. He raised the bet. He did it on his own. I didn't need to advise this arm. All he needed was a signal to know what strategy to play, nothing else.

We played a smooth twenty minutes. Then the Boss left the table. He gave me the cash-out sign, and we headed back to the house. At that point, we packed our bags and headed for the Tahoe airport.

But, it turned out, this was not going to be a trip home. We embarked on a short, quick hop to Reno. The Boss wanted to take a look around.

We checked into a low-profile hotel and ended up playing for low stakes at a smaller casino. We played small casinos for a lot less money for the rest of the weekend.

I could see it coming. This new operation was going to consist of a large number of small outings, mostly away from Vegas. For me, though, it was a nerve-wracking run. It demanded all pistons to be firing hard, every second of every minute.

The new adjustments to playing without the support of a screen, or a field marshal, mandated that I operate the brain position at a level of proficiency that only the Boss had been able to master before.

It was encouraging that my playing partner—the arm of all arms, the brain of all brains—was able to play the tables again. It was a big rush for the Boss. Though the stakes were small, he was playing the game—and playing with a solid partner.

The Boss had been through the best and worst of both roles. He had worked with, and had learned from, others along the way before putting his own brilliant scheme together. He'd been through spooking and card counting. And then he found a way to bring the mirror back from the ashes, as only he could do it.

I had the pleasure and responsibility of playing as part of this dynamic duo for an entire weekend. But the Boss couldn't risk the heat that would come with playing the tables day after day, week after week.

Our few outings on that weekend, though, were enough to convince the Boss that he did have something left to build on. With me working three jobs in one, all he really needed was an arm to bet the money—an arm that didn't have Steve Kammeyer's face attached to it.

The Boss found that he could field marshal from a distance and have a revolving stream of rotating arms come in to bet the money. In the long run, it worked in the operation's favor. The newspaper articles, along with reports from law enforcement research, had identified that Kammeyer Group used a consortium of blockers who worked around the table. With just two people playing, the missing screens actually helped to keep the heat away.

Of course, this didn't lessen the stress for me—just the opposite. I was throwing myself out against an opponent that could chew me up like a ship plowing into a coral reef.

Playing without any support was tough. I missed not having my friends around. The Boss realized how tough this was, so he offered some of his deepest insights to help handle the challenges—that, and to keep the scam alive.

To me, it seemed incredible for us to still be going. To find play at all, after the recent fallout, was a small miracle in itself. To be laboring under this heavy load was one thing, but I was actually learning and growing under the weight.

During this period, the Boss taught me a lot of things. He told me that his best security was his concentration, along with the maximum use of his senses—all six of them.

"Field marshals and screens actually provide a false sense of security," he said to me one time. "A brain needs to work inside his own head. He needs to monitor his environment, while he puts forth an innocent, naive front.

"Presence of mind every second in every situation is essential," he said. "You need to read the opposition before they can read you. You have to have the ability to know your own whereabouts at all times, and to know every possible escape route too."

I digested all of this information. It was like I was the only student in the class, and Socrates was my teacher.

"It's kind of like the lyrics to the song—*You've got to know when to hold 'em/Know when to fold 'em*," the Boss said on another occasion. "You have to have the ability to run when the heat is on. But you have to be better than that. You have to know to run a split second before the shit actually hits the fan."

The Boss told me that I would have to learn to feel someone looking at me. "We all do that, to some degree," he said. "The trick is to do it and resist the temptation to turn around and look back at your observer."

He said I'd have to develop the ability to look straight ahead and still see everything within my peripheral vision at the same time.

"At the height of one's senses," the Boss said, "a person sees beyond the senses—it's like reading between the lines. Sometimes it boils down to reading another person's body language, and possessing the ability to react to that in a matter of microseconds."

Another time he said, "Gut feelings and natural instincts are important." We began to talk about human nature. If a pit boss were staring at me from a distance, I would stick my finger in my nose and monitor his reaction. Nobody watches someone pick their nose. If the pit boss looked away, we were clean, but if he kept staring at me, I would turn my head away and head for the door. He was looking at me for some other reason, none of which was good.

I came away with the feeling that the Boss wanted me to relearn all of the things that mankind lost through the process of becoming what we now laughingly call *civilized*.

I had come a long way, and I knew that the Boss thought so too—but casino defenses had come a long way as well. The dealers were tighter. The pit bosses were smarter, and the authorities were constantly on the lookout for some of our long-lost members—any members, actually—from our infamous and cagey crew. Speaking of cagey, the Boss had also taught me to decoy the people chasing me. "When you're running from security, Red, once you get around the first corner with a decent lead, stop, turn around, and use a tourist for cover. You need to act like you're having a conversation with the tourist. Stay one step behind them and use your hands in conversation with a pleasant expression on your face. In most cases they'll run by you. Do it quickly and pay attention and make sure they don't see you before you slip back around the corner."

CHAPTER FORTY

Several months passed with the Boss and me working the weekends. We would rotate in one fresh arm each week. Despite the odds, I was able to hold up under the pressure. During the weekdays, the Boss and I had become pretty good friends. We went to the gym three days a week to keep in tiptop shape.

He didn't stand still on the new arrangement either. He made one additional big move. He called in his ace in the hole—Wall.

Wall managed to finish up his business at the family ranch, and he was ready to get back to work. With me in top form, the Boss had Wall on his way south with one single phone call.

In the meantime, besides the Boss, I'd been also hanging out with the Kid on the weekdays. We'd both been through the same intense procedures to become brains, and after all the battles we'd managed to survive to reach that status, we felt like two lonely generals at the top—or maybe two warrant officers would describe us better. Anyway, it was nice to have someone to relate to.

The Kid had been to court twice by that time—for both the arraignment and the preliminary hearing. The evidence had mounted against him, and it looked solid enough to earn a conviction for possession of a cheating device. A conviction brought a penalty of three to ten years in the Nevada State Penitentiary.

His attorney advised him to cop a guilty plea, which

could be traded off for a gross misdemeanor charge and a $2,000 fine. The Kid decided to take the fine and probation. The court recognized that he had no prior arrests of any kind and the judge showed leniency. Although, it scared the crap out of the Kid and me both.

Sadly, though, he was history as far as playing cards was concerned. Still, we crossed paths during the week. The Boss had paid his bail and attorney fees, along with the fine that went with the conviction, but the Kid knew he had to stay away from the tables.

As time passed, the Boss's quest continued, with his one and only brain, namely me, carrying the torch. I'd been pushing my solo brain status for upwards of six months by that time. I'd endured long hours under pressure with no substitutes off the bench to give me a break. I was the first string; I was the only string.

Just to get through a weekend was the sustaining force of my legacy—everything was on my shoulders. If the crew lost me, it would set them back at least six to eight months. In fact, if that happened, they might never recover—and there were times when we were faced with some very close calls.

Often plays would go down to the final card before I had to bolt from a casino, just seconds ahead of the heat. There were several classic casino-chase scenes. But in spite of the stress on me, I would often think of the stress on the Boss. Time after time, he had to watch the only brain he had run out into the streets, one short step ahead of security.

On one occasion, the Boss said to me, "You're one of the best runners the crew has ever had, Red."

I couldn't help but wonder if he might have said that

simply to keep me running. But I had no choice. I was operating as the brain, the runner, and the field marshal.

The Boss didn't say anything more. He didn't have to. I knew he was proud to see his protégé perform so well under pressure—the kind of pressure no other crew member had ever faced—except, of course, for the teacher himself.

Arms would be shuffled in and out, with Toosh, Fats, and Spanky alternating. We made some decent runs too. I logged in more minutes of play than I ever thought possible. Someday, though, I knew the jangled forces of energy and raw nerves building up inside me would have to come out. I knew it intuitively. But I didn't give a shit about it at the time. I had enough to worry about, both at the tables and on the streets.

Fats and Toosh really came into their own as arms during this stretch, too. When they were first being trained, they didn't even know a mirror was being used. They just drilled at the practice table thinking they were playing with the smartest blackjack players in the world—they had no plausible way to explain it. The brain just always seemed to know the exact right moves to make.

As I recall, they were eight months into the game before one of them happened to catch a glimpse of the gaff. In the end, though, knowing about the gaff on the table helped them to play their part better.

It was like when a kid first realizes Santa Claus isn't real. Fats and Toosh understood why they weren't told about the mirror earlier on. But on their day of discovery, they came to realize the brain really had more balls than brains.

Wall coming back was a big boost.

He flew back to San Diego to join up for another hitch, and his return touched off quite a reunion. The Kid and I picked him up at the airport two days before the next trip to the tables, which gave us a night to catch up.

We hit a beer joint and got right after it. We talked about everything new, a lot of the old. And we talked about the trials and tribulations we'd all gone through. There was plenty to laugh about.

We finally ended up at my place above Mission Bay, just north of the city. It was a one-bedroom flat that looked down on a quaint little golf course. Wall decided to bunk there, and to use the next day to get himself ready to head back into the fire. He hadn't been in a play for six months by then, so he drilled and practiced with the Kid and me.

The hand signals were burned into Wall's memory, but he'd become rusty on the crew's language—it had evolved somewhat. So, we used hand signals and talked "crew language" everywhere we went.

I continued my workouts on a daily basis, even though Wall was in town, and today was no different. One day, it was around four o'clock on a Thursday. I was in the middle of my daily workout, jogging along the beach on the boardwalk.

After a short warm-up, my routine usually started near Pacific Beach, and I ran in the direction of La Jolla. I was just getting into stride when I thought I heard someone yelling from a distance. The sound was faint. I wasn't sure if it was a human voice, or just something blowing in the breeze. I ignored it at first, but after a few more strides I heard it again, a distant cry for help, maybe.

I stopped, looked around, and started walking, listening. I moved away from the surf, which allowed me to hear better, and there it was again. I looked out across the sea. There was something out in the water, something bobbing up and down. Then a hand went up, and I heard a distinct cry for help. Someone was in the water, a long way out from the beach. It sounded like a woman.

I headed for the water on a full sprint, looking around for other people as I went. There was a lifeguard tower about two hundred yards to the south, but there was no time for me to get there. Then I saw a man and a woman walking near the water. I altered my course to get close enough for them to hear me, and shouted, "Go get the lifeguard. Someone needs help in the water."

They were too close to the crashing waves to hear the distressed swimmer, but they must have heard me. When I saw them turn and hurry toward the lifeguard station, I took off my running shoes, socks, and T-shirt, and headed into the water.

She cried out again, but the cry was muffled by the surf. She was a hundred yards out, but I was in good shape. I could swim the distance.

Once I got started, though, I realized she was in a riptide, and so was I. Swimming away from the beach was easy. I was going with the rushing current, but once I got to her I needed to swim perpendicular to the current to get away from the riptide. I could see the girl only when the ocean swells would buoy her up from time to time, but I could tell she was losing the battle to stay afloat. She would go under the water for a few seconds, and then come back up. I needed to hurry if I was going to save her.

When I finally caught up to her she was completely underwater, one arm barely breaking the surface of the sea. I grabbed that arm and pulled her toward me. She'd nearly gone completely limp before I could pull her to the surface. I held her head up for a few moments so she could breathe. Using one arm to hold her up, and the other to keep us both afloat, I began to kick my legs as fast as I could.

She coughed, took in some air, and said, "Oh my God. Oh my God."

She was too tired to struggle. I put my forearm under her chin and pulled her up, allowing her to breath, hoping she would float on her back.

"Thank you," she said, sounding like someone in the final stages of pneumonia. "Thank you. Oh my God, thank you."

I was out of breath, but I managed to sputter, "You're going to be all right."

I started to swim to the south, with the girl in tow, to get out of the riptide. But then a lifeguard on an oversized surfboard pulled up beside us and said, "You're in a riptide; let me take her."

I didn't object as he grabbed the girl and pulled her across his board. "Are you going to be all right?" he asked.

"Yeah, the other lifeguard is coming this way."

I was tired from both the swim and the excitement, as the other lifeguard pulled up. "Grab the board," he said, and he started paddling back to shore.

"Hey dude, thanks for helping me out," I said.

"No problem, man, that's what we're here for," he replied.

A few minutes later we were close enough for me to reach bottom. I got off the board and took a couple of steps, rested for a moment, and then walked over to my shirt and shoes.

My lifeguard paddled over to the first lifeguard, who was attending to the girl. As I sat on the beach catching my breath, I could see her sit up. She looked at me and nodded; I smiled and nodded back. She seemed to be in her early twenties, but that was the only gesture we exchanged.

Paramedics had arrived by then, and they attended to her as I put on my shoes and socks. I grabbed my shirt and headed back to the boardwalk. I needed to get out of here. In my business, the last thing I needed was publicity. My workout would have to wait. I was beat and I still faced a half-mile jog to my car. Knowing the press would be here at any moment, I headed home.

The following morning there was a small article in the newspaper, headlined "Passerby Saves Young Woman from Drowning."

I read the article and smiled, shook my head, slightly, up and down, and said to myself, *Good job, Red.*

That night, the night before we were scheduled to leave, Wall and the Kid and I flashed a few signals in a bar, just for practice. I told them what had happened earlier that day. They both seemed pretty impressed.

Friday morning came and went, but the phone finally rang at about 1:00 p.m.

"Meet me at the plane at three o'clock sharp," the Boss said. "And don't be late, assholes."

The Boss always giggled when he called his loyal crew

assholes. He was stoked up, with Gator back in town. The two of them had been close for a long time, though they didn't hang out a lot together these days.

Wall and I packed our playing clothes and loaded them into the car. The Kid drove us to Palomar Airport, and Toosh was there waiting with the Boss.

Wall and the Boss shook hands and playfully pushed one another around. After some short conversation, we loaded up and taxied out to the runway. I was riding shotgun, while paying attention to the flight procedures as the part-time co-pilot. We had a system: the Boss would take the plane up to cruising altitude, and then have me hold the heading and monitor the gauges until descent.

I wasn't licensed, but we'd been through some interesting moments. On one occasion, I was holding a course out of Lake Tahoe while the Boss was sleeping. It was a routine flight at twelve thousand feet. We were coming out of the mountains towards Las Vegas when the constant drone of the engines was interrupted by a bit of sputter.

The Boss snapped to attention.

The power of the propellers sagged for an instant. Then the engines sputtered and went dead.

"Shit," the Boss said as he woke up.

Then, very calmly, he reached down between the seats and switched fuel tanks. He reacted quickly, but the plane had already gone into a glide. We were losing altitude.

The plane pulled hard to one side as I worked the rudders. Then the Boss sat back, and the engines kicked in and began chopping up air again. The comforting hum returned.

"Take it down to ten, Red," the Boss said, "and keep the

same heading."

After that, he was back to sleep, hardly missing a beat. His instinctive reaction never seemed to bring him fully out of his slumber. When you risk your life, week in and week out, a little glitch in an airplane engine hardly gets your blood up.

On this particular occasion, the landing in Vegas was negotiated in a tough forty-mile-an-hour crosswind. The plane came in like a crab, jerking side to side as it approached the runway. But we landed gently, despite the interference, and then taxied to the tie-down area at the executive terminal.

We grabbed a rental car and unloaded our gear. After the final preparations were made, we headed out with mixed emotions. We were well prepared for what we were going to do, but we knew our opponents were well prepared too.

CHAPTER FORTY-ONE

Wall, with his experience and friendship, was a big addition to our bare-bones crew, but we were all aware of what lay before us. It needed no discussion.

I drove the foursome to a casino on the Strip, where we filed out of the car and headed inside to scout for a dealer. I took heart, knowing Wall was with us, as I watched him walk through the front doors.

I went in a side door and stopped for a moment to absorb the ambiance. I felt confident as I made my way across the casino floor. Being the only brain, I carried a deep sense of responsibility. I was both nervous and ecstatic at the same time. I would always keep my face hidden from the pit area until it was absolutely necessary.

We scoured the pit, but we couldn't find one playable dealer, so we moved out and moved on.

The next stop was more of the same—tight dealers with no chance of getting a consistent peek at a hole card. It seemed as though all of the casinos had retrained their dealers to hide the down cards—just one of the steps that the casino world was taking to detour the crew.

It had been a year and a half since the *Las Vegas Sun* article had come out; at that point, the article had made the scam, our scam, front-page news. Dealers had been schooled to prevent crossroaders from reading their hands. The percentage of playable dealers was down, way down— maybe 1 percent at best.

The Boss gave up on the Strip and moved downtown.

We hit a place called the Union Plaza Hotel—an establishment that was named after the Union Pacific Train Station, a popular tourist connection in the 1940s. It was a tall, concave building that gave a guy the sensation of being swallowed when he first walked into it.

It was also the one place in Vegas that would cash anybody's chips. Say an enterprising player found he had to quickly exit the Hilton with a pocketful of chips, and he knew it wouldn't be wise to go back into the Hilton to cash them in, that player could always go down to the Union Plaza and they'd gladly cash the chips for him. For us, it was a lucky thing that the Union was here.

Wall found a dealer and I got into the hot seat as quickly as possible. I looked at two hands, and then rubbed my chin.

Wall seemed impressed. He hadn't seen me brain in months. And within a few minutes, Toosh was at the table. He immediately laid his bet out at $500, and it wasn't long before two hands of five hundred were on the table. After that, though, we had to weather a lucky run by the dealer. But it wasn't long before we managed to accumulate a reasonable pile of black chips.

I could see that Wall was feeling a little unsure of himself. This was the first time he'd had to field marshal all by himself. I knew the pressure would be intense on him, but he seemed to be holding his ground. He'd been away from the game for a while, and things had become a great deal more problematic during his absence. The game was moving at a much faster pace these days.

I began to get that old gut feeling that something bad was about to happen. I called for the cash-out and sent Toosh on his way to the backup casino.

I could see Wall. He was watching me leave the area. There had been no incident, so he slipped in behind me, coughed, and gave me the *cool* sign.

I wiped my forehead with a casual swipe and headed for the car. We picked up Toosh a few minutes later and decided to grab a bite to eat. It was nearly midnight. We'd been at it for six hours.

As efficient as our veteran crew was, it still took time to get in and then get out of the casinos. In all of those hours we'd netted only one play.

After a light meal, we headed back to the Strip and promptly went zero-for-two in the first two joints we scouted. I'd gotten to the point where I could work some tough dealers, but it required a lot of scouting to find one that was even marginal.

CHAPTER FORTY-TWO

When two o'clock rolled around, the Boss decided to give Vegas World a try, a casino that was built around a space theme—a place we would play from time to time with mediocre success. Minutes later, we were in the pit and I managed to come up with a blue-chipper—a careless, unsuspecting, very beatable dealer. They were tough to find, but well worth the search, and Toosh and I were working well together.

Of course, the Kid and I had trained Toosh, so we knew each other's movements. One hand of five hundred hit the table and Toosh was soon engaged in a grand performance. The more he played, the better he worked the role.

"Hi, I'm James Rothrock the Third," Toosh said as he shook the pit boss's hand. He played several give-and-take rounds, while four pit bosses migrated his way. Toosh was not only handling the close, high-roller attention, but he milked it. The perfect part for this performer.

Toosh had confided in me one time—late at night, over a beer—that he had aspired to be an actor at one time. He could recite various passages from Shakespeare word for word, and on this occasion he bellowed out a few lines from Macbeth for the large crowd that had gathered.

The table area had taken a liking to him, from the pit bosses right down to the tourists. All systems go, with the exception of the cards. They were falling the dealer's way. Even knowing the hole card was no guarantee of a payoff. Normally, the crew lost nine hands out of every twenty.

This round was way above that. We lost $5,000, and it didn't look like things were going to change any time soon.

I kept eye contact with the Boss for instructions, but I kept getting the green light. A mistake in this situation could cost thousands more. My head was motionless, as my eyes moved to the gaff once a minute.

We took a forty-five-minute beating before the dealer took a break. *Luckily*—I thought at the time—*this is a yo-yo joint.* The dealer would be gone for fifteen minutes, and then she would return to the same table. *Scatter joints* were tougher to handle. With scatter joints, the dealers rotated randomly.

Anyway, we held our positions and played through the relief dealer.

As far as we were concerned, the playable dealer couldn't get back fast enough. Toosh had dropped sixty-seven hundred, and Wall had to signal him to the restroom to give him ten thousand more. That would give him thirteen-three to work with.

Once they were in the restroom, I knew how it would go. Wall would take one stall, and Toosh would take the one next to him. Then Wall would toss a ten-grand packet under the divider, and Toosh would pick it up and put it in his sock.

While all of that was going on, I held my spot at $5 a hand. I kept playing and watched the surrounding area, waiting for the original dealer to come back.

Toosh arrived at the same time she did. I settled back in. I was picking every card, but the losing skid continued. After fifteen minutes, though, I felt things were about to turn our way—and still, they didn't.

Another entire shift had almost passed with Toosh

pumping out the dough. The crew had one more hand before the break and we needed to win it. The dealer had a sixteen and Toosh had a pair of eights. He split and got another eight. He pulled tens on all three hands of five hundred and sat on three eighteens.

The rest of the hands were dealt out and dealer exposed her sixteen. She hit it with a five for twenty-one and headed for her break. We were down fifteen-six after two straight hours of play.

Wall hadn't pushed it like this in months, and I wasn't feeling fresh by any means, but we had no intention of quitting.

I left the table and headed for the bathroom to splash my face and rinse my sweaty hands. The cool water helped tighten my pores, snapping me back to alertness. After a short glance in the mirror, I split for the snack bar to grab some instant energy. A Snickers bar was enough to fill that void. The whole process took just over ten minutes. I felt a second wind coming as I headed back to the table.

The dealer came back a few minutes later, and round three was underway. The crew was down two rounds to none, but when the crew was losing there was usually very little heat on the play. With the money rolling the casino's way, they had nothing to suspect. But we were determined to stay with it until we'd made a complete comeback.

At first, Toosh dropped cash on every hand. Three hands later, though, he won a double down, then another right behind it.

Finally the cards were starting to come our way. I pumped the bet up a couple of times; we were betting three hands of seven hundred. Thirty minutes later, we had thirteen grand piled up. It was past three thirty by then and everyone was close to shot. There were five minutes left in the dealer's shift, so I signaled Toosh to crank it up to three hands of eight hundred.

The next two hands resulted in Toosh doubling down two out of three. The dealer busted on both occasions. The big payouts brought the deficit to a close, and put the crew up by about three thousand. The pit was still cordial and everything seemed fine.

But then—*wham*—my face was slammed into the green felt. I was clobbered from behind without warning. A Griffin agent stuck his shoulder into my backside and pinned my left arm to the table. Then he plucked the gaff up off the felt.

He handed it to the dealer and said, "Don't lose this."

A pair of two-hundred-pound men had me pinned to the table. They'd gotten the drop on me. I never had a chance to run. I couldn't even squirm. The big agents were making it hard to even breathe.

With my left eye mashed down onto the table, I could still see Wall heading for the exit. He had agents picking up his trail, though, before he even hit the door. The chase was on.

I noticed that the Boss had been spotted in the slots, and I could see a couple of heaters going after him. For me, it was all happening in slow motion.

The two that were holding me down stayed at the table, while a number of the others joined the pursuit for the Boss and Wall.

CHAPTER FORTY-THREE

When the agents made their way over to Toosh, he offered no resistance, but when they attempted to take him into custody the pit boss stepped in front of him.

"Not this gentleman," the pit boss declared. "He had nothing to do with it."

I watched the officials brush the pit boss aside and grab Toosh. I was still struggling to get myself up out of my seat, but the agents had a strong hold on me. I couldn't free myself.

Then the two big guys that were holding my head down suddenly pulled me up. A third man stepped up behind me to work the cuffs.

As soon as I felt the handcuff pressure on my wrist, I freaked out, turned, and headed for the door. They'd only been able to get one cuff on, so I still had the use of my hands, and I burst forward with every ounce of energy I could muster. But word seemed to have gotten around about my escape acts. The agents had been warned. I didn't let that stop me. I drove forward through the casino aisles, dragging three would-be tacklers with me.

I could see tourists with mouths and eyes wide open, as they watched the action play out. I got enough yardage for a couple of first downs, but in this league only touchdowns would count. It did, however, take some help from the secondary to bring me down.

I was within twenty feet of the door, and I still had two opponents left on my back, when the agent assigned to the exit that I was headed for rushed forward. He threw his body into my knees, and I went down hard, with two men still on my back. Another grabbed at the still-swinging handcuffs. The others pinned me to the floor, wrenched my arms behind me, and snapped the cuffs shut.

Wall, it turned out, was able to get to the streets and outrun his pursuers, after a very long sprint.

I found out later, the Boss had made tracks through the parking lot, but he was picked up by another agent who'd joined the chase. The agents all knew that the Boss would be the prize to catch, and they wanted him badly. So badly, in fact, that one agent went right over the hood of a moving car to block the Boss's path.

He managed to knock the Boss up against an old Plymouth that was parked in the lot, which slowed him down enough to allow help to catch up. Then they wrestled him to the ground and cuffed him as well.

But Wall was still out there.

He told us later how he headed over to the backup joint and waited for word from somebody. If no one contacted him in an hour, he intended to head for the hotel and get ready to start the bail procedure. He didn't have any bankroll left to speak of, so he'd just have to wait it out and do what he could.

Anyway, back at the casino, I stood by helplessly and watched as the Boss was ushered into the main security office. After that, they marched me down the hall and sat me down on the stairs leading to the second floor.

We all knew the drill. They would question each suspect in a separate room. The Boss was being managed by the chief of security, while Toosh and I cooled our heels in other rooms, with two big guards on each of us.

I gathered from the bits and pieces of conversation that I was able to overhear between some of the agents who'd been involved in the bust that they were upstairs with the owner of the casino, reviewing the videotape that had been rolling on the hot table—our table.

Half an hour dragged by, and my hands were getting numb. The cuffs had been clamped on pretty tight. I'd also acquired a nasty gash on my left wrist. The sharp steel of the cuffs had dug deep into my wrist when I'd dragged the agents along.

Nothing happened for over forty-five minutes, and that turned into an hour. Finally, I heard somebody behind me coming down the stairs. It was two agents and the owner. When they got to me the owner purposely stepped on my handcuffs, while sticking his knee in my back at the same time. Then they walked on by and headed down the hall.

My heart was still pumping fast from the commotion, but I was starting to realize that this was probably the end of my career—and maybe my life. It was a total fear of the unknown.

A few minutes after the group in the hall disappeared, the owner and the two agents came back. The owner just stared at me.

"What are you going to do, rough me up some more?" I stared straight back at him.

"No, no. I'm really sorry about that." He brushed off my shirt with the back of his hand—two gentle swipes as if to brush the dust off.

"How would you like to take those cuffs off and walk out of here?" the owner asked

"What do you mean?" I replied. I couldn't believe what I'd just heard.

"We're just going to pretend that you walked in the door, rolled the dice once, and lost. We take all your money, and let you go free."

"I can't make that decision. You'll have to ask that big man in the room down the hall," I said, not meaning to break protocol or admit conspiracy.

The owner left for a few minutes. Then he returned. He took me by the arm, stood me up, and led me back to my partners. They removed the handcuffs from all three of us.

I figured the Boss must have cut some kind of deal with the owner.

One of the Metro officers was staring at me with his chin resting on his hand and his finger across his lips. Obviously, he thought he recognized me from somewhere. I recognized him too, but I couldn't figure out where.

My wrist continued to bleed. One of the guards noticed and ordered a first-aid kit, and went to work patching up the gash on my left wrist.

Strangely, the air of adversity seemed to have dissipated, and the discussion turned to a more-friendly conversation. At one point, college athletics was mentioned, so I told them I'd played baseball in the Pac-10.

One of the beefy guards had been a down lineman for the Nebraska Cornhuskers. We traded stories. There were impressive athletic credentials all around—each side tried to solidify its worthiness, but it was all done with a measure of respect.

It turned out, the casinos and agents weren't having much luck in trying to stop our crew through the judicial system. Besides, it was expensive to hire attorneys. The owner figured he'd rather save the money than give it to the system.

By the time I was patched up, players from both sides were talking like fraternity brothers at a college reunion. The Boss was taken into another room with Metro, Griffin, the Gaming Commission, and the owner to wrap up some loose ends.

The bullshit session ended when the top dogs returned.

The deal was done. It was mentioned that this was to be a word-of-honor contract, which meant that we were not to ever play there again.

The Boss sacrificed the bankroll for the freedom of his crew, and we were separated one last time for a final talk.

After shaking hands with the Boss, the owner turned and stepped in front of me. "We know who you are now," he said. "You seem like nice young men, but if I see you in here again, we'll have to go for a ride."

"I understand, sir," I told him. "You have your job, and I have mine."

My tone seemed to suggest that I would do it all over again, given the chance. I'd been at this for more than three and a half years by now. I knew what I was up against.

The casino staff and the gaming agents were there to prevent cheating. That was their job—to discourage any players who threatened the casinos or tried to alter the odds. My job was to take their money.

When it came time to leave, the cop who'd been staring at me removed his hand from his face and said, "I know where it was. You were the guys on the east side of town that were held up at gunpoint a couple of years ago."

Then I remembered.

The cop continued. "I was the one that questioned you guys. If I remember correctly, the robbers took all of your money back then."

I nodded to say yes, even though the robbers didn't really get the money.

"Man, you guys are taking a beating," he said with a smile. Everyone in the room heard the statement from the cop.

"Yeah, we're taking a beating all right," I said, while thinking—*If you only knew.*

The owner had one final request. "Would you mind leaving through the back door?" he said, with a smirk on his face. "We don't want the tourists to think we treat everyone this way."

As we walked down the hall, I could hear the head Metro officer say, "Can you believe those guys? Putting a mirror right up on the table—who would think you could get away with a move like that? They're nuts."

We continued on towards the rear of the joint, and once outside, we began to walk faster.

Of course, we were elated with the turn of events. The Boss could care less about the money—somewhere around twenty thousand, I figured. Bail and court costs would have been much more. Even the Boss was surprised that a deal like this had been offered, and he didn't hesitate to jump on it. The judicial process would have cost upwards of $50,000.

We walked a few brisk blocks, and then we flagged a taxi. We couldn't wait to see Wall. I wanted to see the expression on his face when we walked in free men.

As we rode along in the taxi, the Boss broke into a soft giggle. He turned to me and said, "Well, Red, you've still got your freebie."

"Unbelievable, too," I replied, shaking my head in bewilderment.

We rode the rest of the way in silence, each of us sorting things out for ourselves.

When we arrived at the Desert Rose Motel, Wall was peeking through the curtains, probably wondering if the heat had come for him. Needless to say, he had a shocked look on his face when he saw us all file out of the taxi with no escorts and no flashing lights.

He demanded an explanation, but all he got was a smile from each of the three of us.

CHAPTER FORTY-FOUR

Toosh walked up to Wall and began to give him a blow-by-blow rendition of what had just happened back at the casino.

"You should have seen it, Wall," he said. "Coming out of absolutely nowhere, these three huge guys jumped on Red. Then one of them grabbed the mirror and handed it to the dealer. The people standing around the table looked like they were shell-shocked—all standing around with their mouths hanging open, like big, gaping holes. And Red managed to drag the three men clear across the casino floor. It was awesome. They weren't able to tackle him until he got right up to the door."

Toosh was back on his adrenaline edge for the moment, reliving the rush, as he told Wall the entire episode.

The stunned look never left Wall's face. "How in the hell did you guys get out?"

But nobody answered. We all moved inside, so we wouldn't be airing any dirty laundry in public.

"They took all our money and let us go," I continued the conversation, once the door was closed.

"Noooo," Wall shot back, more stunned than ever. Then he turned to the Boss. "No shit, Boss?"

The Boss simply nodded and sat back with a faint smile on his face. Then the three of us hashed out every last detail—including the friendly talk we had before they finally let us go.

Thinking back on it later, that entire episode came to

feel extremely unusual—weird, actually. Even now, years later, I can't believe it. It seems like a dream.

Anyway, we went through a complete play-by-play of the bust. The crew had the pit covered, and it was obvious that the pit boss didn't know what was coming down. Toosh told Wall how the pit boss stepped in front of the agents and tried to protect him.

"Not this gentleman," Toosh imitated the pit boss's loud and direct delivery.

We all laughed when Toosh told Wall how the agent stepped in and cuffed him anyway, barely acknowledging that the casino man had even spoken.

Then Wall told us what he saw, just before he'd made a break for it.

"They drilled you from behind without any warning at all," he said, looking straight at me. "There were agents everywhere. I couldn't do a thing for you, Red, not one thing, so I finally split. Sorry, man."

I quickly put him at ease. "Shit, Gator, you had the pit covered. The whole thing was a setup."

Then the Boss volunteered some inside information. "Yeah, we were set up. One of the Griffin agents' wives was working the eye in the sky. She recognized one of us when we first came through the door and called her husband. He was the one who assembled the National Guard. So they had all the bases covered before they ever made their first move. It was a fluke, Wall. Not your fault at all."

"All I know is I was nailed from behind," I said. "I freaked out and tried to sprint away, but they had me. It could have turned out much worse."

"I wonder if that blue-chipper dealer was part of the setup," Toosh asked, reflectively.

"That agent did hand the gaff to her," I offered.

"She wasn't part of the setup," the Boss said. "The gal in the camera upstairs didn't tell anyone except for her husband. Then the agents snuck into the casino, stayed low to the ground, and got the jump on us."

The conversation trailed off after that, as the twenty-four-hour workday began to catch up with us. Twenty-four hours was not an uncommon stretch for the crew, but this day had been filled with stress above and beyond the call of duty. First there were the frustrations of not being able to find a dealer. Then the bad run of cards that kept us at Vegas World for such a long time, and then the bust.

Even by our standards, this had been a hectic day, and it had been quite a while since we'd faced this kind of intense heat. As it turned out, though, it had been an experience for us to grow from.

We'd been through more angst and frustration in our early twenties than some people face in a lifetime. But that day, after all we'd gone through, we were shot. Even the Boss felt it. He'd been chased down for the first time in quite a long while. He was feeling spent too.

The Boss knew we needed rest, but he also knew we wouldn't be able to sleep after that ordeal.

"Pack it up," he said. "We're out of here."

I kind of figured we weren't going home, so I asked, "Where to, Boss?"

"Bullhead," he replied.

"Let's do it," Wall said, with enthusiasm.

"Yeah," Toosh added.

I was the first one packed. I was ready to go, ready to lead the charge, and I rode up front with the Boss in the airplane. I thought briefly of Teddy Roosevelt—always up front where the action was.

We badly needed sleep, though, and by the time we flew the thirty minutes into Bullhead City and got checked in, we had no problem dropping off. The adrenaline was finally gone. The Boss had taught us some relaxation techniques, taught us how to sleep under stress. We got in six solid hours.

After sleeping on the events of the previous day, the big picture seemed a lot less overwhelming. We got up and went out for breakfast. We had endured; it was a great feeling. We were rested and fed and nobody was in the slam.

Then the Boss sounded the battle cry. "Let's play, Red."

Actually, though, I felt like I'd been on the losing end of a fifteen-round fight. I had carpet burns on my chin, my cheek, my forehead, and elbows, and I was still sporting a Band-Aid around my wrist.

"Let's go look around first," I said, feeling a little worse for wear.

"If you fall off a horse," the Boss added, with his ever-present wry smile, "you have to get right back on."

So, our fearless foursome played for two solid days in Bullhead, and it all passed without incident.

We managed to make back some of the money that we'd left behind at Vegas World, but not enough to break even. And when Sunday evening arrived, we knew we'd given it our all.

We didn't lose very often, but we called it a weekend and dragged ourselves back to California, totally exhausted.

I needed some time to recover. I took the following weekend off to heal up and refocus. Wall and the Kid and I played around on the beach. We became one with the sand

and the rays. We knocked off a beer here and there as well, and I caught up on a lot of needed sleep.

Wall went over the details of the Vegas World caper for the Kid. It seemed to pain him that he had not been there to help.

The Kid had to digest the incredible *non-bust* story slowly.

"I wish I could have gone down in a casino like that one," he said. "No arrest on the old record. Red, you are one lucky fucker."

"I guess I am, at that," I replied humbly.

But a big chore lay ahead of us now. Now we had to begin the process of scouting out new places to play.

CHAPTER FORTY-FIVE

We'd finally come to the point where the mainstream casinos were onto our scam, all over the state of Nevada. They were keeping an eye on how their dealers were handling the cards. Playable dealers in the old joints were down to about one in two hundred. We had come to understand that some considerable effort would have to go towards scouting new locations, and we would have to work longer hours in order to find new weak spots in the casino system.

We did come across a place in Tahoe that seemed a little naive. It was the Cloud's Cal-Neva at the north shore. A Sonoma Valley vineyard owner had recently bought the place. The new owner, Ron Cloud, loved to gamble, and would even take over for the dealer in blackjack games and deal himself when a high roller was playing. He was a very good dealer by our standards, and he didn't have a chance.

It took some work, but this joint offered some playable dealers and a low-key security force. So, we played the Cloud's Cal-Neva Club a couple of times, but we needed a better plan of escape. The casino was located at North Lake Tahoe, right on the California border. We felt like we'd uncovered a gem and there was no heat from the house at all. We wanted to save it for the New Year's weekend.

We also heard a rumor that Skate was playing on his own, in the Tahoe area, but there was no sign of him in the Cal-Neva. The Boss wanted to keep it that way. He didn't want to share the place with anyone. In the end, he decided to try to contact Skate, to see if he wanted to arm with the old bunch again.

Skate did not hesitate.

The Boss had always liked Skate, even though he quit the crew. He was one of the best players we ever had. We treated him like a brother.

There were ulterior motives, too, behind this welcome back. Skate's face would get worn out around here, working for the Boss instead of for himself. But he would make more money working with us. Anyway, we had a short reunion and went out to play.

The Boss got a lot of satisfaction watching us perform together—a union of his very best products. As the brain, I benefited from the strength of this combination as well. With the Boss, Wall, and Skate supporting me, I was able to play even better, and with a stronger brain the crew could rack up major dollars.

Skate was worked into the rotation cautiously, and he worked the biggest plays the crew could find. Wall had stepped it up quite a bit since returning as well. He was getting back into the groove quickly. It's funny, though; some guys come back from a break and they're never able to get it going again—it's like they lose their nerve, and that was understandable.

But Wall was able to function as an all-pro field marshal in pretty short fashion. He protected me with all his heart, looking beyond the pit action for some brewing trouble. Things were looking up again, and Wall was a big part of it.

The Kid got a break when his probation ended six months early, too. The Boss gave him a shot at playing again. He agreed to come back, but he wouldn't carry a gaff, which was okay with the Boss.

The Kid's positive attitude, experience, and friendship made the crew stronger, even though he wouldn't work the gaff. An extra man in the casino, looking out for the brain, would cost the Boss a little more money, but the Kid was worth every penny of it.

We'd been split up by a series of circumstances, but losing members from time to time was part of the game. Once a guy was busted or burned out, he wasn't supposed to be able to come back. But then we weren't supposed to use mirrors on the blackjack tables either.

We'd all shared some big wins and some hard falls together. We never counted on Skate ever coming back, or the Kid either. Getting a second chance to work with the best blackjack crew ever assembled was extremely rewarding. These guys were all seasoned, skilled, experienced, and professional blackjack players. They were the best in the world, and I was extremely proud to be part of it.

For the Kid, being back on the crew replaced a void in his life. He'd been far from ready to hang it up when the law forced him to the sidelines. This gave him a chance to finish the job he'd set out to do, a chance to bring this segment of his life to a close on his own terms, though he did have a regular job during the week to supplement his income.

Wall was dedicated to his family and the hog ranch up in Idaho, but he longed for this other side—this wild side of life. Only friends who went through many battles together knew the warmth and the feeling of accomplishment that came from working together—all the time, having to rely on one another so completely.

The Boss seemed to be loosening up a bit too. He'd crank up the tunes in the car on the way to a play. He loved the Blues Brothers and a song named "Eye of the Tiger" by Survivor. He was becoming more open and friendly. He was always conscious of not letting himself get too close to the employees, but the group he had now just would not go away. We'd been through some searing firefights, and we kept coming back for more. Back when I first started, I watched the brains at that time burn out quickly—gone within the first year—and here I was four years later, still at it.

The Boss began to show his appreciation for our progress, a warm smile here, a joke there. He was much closer to the crew, and we felt it. In fact, he started to go places with his three lieutenants during the week, having lunch with the guys, instead of seeing us only during training sessions. He even enjoyed a beer with us when the weekends were over.

This period of time was the dawning of the *McCloud Era*, the name we used for ourselves in the casino: Red McCloud, Wall McCloud, and so on. It was a name that was reserved for a chosen few: the Boss, Wall, me, Skate, and the Kid. Only a few others even received consideration of McCloud status: Dog, Fats, and Toosh. Others were loyal enough, but they didn't seem to have all that it took, for one reason or another. Anyone who invested time with the crew, and who had any sand in their ass, strove to earn the McCloud title.

By the time Thanksgiving rolled around in 1984, there was a lot to be thankful for—just the fact that we were still alive and not in jail was good enough for starters.

CHAPTER FORTY-SIX

When the Thanksgiving holiday weekend came, the crew was ready for a break, and we got a good one. The Boss, Wall, the Kid, and I spent five great days together. I even made a full-course turkey dinner for the crew. We didn't plan on playing again until New Year's Eve, so the pressure to perform was off.

After some filling meals and a relaxing weekend, we split up and went back to our hometowns, mostly little towns scattered throughout the Pacific Northwest. We planned to reconvene on December 27 in Tahoe. That would give us time to tune up for the biggest weekend of the year, New Year's Eve.

We didn't communicate with one another during the break. We simply enjoyed the slow, simple pace of our small hometowns and rested up.

But the Boss arrived in Tahoe a day early. He had a plan up his sleeve that he didn't want the crew to know about. He remembered stashing some flash cards away in a bedroom closet—cards that I'd used to train with four years earlier. He got them out and used them to refresh his memory. He'd also brought an old gaff along with him. He intended to use it for practice as well—taking it out of his pocket, putting it on the table—a routine that he hadn't gone through since I joined the crew.

In the hours he spent practicing with the flash cards and the gaff, he managed to retrain himself to be ready for the tables. And, although one day might seem like a really short training session, it was enough for this seasoned professional to get back in the game.

After his on-the-sly practice session, he put the training materials back in the closet, so no one on the crew would be any the wiser. The Boss wanted to play the tables again, and he'd already done some scouting by the time the rest of us showed up.

By the time the entire crew managed to arrive, the Boss was excited, and happy to see us back together again. His enthusiasm was infectious. Everyone was itching to go.

The break had been refreshing, but too long away from the mirror can take the crew out of sync—we all knew that. The Boss, however, had already targeted a couple of dealers. He knew what shifts they worked. He even knew their names.

He also had a couple of arms lined up. Wart was flying in from Idaho and Toosh was on his way up from San Diego. A solid crew would be in place.

The Boss was even considering braining a little himself, at the new place he'd been scouting. He told us that he might even put together a double whammy and work two crews at once—something we hadn't done in over a year.

We spent a few hours at the practice table to touch up our skills, and then it was time for action. Once the crew was finally dressed and ready to go, the Boss went over some final contingency plans, in the event something went wrong.

This particular casino, the Cloud's Cal-Neva, was out of the way, so backup plans were a little different. We went over the final pre-play preparations and hit the casinos for what would hopefully be the biggest weekend of the year.

We went to the Cal-Neva first, and started scouting.

The Kid and I grabbed party hats, hoping to fit in with the New Year's Eve tourists. We were like chameleons; we blended in well with any crowd and nothing seemed out of the ordinary.

The Boss was with us, but he stayed out of sight, not wanting to expose his face any more than necessary. If I was playing, the Boss said he might try to find another dealer. He might want to take a shot at the tables, but only if things fell into place. If that did happen, we would play two-man crews and work across the pit from one another. That way we could watch each other's backs.

If the two-brain event came to fruition, Wall was to field marshal for both crews. Whichever way things came down, though, we planned to be playing hard come midnight. Midnight was when the pit bosses broke out the champagne and let their guard down. Sometimes they got downright tipsy, on this one night of the year—the only night we could count on the folks in the pit slacking off a bit.

Our crew, of course, didn't touch a drop of alcohol—none whatsoever. We had to stay sharp all the time, every time out. There was no party atmosphere for us once the mirror hit the table, with the exception of the arm. The arm could have a cocktail at the table. In fact, he almost had to have a cocktail at the table in order to play the part.

The dealers would be scattered on this night, meaning they would not work the same table for more than forty-five minutes. I wanted to be on top of it all, so I was in place at a table before a pre-chosen dealer showed up for his or her shift.

Wall and the Kid and I all staked out brain seats at three different tables, hoping to grab a shift with a playable dealer. As it worked out, one came to my table. At that point, Wall got into position while the Kid moved to a spot where he could oversee the action.

The only problem on this occasion was the table was full. I had the gaff out, I was calling for the arm, and the Kid was trying to buy the arm seat, but the woman who had it simply would not budge. Wall had already signaled Wart in from the bar, but when he arrived at the table, he had no place to play.

Wart, though, was a seasoned arm. He knew the crew depended on him to cut a deal. He offered the lady fifty bucks and got no response, so he came back with a hundred. He'd finally found her price. She'd been stubborn, but Wart stuck to his guns. As the lady got up to leave, he flipped her a black chip and said, "Here, go buy yourself a pack of gum."

Wart stepped up to the table and laid a $500 bet down in the circle.

"Money plays five hundred," the dealer called blandly.

The pit bosses didn't even waste a glance at the table. Fifteen minutes went by. No one seemed to be watching. Wart was on fire and the dealer was cold. He went up eight grand in twenty minutes, and he still seemed to be rolling. The play was on autopilot.

Wall noticed how cool it was, so he began to set up a second play, right across the pit. This time the Boss got the call. Needless to say, he was jazzed. It looked to me like his feet hardly touched the floor on his way to his seat. The Kid wandered over to help set up the second play. The Boss only looked at one card before he called Toosh into action.

Wall and the Kid had their hands full, with two plays going at once. The casino was jammed, and there were only two field marshals to monitor the entire scene. But on this particular night, it turned out to be the perfect setup. The crowd was large enough that the crew just got lost in the shuffle.

Both arms were winning and the casino staff seemed completely relaxed. I couldn't believe it. The pit bosses were more into the party scene than the action on the felt. They were playing grab-ass with the cocktail waitresses, and they were drinking champagne, enjoying a working night off.

The first forty-five-minute session came and went without incident for either crew. Then Wart took my cue and left the table. He retreated to the bar. Toosh got the signal from the Boss at about the same time, and he exited the pit as well.

It was eleven o'clock by then, so the crew regrouped and went to work on setting up another play. We wanted to be in place and playing at the stroke of midnight.

The Boss wandered back to a seat in the slots and watched his crew go about its work. I could see that he was basking in the glow of this precious moment. It seemed to warm him inside. His crew was playing his system with an unshakable faith, and with all the class in the world.

Then the Boss seemed to snap himself back into his work mode.

There was a good chance that a playable dealer would come to my table. We knew which dealers were about to go on break, so we set up at those tables. I was ready for more. Toosh was scheduled to arm for me this time. That way, Wart and I wouldn't be seen together at the same table again. When the alternate dealers wrapped up their shifts and went on break, the dealer I was hoping for came to my table.

I didn't even wait for a hand to be dealt. I simply rubbed my chin to bring in the arm. Another play was underway. This time a pit boss actually took the time to stop by and introduce himself to Toosh, but it was a half-hearted effort at best. He stayed for only one hand and then strolled off to mingle with a party that was priming itself for the midnight hour.

Toosh knew things were cool, and we began to kick ass. The totals soared. No one seemed to notice or care. I played it to the limit, going the full forty-five minutes, and Toosh was betting the table limit.

When the dealer's shift ended, I got up and gave the cash-out sign. I followed that with the head-to-the-car sign. Wall had been well removed from the action this time. He wondered why I was calling the play off.

But when he moved forward to relay the signal to Toosh, he could see the massive pile of chips on the table. He wouldn't be able to tell how much it was, but a quick glance would tell him that fifteen grand was a conservative estimate.

Wall gave the cash-out signal to Toosh, and then signaled him to head for the backup joint. Toosh acknowledged. Wall then signaled Wart at the bar. We both noticed that the Boss and the Kid were already on their way out.

We got together at the car with no heat. Then we left to pick up the arms and to confirm the size of our wins. We were really pumped up—way up. We'd come to town hungry to play, and we'd been boosted even more by the fact that this seemed to be our night.

Things had started fast, and we were primed to keep

the roll going.

"How much, Red?" The Boss asked.

"Well, Wart won sixteen grand the first play, and Toosh was around twelve thousand the second round."

"Toosh won eleven grand with me earlier," the Boss shot back.

It had been a huge take.

I put the car in gear and took off to pick up the arms.

"What a great play," the Boss belted out. "I've never seen such fantastic cards in all my life."

"Not one speck of heat, to boot," Wall noted, "on either one of you. It looks like another freebie for you, Red."

CHAPTER FORTY-SEVEN

We pulled up to the Hyatt Regency to pick up Toosh, and Wall went in to clean him up. He would watch Toosh's back as he made his way to the car. When we saw Toosh come out a side door, Wall was right behind. Wall was rubbing his forehead, to signify everything was cool, and I cruised over to pick them up.

"How much, Toosh?" the Boss asked.

"I won eleven grand with you, Boss, and twelve two with Red, for a total of twenty-three two."

The Kid had been quiet in the back seat. "Great job, Toosh," he said.

The Boss didn't want both arms to come to the same backup place, so I put the car in gear and headed over to South Lake Tahoe to pick up Wart. The Boss had a new stereo installed in the Tahoe crew car, which was a 1970 Bonneville four-door sedan. He had some new CDs in the car, and he cranked up the Blues Brothers on the way around the lake. We were all pretty stoked.

Wart was supposed to be waiting at the bar in Harrah's. Wall went in to get him.

Wall walked around the corner, and the veil of safety that seemed to have been hanging over us that whole night was shaken. "I saw two Griffin agents talking to a pit boss. I went into intense surveillance mode," he told us later. "Then I cautiously made my way over to the bar. The agents didn't see me.

"I found Wart and gave him the heat sign and nodded

in the direction of the agents. Then I gave the head-for-the-car sign. He acknowledged and headed toward the side door, away from the heat.

"I was on full alert by that time," Wall went on. "I knew the whole night's progress could hang in the balance. So, I watched Wart make his way around the corner. Then I scanned the casino to see if there was any pursuit. After that, I fell into line behind Wart. I could see that everything was cool."

Of course, we were all sitting in the car while all of this was going on, running the heater to fight off the winter cold. We saw the two of them come out of the casino, and when Wall finally rubbed his forehead, I drove over to pick them up.

"How much, Wart?" the Boss asked.

"I was in for nothing and cashed out sixteen one."

The crew was laughing and high-fiving while I drove them back to the Boss's place to fill out the sheet. This was going to be a sheet worth framing. The crew had put together its best night ever. The total was already thirty-nine three, and the weekend was young.

The Boss went right to work on plans for the next day's assault, while the crew enjoyed the thrill of running up such big numbers.

But we didn't get too jazzed. We knew how quickly things could turn. Then too, it was still early in the workweek. There would be a lot of action ahead to deal with. The big numbers on the sheet weren't really safe until the weekend was over and the crew was completely out of town.

The next morning, the Boss asked where we wanted to eat. No one had any great preference, so he took us to Lion's

Restaurant on the California side.

On the way, the Boss said, "Red, jack up the bet for the rest of the weekend."

After breakfast, the crew went to Harrah's to set up a play. The Boss stayed way back from the pit to make sure he didn't draw any unnecessary heat. The Kid found a dealer, but the table limit was only $200. There were four different table limits: $2 to $200; $5 to $1,000; $25 to $1,000; and $100 to $2,000.

Each table had a limit marker in one corner. The more crowded a casino got, the higher the limits were raised.

The Boss couldn't afford to play at two hundred a hand. Playing time was too hard to come by, so the risks were just too great to play for such low stakes. After a little deliberation, the Boss decided to alter the numbers. A simple, logical decision from an analytical angle, but it was a little tougher to actually execute than a guy might think.

Changing a table marker was the only choice. Not so difficult if you worked for the house, but of course they discouraged the patrons from doing such things.

With a newspaper in hand, the Boss sauntered over to an unoccupied table with a $5 to $1,000 marker. Then he sat down at first base and began to read his paper—at least, it looked like he was reading.

Wall and I were following the Boss's every move. We wondered what he was up to. A few minutes later, he got up and wandered back over to the slots. He didn't stay long, and then he headed back toward the pit. Three people were playing the $2 table.

First base was open, so the boss sat down. He slouched and opened up his paper. A hand or two passed before he pulled out a twenty and started playing $2 hands. He played a couple of hands, with the crew keeping a close eye on him.

Suddenly, Wall caught on to what the Boss was up to. He saw a $5 to $1,000 marker in the Boss's hand. He was about to replace the $200 limit sign at that table.

Wall jumped in to help.

He came up to the other side of the table and spoke in a loud voice, "Hang on. I want to play this hand."

He fumbled through his left pocket, and then his right.

The dealer waited as she watched Wall dig through his pockets. He had all the attention on the third base side of the table, and that allowed the Boss to finish his mission.

Just as the Boss went to slide the new marker in, Wall got loud again. "Here it is," he said. Then he pulled a crumpled $5 bill out of his pocket. He was acting like any other obnoxious tourist, and he played the scene to the hilt.

He put the five on the table, played it, lost it, and then hit the trail. The Boss was gone as quickly as he'd come.

The Kid and I watched with admiration while shaking our heads in astonishment, as all of this went down. The Boss and Wall would have to stay away from that table after the switch was done, but they'd completed their task. The Boss was remarkable when it came to that type of ingenuity.

I sat down in the brain seat and the Kid, without a signal, took up the arm slot. It only took one card before I had Wart on the way.

Wall moved into position across the pit, facing my front and the dealer's back.

The Kid moved out when Wart came in. Then he moved away from the table to help Wall field marshal.

Wart put down a $1,000, and the dealer started to say something. But then she checked her table limit marker and continued about her business. She picked up the money and counted it, and then she notified the pit, "Money plays one thousand."

She went right on to the deal. Nobody was aware that the switch had been made.

Wart started out on fire, winning several hands in a row. A pit boss came right over to introduce himself. Wart was cordial and shook his hand, but then he went right back to work on his cards.

The play rolled on for twenty minutes. We would get ahead, and then fall behind. After that, we'd get back up again. The pit boss was smart. He'd been schooled in the game more than most. He noticed when Wart would hit a fourteen with a six up and then stand on fourteen with a ten up. He took notice of the way the cards were played.

But as the play went on, a strange thing happened. A tourist walked up to the table and slapped down a $100 bill. When the dealer grabbed it and started to put it down the slot, she suddenly stopped. Then she snapped the bill a couple of times, between her fingers, and set it off to the side.

She gave the tourist change and motioned for the pit boss to come take a look. The pit boss stopped monitoring Wart for a moment, leaned over to the dealer, and whispered something. She whispered something back, but no one could hear it. The tourist got his chips and began to play as if nothing were going on. Wall saw the pit boss get on the phone and dial a three-digit number—an action that caused him to become very cautious.

I knew the pit was responding to a counterfeit $100 bill, but there was no way Wall could know that.

After a few minutes, Wall saw security heading toward

the table. He coughed and gave me the signal to get out fast.

But I knew what was going on. I ignored Wall on purpose, just to fuck with him. I looked the other way as Wall coughed louder and longer. He was beginning to panic as security closed in. He wanted me to get out.

Wall was about to go nuts with frustration. I finally looked over at him and winked. He stopped in his tracks, and two seconds later, security reached the table, tapped the tourist on the shoulder, and asked him to come with them.

I watched as Wall stood there and shook his head in disbelief while they hauled the counterfeiter away. I didn't do that sort of thing very often, but I couldn't help but seize the opportunity.

I had a big smile on my face. Wall went back to work.

Play continued. Wart's bet was up to three hands of a thousand—not your average run at the table. A few tourists had gathered to watch the big-money player.

As the relief dealers began to move around, I knew this would be his last hand. The final hand was dealt just as the break dealer showed up. Wart won all three hands and I was gone before the payout was completed.

Wart cut his bet dramatically and played a few more hands before Wall signaled him to the backup joint.

The Boss and the Kid followed me out to the car, keeping an eye on my backside all the way.

Everything checked out cool, and we left to go pick up Wart—another successful play.

CHAPTER FORTY-EIGHT

Things were going so well that night, we simply moved back into attack mode and got after another play. The opening rounds of the new season were beyond our highest hopes. We had amassed staggering totals, while playing unnoticed, at a time when we thought Tahoe held out very little potential.

Not many places in Nevada were even playable anymore, so if we could find a lax night like this, we had to go for the gusto. On a few occasions the Boss told to me to open the play with three hands of one thousand.

For the most part, playable dealers had become hard to come by, especially in South Lake Tahoe. They'd been schooled in the way that they dealt the cards—the crew called it *Harrah's style*. They would pull the card off the deck between their fingers, and their hand covered the entire card. There were rookies to be found, though, among the masses, and we kept after it until we found one.

The Boss had been in contact with Spanky for the last couple of months. He had finished up his baseball season in October. When he arrived home his wife was gone. She had filed for divorce a month before, and he wasn't taking it very well. He was going to be delayed in getting to Tahoe, for that personnel reason, and we expected him to be at the house by now. Our two arms were winning so much money that the Boss decided he needed to throw a new face in the mix. He got on the phone and called the house to see if his brother was there. Spanky answered the phone and the

Boss told him to take a cab to Caesars and meet us at the bar. The Boss told us that he was getting over his divorce and he was ready to play.

We readied ourselves and headed for Caesars at South Lake Tahoe. I found a dealer who looked impossible to the rest of the crew, but I had a little different slant on things than the others. For us brains, hole cards had become no more than a flash, but as the dealers got tougher, I simply got better with the gaff. Besides, I had really good eyesight.

In the beginning, brains could look long and hard at the glass. These days, though, every pit in the state was on the alert for mirrors. It was an era where the brain only got a glimpse of the card at best. When I said I thought I might have a shot at this guy, the crew was ready to back me up.

I moved in and got the gaff on the table. The Boss got as far away from the table as he could and still be in the same building. Wall set up to field marshal and the Kid began a foot patrol around the general pit area.

I was set up, and I had Spanky on the way. Two spots were open and waiting when Spanky stepped in. He plunked five hundred down on both spots. I coughed to get Spanky to raise the bet, but it was too late, the cards hit the table.

I looked back to catch the hole card. The dealer was fast and low. I heard Spanky above the din say something about Wild Turkey, as the hole card snapped off the deck. The card hit its low, quick apex, and then flashed out of sight. If you could position a two-foot mirror on the table, you'd have a hard time picking up this dealer. The brains saw so many cards in training, though, they could make sense of a blur—and a blur is all I could see in the mirror. I had to close my eyes and replay the subliminal message in my mind.

Spanky was ready to play, though, so I had to decide on the card in a microsecond. I signaled with my hand before my eyes were even open. I'd processed and distributed the vital information in less than two and a half seconds.

As the dealer worked through Spanky's hand, I smiled to myself. I was listening to a veteran arm work the staff and the crowd. He was gobbling like a turkey, and showing his turkey-skin boots to the cocktail waitress, who had brought him a shot of Wild Turkey.

This mastery of character should have gotten Spanky an Academy Award nomination. When an arm can take his position to the level of drawing attention to the cocky image he was presenting, he is helping to keep heat off the gaff. Gobbling like a goddamn turkey with—now—$1,000 out on the table was a masterstroke.

Whether the tourists loved him or hated him, he was playing the part of the high roller to the hilt. A high roller, the way that Spanky was playing it, was noticed. Of course, that was his job—taking all eyes off the brain. On this occasion, the dealer busted and had to pay on both hands. Spanky was shining like never before. He was piling up chips on the table while talking more about his boots than the cards. I must have seen the turkey boots half a dozen times by that time—and they were even giving me confidence. I signaled him to raise the bet, two hands of $1,200. We ended up with a productive twenty minutes of play.

Spanky's performance had been so engaging that he'd assembled a huge audience. Among those who stopped by for the show was the Boss. Wall had also moved in. He was positioned behind me. The Boss watched one hand. Then he made his way over to Wall. He'd noticed something a little more interesting than Spanky.

Of course, they were right behind me, so I could hear them talking.

"Fuck, Wall," the Boss said in a stern tone, "how could you let Red play that dealer?"

Wall looked straight ahead with his arms folded across his chest and let one more hole card go down before turning to the Boss. "Red hasn't missed a card yet, Boss," he said with a smile.

Spanky was up eight grand and had three hands of twelve hundred on the table. The Boss shuffled away—he could see that I was taking care of business.

The dealer ended his shift and we all left without incident. The biggest New Year's ever kept getting bigger, and the heat was kind enough to stay away.

We played the next day and lost four grand without mounting much of a charge. No big deal. We were tired and ready to call it a weekend. No one likes to lose, but if four grand went the other way at the end of a run like we had on this outing, it was nothing to cry about. We had amassed a $48,000 New Year's Eve weekend—*awesome.*

I handled the payoff for the crew, and gave the rest to the Boss. Instead of heading off on his own, however, the Boss wanted to savor the weekend.

"Come on, Wall, let's go eat some scampi," he said, knowing scampi was Wall's all-time-favorite meal. So that's where they headed. To Christiana's, a top-notch, five-star restaurant on the mountain, right at the base of the Heavenly Valley ski area.

Then the Kid, Toosh, Spanky, Wart, and I decided to join them, for a full seven-course meal with all the trimmings. It was a celebration fitting for the great start of the New Year, and it would be a hard meal to top.

The Boss paid the $1,800 tab and left a $400 tip. We were laughing and kidding as we thanked the Boss on our way back to the car. For a bunch of small-town Podunkers, we were having the time of our lives. The Boss turned in, after that, but the rest of us went out to blow off a little more steam.

On the following morning, the Boss got up early and called a snowmobile rental place to rent five snowmobiles. He lined them up for ten o'clock. Then he had Spanky, Wall, the Kid, and I up and ready to go by eight thirty.

CHAPTER FORTY-NINE

We arrived at the snowmobile park and proceeded to fit ourselves with the proper gear. While we were occupied with these activities, the Boss was lining up the machines. We were going to have to put up with a guide, because none of us had ever ridden one of these machines before. And, of course, the Boss wanted to operate the fastest machine so he could outrun the rest of us.

As we followed the guide up the northwest side of Heavenly Valley, the Boss was getting a little antsy. True to form, he was looking for a little more action.

When we arrived at the top, where the trail and the trees gave way to a huge open area in which the crew could play, the Boss took off first and the rest of us followed. These machines had a lot of power. They would reach speeds up to seventy miles an hour, and after some experimental jumping and racing around, the Boss started to get a little crazy.

He began to chase Wall around, trying to hit him with his machine. He finally caught Wall as he was making a wide, sweeping turn. Then the Boss rammed Wall from behind, smashing out his taillight. After that, he snuck up on the Kid and smashed out his taillight. As I watched all of this unfold, I became wary of the Boss and his agenda. So I went after the Boss from a side angle.

I missed hitting his machine by inches, but just as I went by, he cut Wall off and shoved his machine over the bank. I stopped to help Wall get his snowmobile upright, and the Boss took that opportunity to ram my machine from behind, knocking out my taillight.

The Boss was laughing and giggling like a little kid. He was having the time of his life, and then he went after Spanky.

But the die had been cast. By this time, the rest of us were all after the Boss.

It was getting a little out of control, so the guide stopped the Boss and reprimanded him for his careless activity.

The Boss reached in his pocket, took out a ten-grand packet, and handed it to the guide. "I'll take responsibility for all the damage and insurance," he said.

The guide took the money, put it in his pocket, and he let the crew run wild.

The Boss resumed his pursuit of Spanky again while the rest of us went after the Boss. But the Boss was determined to smash everyone's taillight before he finally gave up.

After an entire afternoon of chasing each other around in the snow, it was time to go back down the mountain. Wall's machine didn't have one piece of fiberglass that wasn't cracked or shattered; we all had more than a few dings, and there wasn't a taillight left standing—including the guide's. The Boss nailed his taillight on the way back down the mountain.

When we arrived at the bottom, we were all exhausted. The Boss went for a short walk with the guide; a little more money was exchanged for damages, and the guide walked away with a smile and a really nice tip.

We were all talking about what a great time we'd had, as we loaded up the crew car, and when we got back to the house, everyone was hungry, including Toosh and Wart.

We headed out for a bite to eat.

CHAPTER FIFTY

After dinner the Boss had plans to make, so he headed back to the house via taxi. He left us the car, knowing his young crew needed to blow off a little steam. We took the car and headed off into the vast fantasyland of the Tahoe New Year's weekend party scene. We were trained not to party in or near any casinos, for obvious reasons. We knew that our semi-famous faces were our own worst enemies. We also knew that the authorities would be on the lookout for us. Besides that, we'd been drinking and our guard was down.

We found a nightclub in South Lake Tahoe, a small resort town on the California side of the lake, a place where there were no casinos, and consequently no heat. The entire crew quickly mingled with the crowd. Spanky and I had done a little partying in college, and he'd developed a bit of a wild side away from the Boss. Of course, I could slide over to the wild side too, when I wasn't saddled with the discipline that was demanded of me as a member of the crew. None of the four of us were teetotalers, though, and when it was time to party, we could keep up with the best of them.

We were all in our early twenties. It was New Year's weekend. We were in Tahoe, and we all had a pocketful of money.

Anyway, we were all sitting at the bar drinking when we met up with some girls from the Bay Area. The girls were pretty buzzed, and when one of them came back from

HEAT IN THE VEGAS NIGHT

the restroom with a little white powder just below her nostril, I leaned over and told her, "You'd better wipe off your nose."

She quickly wiped away the powder residue. Then I asked, "Do you have any more of that stuff?"

"Let me go ask," she said. Then she got up and went over to a guy at the end of the bar.

She returned a few minutes later to say, "I can get you an eight ball."

I gave her $200 and she headed for the door. I watched as the guy from the bar followed her out.

It's always nerve-wracking, giving a total stranger money for drugs. A guy is just simply asking for trouble. But she came back in, walked over to the corner of the room where I'd moved to, sat down, and handed me a little packet under the table.

Wall, the Kid, and Spanky saw what was going on, so they all came over. Spanky said, "Come on, Red, let's go party. We can come back later."

We told the girls we'd be back shortly, and we headed for the door. After all, it was the 1980s and Pablo Escobar made sure that there was plenty of cocaine to go around. Cocaine wasn't something we did often, but we had done it in the past. It was something that the Boss would frown on, heavily. We all knew that, so we kept it a secret amongst the crew. The Boss did not approve of any drugs of any kind. We all swore not to say a word about it later.

We drove to a quiet place deep in a parking lot, intending to do a couple of lines of coke. I reflected on how vulnerable we would be if the cops should happen to show up, while the others got out a pocket mirror and a one-sided razor blade to prepare the coke.

Snorting blow is a situational circumstance that even the greenest rookie coke user quickly becomes familiar with. The members of the crew were no exception. In this case, as we all went through our first line of coke, Wall was the last to indulge, and he was anxious to catch up. He took the little pocket mirror from me, along with the razor blade. Then he chopped and arranged the white substance into a line.

With a rolled-up $100 bill inserted into his left nostril, Wall bent his head down to the mirror for the purpose of sucking up the magic powder. But just as he was about to draw his breath in, Spanky reached out from the backseat with a swizzle stick he'd cabbaged from the bar. Then he tickled the bottom of Wall's left earlobe. Wall barked, "Hah," and blew the white crystalline powder into the interior of the car. It stayed suspended in the air for a moment. Then it drifted down to cover the seats, our clothes, and the dashboard of the car, like snow.

Everybody laughed, except for Wall, who was kind of mad about the whole thing. But then he developed a sheepish grin, and simply prepared another line. "Keep an eye on that goddamn Spanky, Kid," he said, as he bent down once again to pull in the ecstatic powder. This time his snort was successful. Within a few minutes, he was laughing and talking just as rapidly as the rest of us.

The coke had induced a lot of chatter as we headed back to the bar, but when we got there, the girls were gone— probably the result of having just sold an eight ball of coke to a bunch of total strangers. I figured either paranoia had set in, or they'd found something more enticing to do.

Anyway, we stayed a while longer. Then we decided to head back over to the Nevada side, where the partying would go on until three or four o'clock in the morning. We had to be extra cautious in Nevada, though. The authorities there had no sense of humor at all when it came to illegal drugs.

We entered a little bar off the main drag and continued to party. We found another group of girls to hang out with. After all, we were buying the drinks and spending money on everyone in the place. We quickly became the life of the party.

We continued to dance and socialize until four o'clock or so. Then we thought we'd better get back to the house and try to get some sleep. After all, the Boss would expect us to be bright-eyed and bushy-tailed in the morning.

But just as we were turning up the street to the Boss's house, the Kid piped up with, "Did you ever hear the one about the Irishman who sneezed away his last line of coke?"

We all burst out laughing.

The Kid tried to go on, but he was laughing so hard himself that he couldn't talk.

But by then we were in the Boss's driveway and everyone began to get out of the car. The Kid never got to finish his story, if there really ever was a story.

CHAPTER FIFTY-ONE

Later that day, Wart headed back to Spokane while the rest of us flew to San Diego. When we touched down in California, Wall went with the Boss to stay at his place for a few days. The Kid and I went back to our pad.

The Boss and Wall seemed to be enjoying a new level of friendship—a deep respect for one another rooted in their long-shared past. They would have time to talk things out at some length.

I ran into Wall a few days later, and he told me that the two of them had talked about me.

"The Boss says you're getting pretty good," he said. "I told him that I thought you were better than him."

Wall didn't say this in a disrespectful way, though it did sound like there was the hint of a challenge in there someplace.

Wall told me that when they got back to the house, the Boss went straight downstairs to the practice table, grabbed a gaff, and started working on his skills again. "This went on for several days," he said. "The Boss worked with his flash cards, the brain cards, and the gaff."

When the time came to go back to Vegas, the Kid and Wall and I met the Boss and Spanky at the airport. We headed up into the friendly skies, destined for the not-so-friendly welcome that most certainly awaited us in Vegas.

Over time, I'd discovered the extraneous mental tasks that went along with braining—tasks that were carried beyond the tables. I'd come to recognize that in between plays I had to relax and catch my mental breath before whipping up my energy for the next play. It had become a job I took home with me during the week. I ate with it, slept with it, played tennis with it, and dragged it around on both the golf course and the dance floor.

The Boss was beginning to have other kinds of troubles, too. For some reason, frustration from less playing time seemed to be getting the best of him. Trips to Las Vegas were especially tense.

He seemed to be having fun, but he appeared to be showing signs of fraying around the edges, driving up on the sidewalk and over people's front yards, or performing scary airplane acrobatics.

Driving over curbs and through yards was a bit out of character for him. Stuff like that was hard to read. The crew enjoyed seeing the Boss loosen up, but they didn't like him too far out of character. It was kind of fun, though, when he drove through that flock of plastic pink flamingos, and to hear him giggling out loud while he was doing it.

When all that had happened, simply heading out to the action on any individual night had an uneasy feel to it. I was well aware of how dangerous Vegas had become, but I was still anxious to test the water. If a brain didn't remain aggressive, he was done.

For the public establishment, the crew we'd assembled was the most pressing problem in Nevada, as far as the Gaming Commission and the anti-cheating squad was concerned. A guy walking into a casino with the Kammeyer Group was known to be a man who was traveling with the hottest bunch in town, and the anti-cheating security forces in Vegas were sharply tuned in to stopping our shiners. But we continued to find cracks in their security walls, and somehow, we always managed to slip through.

On one particular night, the search for a table started out in typical Vegas fashion. Two casinos searched, and two casinos without the slightest hope for a play. Finding a weak spot in the more organized houses had nearly become a thing of the past.

So, the Boss decided to take on an experienced pit crew—a run against the most aggressive defensive effort the crew had seen yet.

He pulled into the parking lot of the Tropicana Hotel and Casino for the first time ever. Without a word, he opened his door and got out of the car. The Tropicana was well-known for its razor-sharp and vastly experienced pit crews. They'd been around for so long that they had firsthand experience with mirrors—from years and years before. It had been the Boss himself who'd instilled into the crew an almost legendary respect for the Tropicana. Seeing him ready to buck his own advice was against all of our instincts. No one, however, could imagine telling the Boss where to play.

"Where to, Boss?" I asked, before anyone else could formulate the question.

"The Trop," the Boss replied in a stern voice.

Driving on the sidewalks and stalling his airplane at ten thousand feet were things we could tolerate, but this was not a place where the crew wanted to go. However, overruling a call from the top was unthinkable. Still, I knew I was the crew's only hope.

"I'm not playing in there, Boss," I said.

"Oh, you're not fucking playing here, huh?" the Boss yelled.

"You want to play there, Boss, here's the fucking gaff."

I tossed the little mirror to him in a defiant manner.

The Boss came back with some heavy artillery. "Okay, *Johnny*," he said—referring to his one-time friend who had stabbed him in the back. He said this with bitter venom dripping from his words.

Then he turned and took three steps in the direction of the casino. He called back to the rest of the crew without turning. "Come on, you assholes." Then he continued on without any support falling in behind.

At that point, he stopped, turned around, and walked back to the car.

"Here, Red," he said, as he handed the gaff back to me.

He slid back into the car, without any show of distress, and asked, "Where to, Red?"

"The Maxim," I replied.

We operated for the rest of that evening with me calling the shots. I managed to make some solid calls and we got through a decent evening's work.

By Sunday I was feeling the roll, so I made an aggressive call of my own to take a look inside the Sahara. It was a casino that had spelled trouble for the crew in the past, but we'd come a long ways since those incidents.

Once we got inside, Wall found a dealer that was ready-made to play. I got it set up and called Spanky in to arm. He got to the table and things were up and running. The Boss found a spot in the bar for himself, right behind the table. After that, he noticed two men with beepers on their hips and signaled for Wall to follow them. But with Wall gone, the Boss became the lone field marshal.

Moments later, the pit boss hopped on the phone. I was concentrating down low to the table, but I did notice that the Boss was moving into the pit area.

The Boss positioned himself right in front of the pit boss's face and asked for a Kleenex. He was creating a diversion. It would last for only a second or two. A desperate move on his part, but I didn't have to think too hard to make the connection. I needed to get rid of the gaff.

When the Boss stepped in front of me, I pushed the gaff off the table and into my lap. Then I took a slow drink of beer, exposing both of my hands. The pit boss could see there was nothing on in front of me, but he made a beeline for the table to examine things further. Then he took up a position behind the dealer.

I knew what he was up to, but I didn't panic.

At that point, I casually stood up to leave, but I didn't get far. A houseman slammed into me from behind and pinned me against the table. The pit boss moved forward to help. I slipped the mirror into the purse of a woman sitting next to me.

The pit boss and his helper had me under control, and they began to yell, "Where's the shiner?"

One of them had a high tenor voice, while the other shouted with a deep bass rumble. They sounded like the basic formation of a barbershop quartet. I was reminded of the old Disney movie *The Lady and the Tramp*.

Then a mezzo-soprano voice screeched forth, drowning out everything else: "Here it is. Here it is," the shrill voice shrieked. I wanted to cover my ears with my hands, but the houseman and the pit boss had my arms pinned down. Then I noticed the obnoxious noise was coming from the lady with the purse.

I looked down and saw the mirror. It was in plain sight. The paper clip on the gaff had caught on an edge of the lady's purse—an easy find for the most amateur of detectives.

When I put it there, I was hoping she wouldn't find it until she was safely back home in Wisconsin, or wherever she came from.

At this point, I had nothing to lose, so I grabbed for the gaff, but the paper clip foiled me again. It caught the edge of the purse, and flipped the mirror up onto the table. Being in a crowded casino, a little mirror showing up in the center of a blackjack table drew a loud collective "Ahh" from the crowd. Not even Houdini could have escaped from this trap.

Still, I kept after it. I managed to rip my arm out of an iron grasp of the houseman, and in my last moment of freedom, I flung the gaff away in the direction of the slot machine section—a final effort to rid myself of that frightful piece of evidence.

The crowd around the table had swelled to capacity, as two uniformed security guards put a firm grasp on each of my arms. Then they led me away from the table.

Totally unaware of the circumstances surrounding what had happened at the table, the guards didn't cuff me, so I put forth an air of complete submission. As I was being whisked away, the scene around the table got busier. I could see that Spanky was being detained, along with the Kid at third base. And while that was going on, the houseman and the pit boss were over by the slots, desperately searching for the mirror.

CHAPTER FIFTY-TWO

The uniformed guards kept me well away from the table, and they seemed to be unemotional in their escort. Other security personnel set up a perimeter around the area. Then they moved in to take over. Eventually, the two guards who had me in tow to the back room began an impromptu interrogation.

"What happened back there?" the older of the two asked. They obviously didn't know who they had, so I played along.

"I don't know for sure," I told him. "This guy at the other end of the table was betting $600 a hand. Then, out of nowhere, the lady next to me started screaming and they closed the table down. They damn near knocked me over."

I was trying to sound like an innocent young tourist caught in the crossfire.

"Well, come on down to the security office with us. We'll straighten it out there," the older guard said.

At that point they fell silent and I felt their grip loosen up just a bit. I thought to myself—*these two don't know who I am.*

Right then, out in front of me, Wall came around the corner up near the escalator. He could see the bad news, but I was trying to look nonchalant about the whole thing.

Wall was tapping the last ice cube out of a Coke glass when we first appeared, and I could see him visibly stiffen, ever so slightly.

The younger guard asked where I was from.

"Oregon," I answered, with a naive shrug.

I was watching Wall's face as I felt the guards let up on their grip around my arms. His eyes popped wide open when I made my move.

I jerked both arms free, dropped to one knee, and pushed forward to get away from my captors. I did this all in one quick motion.

Wall's expression of surprise changed to one of astonishment, as he watched me literally slip through the fingers of the unsuspecting guards. There were all kinds of heat in the vicinity right at that moment, so I headed for the nearest exit, which was about twenty yards to my right.

I flew out the revolving door as I shoved several tourists backward. The two guards right behind me were stuck on the other side as I busted the revolving door from hitting it so hard. It had come off the pivot point and wouldn't turn. The guards had to use one of the other doors to get out, as Wall fell in behind them. As I was chewing up the pavement under my feet, I reflected on how the body was able to run so much faster when it was scared—like it had a hidden high gear that could only kick in when extreme circumstances presented themselves.

Over the course of my time with the Kammeyer Group, I'd mastered the feel of this reckless scramble—it felt good, in a way, pulling in big gulps of oxygen while unleashing the energy of an all-out sprint.

I zipped around a street corner and reeled off several blocks on a dead sprint. The guards had fallen hopelessly behind. As I sailed down the street, I was totally surprised that I'd been able to get out of that bind, but I didn't feel like I was out of the woods yet. I ran beyond my potential with a surge of freedom that pushed my physical ability to new limits.

I was in really good shape from training and I wasn't winded, so I pushed on toward freedom at full speed. My cross-country effort turned the tables on me, though. Security guards who were standing around outside the El Rancho saw me on the run, and they took up the chase as well.

So, I veered off in the direction of the Hilton. I was now running through open desert. I went two hundred yards across the open spaces. I had another four hundred yards to go to reach the only chance I had to lose the pursuit. I watched as it rose up before me, taking the form of a big block wall that bordered another little street and isolated the Hilton golf course from the public.

I sized up the eight-foot wall and made tracks straight for it. I kept on pumping. I could see that the extras from the El Rancho were out of their league—two of the three gave up, and there was no sign of the bunch from the Sahara now.

As I got closer to the wall, though, it seemed to grow. At one hundred yards, I recalculated. It now looked more like a ten-foot barrier that stood in the way of my greatest escape ever. At the same time, I noticed a taxi cab was now racing into view. It was about a quarter of a mile away. Then I saw one of the original security guards from the Sahara hanging out the window. He was yelling something that I couldn't make out.

This presented a new challenge. I'd just reached the street that ran along the wall, and the cab had gained an angle to cut me off. That gave me a new charge of adrenaline, and I pumped even harder.

I got to the far curb before the cab had a chance to stop

to let the guard out. I hit the wall at full speed and I felt something rip. I didn't care at the time—I was trying to get over the wall, not knowing if I could find a way over or not. It was an all-out stretch for every inch I could muster. I had to climb straight up the masonry blocks—three scrambling steps—in order to get a finger-hold on the top. Luckily, I was able to hook my fingers over the backside of the wall-cap—it stuck out an inch or so beyond the back face of the wall.

I began to pull with my arms while scrambling for a foothold with my feet.

Finally, with one last final burst of strength, I managed to pull myself up and over the top of the wall, while agents from the casinos were still lunging for my heels from behind. I didn't pause to consider my descent. I simply found myself in free fall on the other side.

It was an extremely rough landing.

A little shaken up from the drop to the ground, I managed to get back on my feet, and headed out onto the golf course. I could hear the guards on the other side of the wall as they yelled orders amongst themselves. What I got from it was that they were getting ready to boost someone up over the wall, but it was proving to be a harder task than they'd thought.

I made my way over to a huge Arizona ash tree, probably planted there years ago to provide shade for aged golfers. I sat down directly behind it. That way, if my pursuers did get a peek over the top of the wall, they wouldn't be able to see me running away. I listened and heard voices coming from behind the wall, but I stayed put. I didn't even dare to peek around the trunk of the tree. My heart was pumping like never before, and my breathing was heavy. A few moments later, one of the guards was finally boosted up to peek over the crest of the wall.

I held my breath so I could hear better and waited. Then I heard the man say to the others, "I can't see anyone out there. Let me down."

I rested there for a few more minutes, behind the tree, desperately needing to catch my breath. My throat and lungs felt like they were on fire. Then I looked down, and that's when I noticed my toe. The ripping sound that I'd heard as I'd scrambled over the wall had been the destruction of the toe-end of my left shoe, my prized Nike Air Jordans.

My big toe was now sticking out through the hole in the shoe. It was torn too, and it looked like a bloody stub—a prop, maybe, from an old Vincent Price movie.

The toe wasn't bleeding profusely, but it was noticeable. The funny thing was my toe hadn't hurt until I'd noticed it was damaged. The pain, I assumed, had been blocked by adrenaline, but once I could see it, it hurt like hell.

And when I stood up to move forward, the toe throbbed with a pain that took my newfound breath away.

I stayed where I was, thinking I was probably safe for the moment, but all the time wondering what to do next.

As I crouched behind the tree, desperately trying to come up with a plan, a golfing threesome made its way down the fairway near where I was hiding. When they continued on past me, I shuffled out and took up a position a few yards behind the clueless golfers. I stood a little off to the side.

My presence didn't seem to bother the group, but I figured that from a distance I would appear to be the fourth member of the group.

I stayed with the golfers for the rest of the hole they were playing. But when they began to approach the next tee I wandered away and slipped into the adjoining neighborhood. I was in the clear, for the moment, but I knew enough to move through the streets with extreme caution. I wanted to get as far away from the Sahara as possible.

With me on the move, and two others in trouble, I figured the Boss would head back to the hotel and set up headquarters there. By then he'd have Wall with him, and Wall could fill him in on my escape attempt.

I was still consumed with the need to put more distance between myself and the Sahara Casino, but I wasn't sure exactly where I was, so I continued to walk down little neighborhood streets until I came to one with more traffic. I made a conscious effort not to limp—anything to keep from drawing attention to myself. Eventually, I came to a main artery and found a corner 7-Eleven store.

I went inside and bought something to drink, along with a T-shirt and a hat. I figured I must be a good five miles from the Sahara by that time, which was a long ways to cover on foot. At that moment, however, I was paranoid to even be in the same hemisphere with the agents from the Sahara, and the adrenaline had not totally subsided yet.

The T-shirt and hat would change my appearance enough so the guards couldn't recognize me from a distance, and some of them might be still out there running around in cabs.

Anyway, I got some change from the clerk at the store and went down the street to a gas station to a pay phone. It was located on the side of the building by the restrooms.

I took a deep breath and an exhale with a long sigh of relief. When I thought my cover was as good as it was going get, I made the call.

"Hey, Boss," I said when he picked up the phone. "I'm safe."

"Good," he said. "Did they get the gaff?"

And that was the $10,000 question. Not only that, but I would have given $10,000 to not have to give the answer.

"Yeah, Boss. They did."

"Fuck," the Boss barked out. "That ain't good."

"I did everything I could, Boss."

"I know you did, Red. Where are you?"

"I'm down here on the corner of *Walk* and *Don't Walk,*" I told him, hoping to lighten things up a little.

"I'm in no mood for your Oregon backwoods humor, Red," the Boss admonished.

"Let's see," I said, feeling a little chastened. I had to hang onto the receiver to stick my out to check the street signs. "I'm at the corner of Twain and Eastern."

"Wall will be there in a few minutes."

CHAPTER FIFTY-THREE

The Boss rented a white Chevy Blazer for this particular outing, and Wall was driving it when he pulled into the gas station, fifteen minutes after I got off the phone.

Not wanting to look any more conspicuous than necessary, I'd walked around the block as I kept an eye out for Wall, and also for any prowling guards from the casinos that might be cruising around in cabs. Wall saw me walking so he pulled up to the gas pump.

He paid for $5 worth of gas—giving him a reason to be there—and the Blazer was sitting at the pumps when I caught up to him and slipped in through the passenger-side door.

"What'd you do, sprain your ankle?" Wall asked as he turned into a small strip mall to get turned around and headed the other way.

"No. Why?"

"You were limping like a son of a bitch."

I didn't respond immediately, and we drove on for a few moments in silence, then Wall started in again.

"Spanky and the Kid were a few steps behind you when you made your escape," he explained as we pulled to a stop at a red light. "The guards really clamped down on the two of them after you got away."

"I noticed they'd been pulled aside," I said. But we all knew it was every man for himself once the heat came down on a table.

Wall didn't ask any more about my limp as we made

our way back to the hotel. I didn't mention it, either.

The phone was ringing when we walked into the Boss's hotel room, and the Boss moved to answer it.

"Hello," he said, as he braced himself for the damage report.

He held the phone away from his ear, as usual, so we could hear the entire conversation.

Spanky spoke right up, and he had a hint of promise in his voice. "Boss," he said, "they want to talk to you."

The casino manager came on the line. "Steve," the man said. He spoke in a Midwestern nasal tone. "We have two of your people here and they're in quite a bind. We have them and, more importantly, we have their mirror."

"What mirror?" the Boss said, trying to disassociate himself from the gaff.

"You are well aware of the mirror we're speaking of, Mr. Kammeyer. But I believe we can work this dilemma out. One of your operatives is holding $6,000. We think that it's our money. You give it back to us, and you can have your people back."

The Boss didn't argue. There was no room to dicker in a straightforward deal like this. "Okay, yeah, let's do it."

The casino manager wrapped up the business. "It's a deal, then. And, Steve, it goes without saying, we never want to see any of your people in our casino again. Not ever."

The Boss acknowledged that stipulation, and he hung up the phone. He had a funny smile on his face—*another joint that would rather strike a deal than drag everything through the courts.*

The Boss seemed pleased with the outcome. The whole transaction actually displayed a great deal of respect on both sides. But we all knew that violating the pact he'd just made about not going into the Sahara Club again would be crossing a very serious line. It would be asking for the worst. It was also a casino's best defense against our crew disrupting their cash flow in the future. Forcing the Boss to agree to never come back made their troubles at the blackjack tables much more manageable.

The Kid and Spanky gladly turned over their money, but they were barred from the place, personally, for life. They were able to walk out free men, though, and on top of everything else, they seemed to be thankful that I had gotten away as well.

The Kid was especially fortunate. He really didn't need another session with the court system in Nevada. The authorities had made it very clear—he would pay dearly if he were ever caught with a mirror again.

Later, Spanky told me that he flagged a cab, and the two of them went through another casino to make sure they were clean. Then they carefully made their way to the backup joint, the Peppermill restaurant on the Strip. From there, they called the Boss again.

"Where ya at?" Wall and I heard him say.

"The Peppermill."

"We'll be right there."

The Boss decided to go along for the ride on this one, to pick up his brother. The three of us jumped in the car, and the Boss filled us in on the details of the pact he'd made.

I wondered, as we drove, if my escape had prompted security to free Spanky and the Kid. Without me, they really didn't have much of a case. But another deal had been struck, and I was quietly impressed with the respect that had been shown towards the man I worked for.

"Let's make sure they're totally clean before they get in the car," the Boss said as we pulled into the parking lot of the Peppermill.

"I'll go in the back door and find them," Wall said. "Red, you watch to see if they're being tracked."

I nodded and the Boss watched as two of his top McClouds disappeared into the backup joint.

Two minutes later, the Kid and Spanky emerged out through the lounge door, near the rear of the Peppermill. Wall was right behind. I tailed them to the door, but I stayed inside and then hurried around to exit out the front. Limping all the way.

I made a quick check of their flanks as they made their way around the building. When Wall came into sight, he wiped his forehead—*all was cool*. The McClouds were reunited, and we headed back to the hotel.

The Boss went right to work on breaking down the bust. He figured we were spotted by the eye in the sky, and the pit had been alerted from above. Security must have been on the way before the pit boss even hung up the phone.

I'd been seconds away from getting a jump on the heat. I'd already removed the gaff from the table, and I was standing up to leave when I was slammed from behind.

"We were late getting out," the Boss grumbled in a disapproving tone. "We've got to catch that pit guy on the phone and get the gaff out earlier."

"They acted pretty cool, Boss," I offered. "There wasn't much to read."

But this didn't count for much with the Boss. The bottom line was that the crew had been beaten to the punch.

His voice took on an even sharper tone. "But we have to see that coming." He was nearly shouting at that point. In years past, that would have been the end of the conversation, but I wanted to calm things down.

"Boss, I fucked up. I saw the diversion that you created and I didn't react. I should have taken off right then, but I didn't," I explained.

"Why?" the Boss asked.

"I was so shocked to see you in the pit, I think I froze for a split second, Boss."

"Well, fuck, Red, don't let that happen again."

"Oh, you can bet on that, Boss," I said with a slight smile on my face.

Then the Kid followed up with, "Well, we're not in the slam. Let's break it." He said this with a burst of excitement in his voice.

So, I played off the Kid's remark. "Yeah, let's break it."

The Boss reacted as any great teacher would when his pupils exhibit a growing sense of confidence. He knew we had taken his lecture seriously, and now we were ready to move on.

The Boss caught the spirit. "All right," he said, with a happy smile on his face. He reached for the sheet, and we got ready to wrap up the weekend.

CHAPTER FIFTY-FOUR

The crew headed back to San Diego to rest up for a week, but the Boss was already talking about another visit to Bullhead City. The heat was still turned down low in Laughlin, but we wanted to play it safe. We always looked for the perfect situation before setting up a play.

I'd been limping around on a sore foot for nearly twelve hours by the time we finally got back to the apartment where Wall and the Kid and I were living. Wall helped me get my shoe off. Then he cut my sock away with a pair of scissors. The sock had formed a crusty cast around my toes—a cast that consisted of coagulated blood and white cotton sock.

He got a little plastic dishpan from the kitchen, filled it with warm water and Epsom salt, and told me, "Soak it for an hour." So, I sat through an entire episode of *Bonanza* with my foot in the dishpan.

About halfway through the program, Wall went back into the kitchen, filled a small saucepan with hot water, and warmed up the soaking solution. It felt too hot to begin with. I was about to pull my foot out, but I quickly got used to it.

When the show was over, Wall had me pull my foot out and put it on a towel. The skin on my foot looked all pink and shriveled—except for the big toe on my left foot. That toe was hard and swollen, and it throbbed. It also glowed with a kind of pastel red sheen.

"You're gonna lose that nail, Red," he said. Then he told

me, "Sit there for a few more minutes. I'll be right back."

I heard his car start out in the parking lot, saw his headlights sweep around to the street, and a few moments later, I heard him come back in. He was carrying a brown bottle in his right hand and a box of Band-Aids in his left.

"You need to keep the nail in place until it's ready to come off," he said. "Otherwise, it'll get sorer than hell. It might even get infected." And to make sure it did not get infected, he poured a generous helping of hydrogen peroxide over the entire toe.

Once the liquid quit fizzing, Wall pulled out a Band-Aid. Then he secured the toenail to the toe. "You'll need to change that every day or so," he said, and then he handed me the box of Band-Aids.

After that, Wall, the Kid, Spanky, and I had a really good week together. We spent a little money, played some golf, and chased a few girls for fun. In our occupation, we never really knew when, or if, we might get another day off, so we were always motivated to get the most out of each situation. We all knew, as one day would burn through to the next, the good times might come to an end at any given moment.

On the evening after the great Epsom salt soak, I pulled the Band-Aid off my toe, and I could see that it was getting a little black around the edges. I never had much trouble with it, though, except for one time when I was dancing with this chunky girl at a disco bar and she stepped on my sore toe with her spike-heeled leather boot.

We knew we couldn't stay away from Nevada forever, though it was a living hell to us. The only thing that was fun for us in Nevada centered around the teamwork, camaraderie, and the skill we possessed to pull off such an unbelievable caper.

We did have to check our moral compass from time to time to see where we stood amongst the masses. I was asked one time by a religious girl that I knew, "How will God judge you, when you die?"

I thought for a moment and said, "I remember one time, on the Vegas Strip, we were at a casino at three thirty in the morning. I was waiting for a certain dealer to come back from her break. I sat down at a *twenty-one* table to wait. There was a man, with a small stack of $25 chips, sitting on first base. The man was dressed in a suit and tie and was playing $50 a hand. He looked like he'd been there all night, drinking and gambling. He smelled like alcohol and sweat. The stack of green chips in front of him quickly disappeared.

"As the dealer began the deal, she said, 'Sir, if you're not going to play this hand, you'll have to leave the table.'

"'I'm just waiting for my drink,' the man replied.

"'No, sir. I mean it. If you are not going to play this hand, you'll have to leave the table.'

"The man stood up, checked his pockets and then his wallet. He was obviously out of money, and he sat back down. The dealer repeated herself one more time.

"The man slapped the table with an open hand and said again, 'I'm waiting for my free drink.' The dealer motioned to the pit boss, and one minute later two security guards come over to the table and addressed the gentleman.

"'Excuse me, sir. You need to come with us.' They grabbed the man, one guard on each arm.

"The man said, 'I'm waiting for my drink!'

"The two guards escorted the man to the nearest door and threw him outside and told him not to come back.

"So, to answer your question, if God really cared about who won at the blackjack table, I think he would want us to win—no matter how we did it."

"Why do you think that?" she asked.

"Because the casinos kick the winners out and serve free alcohol to the losers. At worst it would be a toss-up."

She thought for a moment. "Well, two wrongs don't make a right. I think you're all going to hell," she said finally.

"Maybe so," I replied. I wasn't trying to justify our existence, I was just telling the truth. *Which one is the worst of two evils?* I wondered.

CHAPTER FIFTY-FIVE

After almost every outing in the casinos, the Boss needed to regroup. He was one regrouping son of a gun. As a crew, we were all living double lives. We were totally different people away from the casinos. We were fun-loving, polite, and friendly young men—and in contrast to our career, we were honest. We also had many friends in the San Diego area. But when we played cards, we were animals—aggressive, ruthless animals. When we found a weak spot in the casinos, we went for the throat. Consequently, we had to make a mental transition every week, unmatched by anyone or anything that I had ever heard of. We learned to deal with both aspects, and it was livable for the time being.

We planned to stay home the following weekend to let my toe heel. As luck would have it, one of my old friends from Oregon, Bill, was in town and he called to set up a visit. We planned to get together the following day.

When Bill showed up, he wanted to play some golf, so I asked the Boss and Spanky if they wanted to join us. At that point, the Boss set up an afternoon tee time at the Admiral Baker Golf Course in San Diego.

The Boss had recently been in contact with an old accomplice of ours, known to the crew only as Mole, who happened to be Wart's little brother. Mole was a helicopter pilot turned lieutenant commander in the Navy. He set us up with a tee time at the private military golf course that was associated with the base where he was stationed.

When we showed up at the gate to check in, an extensive checking of IDs ensued.

I was still limping around with a sore toe, and none of us were very accomplished golfers, so we began to lose ground on the foursome that was playing in front of us pretty quickly. On the twelfth hole, the group behind us yelled something at us, but none of us paid much attention—except for me.

"Hey, Boss," I said, "I think that old guy is yelling at us."

"Fuck him."

When we reached the fourteenth hole, the Boss hit his ball down the fairway. And though there were signs all along the way—NO CARTS ON THE FAIRWAYS—the Boss, in an attempt to stay ahead of the group behind us, drove his cart out on the fairway anyway.

As he was addressing his ball, the old guy back on the tee was yelling again, so the Boss stepped away from his ball, and a second later a ball from the tee came rolling right past where the Boss and I were standing.

The Boss was pissed off. He went over to the ball and hit it back toward the tee. The old guy yelled something again. Then he jumped in his cart and headed right for the Boss, yelling, "Get that cart off the fairway."

The Boss ran over to the cart path—he had good angle to cut off the old guy's cart. Then the Boss jumped on the back of the old fellow's cart. He began to swing it from side to side. He almost made the old boy's cart tip over. Two wheels were off the ground on several occasions. The guy in the cart looked like he was scared half to death. He was hanging on for dear life.

Then, after the Boss had his fun, he let go of the cart and headed back to his ball to play his shot.

But it wasn't three minutes later that six military jeeps showed up, and they headed straight for us. They pulled up, stopped, and directed us to follow them. With two jeeps in front, one on each side, and two jeeps in the rear, we were escorted off the golf course.

We were shuffled into an office to wait for the brass to show up. One hour later, three uniformed men arrived and interrogated us for over half an hour. It turned out the old guy in the cart was a retired admiral. He had more than a little pull around the base, and after the panel of officers finished with us, we were told that we were barred from ever playing there again.

As the Boss was escorted to the main gate he was laughing—laughing like I'd never seen him laugh before. Once our nerves settled down, the rest of us began to laugh along with him.

My friend Bill was completely shocked over the incident.

But with everything that can happen on any McCloud excursion, Spanky and I were not bothered by the incident. We'd been through the ringer a hundred times before, and we'd become used to this kind of attention, though we didn't really like it much. We just went along with the Boss.

We always got a charge out of reliving some of the past harrowing moments that would crop up from time to time, when things went wrong. We didn't see this rehashing as bragging so much as a form of therapy.

Wall, for instance, kept reliving the Sahara bust—or maybe I should say the Sahara escape.

We were all sitting around at the Boss's place when he sidled up to me and asked, "Is your friend Bill cool?"

I didn't say anything out loud. I simply gave him the

cool sign. Then he knew he could tell his version of the Sahara events in front of Bill.

By this time, the crew all knew what had happened, but Wall was a magnificent storyteller, so we were all willing to hear his latest rendition.

He stood with a beer in the middle of the living room and commanded the attention of everyone in the room. "First," he said, looking at Bill, "the two Sahara security guards didn't have any idea who I was, so I was able to watch the whole thing. You might say I had a ringside seat."

Bill just sat there and listened to Wall.

"Yeah," I said, giving Wall a moment to collect his thoughts. "You were trying to get that last ice cube out of your Coke glass." I was flicking Wall a little shit for not being by the table when the shit hit the fan.

"Anyway," Wall started in again, seeming to ignore my comment, "we were in the Sahara Club playing blackjack, and I was just coming back from following two housemen. I had a glass of Coke in my hand. I was coming around a corner by a staircase when I first saw Red. He was walking through the lobby with the two guards hanging onto either side of him. I was stunned.

"*What the hell happened,* I thought to myself.

"It was like Red said, I was standing there, tipping back my Coke glass, trying to get the last ice cube out of the bottom of the glass, and things looked kind of distorted through the glass. At least, that's the way it seemed at the time. I mean, Red actually looked happy, like he was involved in some kind of a drill or something—like he wasn't actually in any kind of trouble at all.

"Then, just like he was responding to some kind of a cue—a cue that only Red could hear—he dropped to one knee, drove his elbows towards their grasping hands, and bolted away. The guards were reaching to re-grip Red's arm, but Red had broken free.

"You should have seen him," Wall laughed. "He hit the revolving door like a nose tackle going after a tackling dummy, shoving the tourists back out the door. Then he turned the corner.

"I'm here to tell you, Red was this high off the ground." Wall was holding his hand about waist high. He made it sound more like a cartoon chase than a card cheat on the run.

Wall chuckled at that point, and then continued. "Red's little legs were moving so fast you could hardly see 'em.

"Then there was his sprint into the desert. I could see him; then I couldn't. I could see him; then I couldn't. I'll tell ya what, ol' Red, man, he was flat-fuckin' movin'."

The Kid shook his head and said, "Red, you lucky fucker."

Everyone laughed at that—even the Boss, as he shook his head in disbelief.

Bill was just sitting there with his mouth wide open as he listened to the story. We grew up together, playing football in high school. He was the quarterback and I was the fullback for three years running. He was a little shocked, hearing about my new career. But it didn't surprise him that much. He knew me to be a little on the wild side, but this was a little much for Bill.

Wall continued. "Red was getting so far away I could barely see him, but I could tell that he was headin' to the golf course. Then I saw someone climb over the wall at the golf course, and two or three other guys at the bottom of the wall. Later I knew it was Red that had gotten away."

Wall's story ended and we all headed out the door. Bill was still shaking his head in disbelief.

CHAPTER FIFTY-SIX

The rest of the crew took advantage of the twelve-day layoff, myself included, but I had to devote most of my attention to healing.

When Thursday of the second week rolled around, the Boss got the crew together and took us out to dinner. We discussed our plans for the upcoming trip to Bullhead. We managed to settle some hanging short-term business as well. The Boss had another item on the agenda, as well. He wanted to begin training some new people sometime after the upcoming weekend. He knew he would need some new faces soon.

When I took the large Band-Aid off the big toe of my left foot later that evening, I could see that the entire toenail was gleaming back at me. It looked like a piece of obsidian— *blacker than the ace of spades*. I could feel that a new nail had started to grow at the base of the old one. In a few days old Blacky would be dislodged.

After I replaced the Band-Aid, I took a moment to reflect on just where things stood right now, with me and the Boss and the crew.

The McClouds had been operating for a very long time at this point. Our mugs were familiar to a lot of the pit bosses and dealers in both Reno and Vegas. I'd been in the middle of some big-time Las Vegas heat operations, and Wall was well-known too. The Boss, though, he was still number one on the most-wanted list in almost every casino in Nevada. We had become well-experienced, hard-nosed, sought-after card cheaters.

The authorities—corporate, civil, and private—had mounted such an extensive effort to stop our crew that it had become nearly impossible to operate. The cops were extremely thorough in their efforts. They were smart and on top of their game. By this time, I'd been exposed at all the places where the crew had played, and I was the only brain now, aside from the Boss. And, to make things worse, neither of us could realistically expect to last much longer.

As far as Spanky was concerned, he had one more weekend to play before he was scheduled to return to the California Angels minor league system. After that, he would be gone until fall.

The following Saturday morning, the Boss was up and full of energy as the crew packed into the plane for the flight to Bullhead. Spanky and Toosh were going to arm, while Wall and the Kid and I were to set the stage. The way the Boss was acting, it seemed like he intended to sneak in some play of his own if the opportunity arose. He'd honed his brain skills back into shape, and it sounded like he anticipated some action.

It wasn't until later that I found out what was going on. Wall was kind enough to fill me in on the details. On my last sprint to freedom, at the Sahara Club, after I banged up the big toe of my left foot going over that wall, I'd been limping pretty badly. In fact, that very morning, when I pulled the Band-Aid off to inspect the injury, the old toenail came with it. But it was still sore, very sore, and I suppose at that time I was still limping—though the limp seemed to be more obvious to everyone else than it was to me.

In any event, the Boss had determined that I would not be able to brain. I wouldn't be able to run if there was heat.

It's funny how little things can become big things in an enterprise like this one.

I thought briefly about Benjamin Franklin's old adage— *For want of a nail ... the kingdom was lost.* Of course, ol' Ben had a different kind of a nail in mind. I smiled at the thought of it.

On the other hand, the Boss seemed to find my untimely injury to be an ideal opportunity for him to practice up on his braining, though he still hadn't said anything to me.

We landed at Bullhead and checked in. Toosh was the only man left on the crew with a clean name by that time, so he took care of renting some wheels. The crew really needed a car here. We needed some physical object to run to if things went sour. It was a bit of a false sense of security, though—even in a car, a police helicopter could pin us down very easily.

Everyone got dressed and headed to the shuttles to cross the river to the Laughlin casinos—except for the Boss and me. The two of us drove the eight miles around the dam and parked the car in case it was needed. Wall, the Kid, Spanky, and Toosh took the shuttle boats, so they were already there and scouting by the time we arrived.

The Boss and I met up with the rest of the crew in the Pioneer Club. Wall had already found a dealer, and he was rubbing his nose to let his brains know that a play was available. The Boss hesitated just long enough for me to zip past him and slip into the hot seat. Suddenly my big toe had become a nonissue. The adrenaline had kicked in.

Wall left at that point, and I settled in to work. The Boss backed off. I suspected he really wanted to be in the brain seat, but his hesitation showed him to still be a little rusty.

By the time the Boss looked back, I was signaling Toosh in to get the money to work. Wall and the Kid took up their positions. But as soon as the play began, Toosh started to lose. Things continued for thirty more minutes, and the crew kept losing ground. We were down about six grand.

When the dealer finally went on break, the crew was down nearly nine thousand. The pit bosses seemed to take a liking to Toosh, though, as he continued his downhill slide, and they seemed to be getting a little nervous about how much money he was losing.

The federal government had recently passed a law that every transaction over $10,000 in cash had to be recorded and claimed as income by the casino. The pit obviously didn't want to have to record this big cash drop. They wanted Toosh to quit before it reached the $10,000 mark.

But the dealer came back from his break and the play continued its downward spiral. Our losses, at that point, came to $9,300, and Toosh had two hands of three hundred in the betting circle. The pit bosses were verbally pulling for Toosh to win the next hand—and he did.

He won one and lost one for the next three hands in a row. Both Toosh and the pit seemed to be at the point of pulling their hair out. The casino actually appeared to be pulling for Toosh.

As the cards were dealt on the next hand, one of the pit bosses leaned over and put a hex on his own dealer—all for show, of course—nobody at the table really believed in that sort of thing.

But Toosh had a *sixteen* and a *twelve,* while the dealer had a *six* up. I gave Toosh the stiff sign, so he stood on both hands. Then the dealer turned over a *ten* for a sixteen and after that she hit with another *ten.* She had a busted hand.

Everyone cheered, including the pit.

Twenty minutes passed, as the pit continued to worry, now nervous about how much money Toosh had in front of him. He'd been on a roll ever since the pit boss put a hex on his dealer. By this time, Toosh had piled up about $6,000 in chips, and he kept winning clear up to the dealer's break.

The pit boss looked like he'd aged ten years—believing, maybe, that he really had put a hex on the dealer—and he might be fearing trouble from his boss.

At that point, I signaled the last hand strategy to Toosh and got up from the table. The play was over and I headed for the car. Toosh stayed and played for a few more hands, and when he played his last hand the pit boss offered him a free room for the night and dinner.

Wall saw all of this going on, so he gave Toosh the *cool* sign, allowing him to take the offer. Once Toosh was squared away, and on his way up to his room, Wall signaled him to the restroom to relieve him of some money. The Boss didn't like the arms to have too much money on them when they were away from the rest of the crew.

Wall said later that when he asked Toosh about the drop and the cash-out, Toosh told him he was in for $9,300 and cashed out for $13,300, but he still had some chips. He cashed only $9,900 because he didn't want to have to fill out the IRS paperwork for cashing in over $10,000.

Wall took ten grand from him and made arrangements to meet him for breakfast at seven.

The next morning, the crew prepared for another few rounds in the ring. I felt like we could pull off another good day. I'd owned the dealer we'd worked the night before. I was anxious to get in another forty-minute stretch somewhere, and the Pioneer would be a good place to start.

Then the Boss called everyone together to go over the plan of attack. "Red, you, the Kid, and Toosh go to the Nevada Club and scout for dealers. Wall and Spanky will go with me to the Pioneer."

I was ready to play. I was surprised the Boss wanted to bum time scouting.

"Why scout, Boss?" I asked. "I'm ready to ream the Pioneer." But I felt my momentum lose a little steam, and I wondered what the Boss might have up his sleeve. I should have realized that he was thinking of braining himself.

"Well, just take a quick look," he told me, in a reassuring manner.

So, the crew loaded into the shuttle boats and went into their amphibious operation. One of the unique aspects of playing in Laughlin was the flotilla approach. It felt as if we were riding with the Marines onto the beaches at Normandy. We knew a fierce battle lay ahead, and we had only a few seconds of calm before the storm—Betty Grable, apple pie—all for our country, our mothers, and all those poor bastards who dump their hard-earned dollars down the biggest currency drain in the world—the casinos.

Once in the Nevada Club, I headed up to the bar and ordered a Coke. I figured I'd kill some time while the Kid did some scouting. I scanned the overall scene, and I studied the pit area for anything unusual. Fifteen minutes passed before I decided to find a dealer and get some excitement going—and excitement was what I was about to run into.

CHAPTER FIFTY-SEVEN

It wasn't until we were back in the hotel that Wall told me what had happened at the Pioneer Club that morning. Wall began to tell his story.

First, he told me how the Boss had embellished his scouting assignment. "He started back in the slots at the Pioneer with his hat on," Wall said, "the one with the holes in the brim. It seemed to me like he was trying to calm his nerves.

"I felt kind of funny because you weren't there, but I found a dealer and gave the signal; you know, I rubbed my nose. I was standing behind the table closest to the door.

"Then it all became obvious. The Boss had planned on playing all along. I think he was going to play the night before, but you beat him to the punch. It was kinda funny, though; he started for the table, but then he stopped. It was the same kind of pause that cost him his seat at the banquet the night before.

"Even though you weren't around, it seemed like he had to evaluate his courage for an instant. It seemed like a real struggle as he fought his way to the table—like he was walking through molasses. Finally, he jerked his body out of its frozen momentum and moved forward.

"I saw him pause at the edge of the slots. Then he took a deep breath, and continued. The brain seat was open, so he sat right down. He snuck another deep breath as he threw a $100 bill on the table and asked for nickels.

"The dealer counted out the $5 chips and pushed them

across the table in four stacks. The dealer couldn't seem to keep his eyes off of the Boss's weird hat. Anyway, the Boss arranged the chips to his liking, and then something seemed to kick in.

"Suddenly, it was like he was back in the saddle—ready to take his chances and play without inhibition. He had the gaff on the table and he brushed aside his fear. It seemed to shed from his shoulders like a light cover of dust.

"He looked to be beyond fear at that point, oblivious to the consequences and penalties that came with the hot seat. It had been an entire year since he'd unsheathed his sword and set it on the table to do battle.

"And then his recent training appeared to take over. He caught the first hole card. It seemed like he'd become another person—kinda like Clark Kent after changing his clothes in a phone booth.

"I'd taken a couple of steps forward," Wall went on, "before the Boss's hand even made it to his chin. Spanky had a clear view from the bar, and he was on his way. The Brothers Kammeyer were about to be engaged in a rare live performance at table fourteen.

"For the Boss, it was a career-topping show. He could enjoy being the headliner one more time. It seemed like he wanted to show the world that he was still the master of his own game—and the icing on the cake was working side by side with Spanky. I was thinking while I watched them, *This should be recorded in the Blackjack Hall of Fame.*

"Anyway," Wall continued, "the dealer laid the cards down, and Spanky reeled in most of the first ten hands. He started out betting two hands of five hundred, and then the Boss signaled him to bet more. As the play rolled on, Spanky got up to three hands of a thousand each. The dealer was cold and Spanky was getting good cards. Finally, the pit began to scurry around a bit, but they didn't really know what to do. The head pit boss decided to change dealers in order to put out the fire.

"The Boss seemed to be a little bit bummed out about that, but he stayed to see if he could catch the new dealer's hole card too. He was shocked to discover that this dealer was easier than the one before—so he bore down and stayed with it."

Of course, all the time that that was going on, I was next door waiting for the crew. I'd been sitting in the bar for thirty minutes, and suddenly a weird feeling came over me. I began to wonder if the Boss might be playing.

On my way over to the Pioneer Club, I saw the Boss as he was coming out. I watched as he strode through the second set of doors. He was moving fast, and he had an unreadable blank look on his face.

When we met, I asked him, "Did you get heat, Boss?"

"No," he replied, without breaking his long, meaningful stride.

I kept pace with him for another two dozen strides. He held his blank expression just long enough to draw the suspense out to a peak. Then he startled me with a complete change of character. He broke out into a childlike giggle, the kind of giggle that he'd always reserved for his proudest moments. The cat was about to burst out of the bag.

"I beat 'em for thirty, Red," he laughed, "me and Spanky."

"Thirty what?" was all I could think to say.

"Thirty grand."

The pride just oozed out of the man. The total take spoke for itself. The Boss had shown some real balls to play the tables again.

"In twenty minutes?" I asked.

He nodded with a smile and then moved on.

I gathered my swirling thoughts. I'd been set up and worked over by a pro. I was dumbfounded, but equally impressed. This had been a masterpiece effort by an artist.

But now it was my turn. I felt like I had to kick-start myself into action. I moved on with my best effort—which was a slow, unhurried pace at best. I forced my footsteps forward. My thoughts shifted to the triumph of the Boss's moment. Even though it came, in some part, at my expense—the fact that the Boss felt like he had to prove his skills was enough. I took it as a compliment that I had pushed the Boss back to the table.

I started moving a little faster, and I considered that I might have been the key factor to get the Boss to take a look under his hood and see how his engine was running.

Pounding out a thirty-grander in a quick hit-and-run, with Spanky as the co-pilot, was a one-shot deal. A kind of *You don't need to question my standing ever again* type of a statement. And it was received loud and clear.

My long walk took a good turn when Wall appeared out of nowhere and put his arm around my shoulder. He was going to break the news as gently as possible.

"Did ya hear?"

"Yeah," I replied, with a pained tone.

"Don't take it personal, Red. The Boss had something to prove to himself, and to all of us." Wall said this from a genuine heart-to-heart perspective.

"I know."

Wall stuck with me down to the shuttle boats and back across the river. Toosh had car duty this time. He drove back around the dam to provide pick up service.

When the Boss and Spanky were safely across the river, they began to relive their moment to its fullest—laughing and giggling as they replayed the big win. It was a rare pleasure to see the Boss let his hair down and express a sense of contentment.

As we rolled up to the hotel, the Boss excitedly called off play for the rest of the weekend. He was going to savor the moment.

This was another good sign for the crew. The Boss was cognizant enough to realize that pushing things further would be greedy—and probably dangerous.

But he and Spanky were hugging and slapping high fives in the parking lot of the hotel. Of course, some of the show was for me. But I was big enough to give the Boss his due, and I celebrated with them. After all, we'd all become great friends, a tight family of sorts.

CHAPTER FIFTY-EIGHT

The glow that encapsulated the Boss burned strong and bright as the crew assembled for an early, relaxing dinner. We all soaked up the warm rays of his long-overdue sense of fulfillment, and we basked in our leader's aura. We were proud to have played a role in the long road that brought us to this moment. The Boss was still very much the Boss. It had really never been a question amongst any of the McClouds—including me—and it never would be again.

It was impossible to know what to expect in the coming few weeks, though, as we loaded up for the flight back to San Diego. We had celebrated hard, riding the crest of the Boss's wave, and we were totally drained by the time we left town. Except for the Boss. He was as sharp and alert as ever, still riding high. Not only had he violated his own policy against getting emotionally attached to his crew members, his crew had become his family, far beyond anything he'd grown up with.

But the two brothers had to part shortly after the big win. Spanky was due back at training camp. Wall and the Kid shook his hand. The Boss and I hugged him. Then Spanky jumped into his car, flashed us a big thumbs-up, and drove off.

But the time had come. The Boss knew his frontline faces would burn out soon. The casinos had finally had enough of our shenanigans and they'd begun to change the game. They'd educated themselves as to our mode of operation. They knew two things had to happen—they knew we had to bet large sums of money, and they knew we had to use a mirror to win.

The game itself had become a burnout. We suspected the casinos had our pictures in every dealer break room in Nevada. We played for two weekends in a row. One weekend we played a total of five hands and had to run out of every casino. The sheet looked ridicules. Point-one, point-one, and point-one— for twenty plays in a row. I was a tough customer, but not that tough.

We had other information too. We knew that the authorities had reviewed the film at the Pioneer Club, which told them that Steve Kammeyer had been in Laughlin with his crew. We didn't have a chance. We needed to stay away from Nevada for an extended period of time.

The Boss gave the order to train some recruits The Kid and I thought this might be a waste of time, but we followed orders and gave the Boss his due. The Kid took an ad out in the paper and began to wade through hundreds of responses. We narrowed it down to six that might be worth an initial screening. We did nothing but practice with the new guys for a few weeks. It was three full weeks before the Boss even showed his face. Then one day, he showed up at the Kid's apartment.

"Hey, Boss," Wall said.

"Hi, Gator," the Boss answered back. He walked over to the table where the Kid and I were working with the wide-eyed rookies. He watched for a moment so he wouldn't interrupt.

Then he stepped forward and said, "Hi, I'm Larry Williams." He reached out to shake hands with each of them.

The Kid rolled his eyes when he heard the Boss's alias, so he replied, "How's it going, Larry?"

"Good, Kid."

The Boss didn't have to say much. His teachers had done a stellar job with the pupils. The Boss was proud of them. The whole operation could almost roll right on without him, and it didn't take long before he'd seen enough and was ready to leave.

As he approached the door, Wall said, "See ya, Lawrence." This comment had a smart-ass twang to it that brought a smile from the McCloud crew.

None of the new bunch had earned a nickname yet, but they'd been sticking with the training and showing promise. They were actually ready to contribute soon. Nobody earned a nickname until they were on their way to Vegas or some other target for live combat.

The crew continued to work a few plays in, now and then. Sitting at a table with a mirror was really fucking hard for me at this point. I was about ready to give it up. Running out of a casino after just five or six hands was getting old. We played Tahoe and the outskirts of Reno once a month without drawing too much heat, but there wasn't much sense in pushing it.

The Boss seemed burnt out. He didn't carry a gaff anymore. He didn't even go into a casino very often. I was pretty much the foreman by then. I called the shots and the Boss supported my decisions. Wall and the Kid busted their asses to protect me, and I knew how sharp, competent, and dedicated the support team really was. It helped me brain for a little while longer than I should have. But we were working under extreme conditions during that time. The McClouds were well-known, and we had to perform at peak levels at all times to avoid final termination.

The new arms' hard work finally paid off. They were baptized in a casino in Reno called the Shy Clown. Only three of the six selected actually had what it took to run with our group. They were presented with the nicknames of: Violence—a small, soft-spoken guy who wouldn't hurt a soul; Smoke—who smoked cigarettes like a fiend; and Freud—named after the famous psychiatrist. The Kid and I had a feeling these guys wouldn't last long.

But the bugs began to work themselves out, and the new arms worked smoother each time around. We limited ourselves to out-of-the-way casinos as the summer progressed. Sadly, our old veteran arms were all burned out, after taking big chunks of cash out of those small, tightly monitored venues. We really needed the new guys.

The Boss still wanted to find a new brain. I thought that would be impossible, but he was keeping an eye out for any possible prospects. He knew it would take someone really special, if he could even find a guy who would put a piece on the table again. An experienced card cheater is not somebody you'd find in the want ads.

The Boss even set up some evaluation sessions for some hand-picked prospects—guys he'd met at his gym. He tried training them himself. Some of them had the guts, but their character was questionable. Others weren't smart enough to learn the strategy.

By the time midsummer rolled around, every casino in the state was aware of our group. Stress levels were so high that the Boss decided to take a month off, hoping things would cool down a bit.

Wall and the Kid and I headed north to my hometown in Oregon for some rest. I drove my seventy- six Pontiac

Firebird Formula 400 to Oregon, with the two of them in tow. We found a peaceful and therapeutic refuge in the vast, tree-covered forests and the tall mountains with fresh, clean air to breathe. It was a nice contrast to the eye-bulging intensity we'd been experiencing in the desert.

For me, it was refreshing to step out of the pressure cooker for a few precious moments, and to think about my future after burnout—which in our business and in the current climate was inevitable. It was never a matter of *if you get caught*; it was a matter of *when you get caught*. And the consequences were unknown.

But the Boss, he had destinations planned all over the country. Early in his journey he caught up with us. He was on his way to visit his mother in Eugene. From there he was heading to Connecticut to check on Spanky's progress—he was playing Double-A ball with the California Angels farm club.

Steve had nurtured and supported his kid brother all through junior college, and then on into USC. Spanky was now off to a solid start on his voyage through the minor leagues. He had a serious shot at making it to the Show.

The Boss knew that, and he wanted to keep his support solidly in his brother's corner.

CHAPTER FIFTY-NINE

But everything didn't go as planned. And while Wall and the Kid and I were lounging around in Grants Pass, Oregon, I received an overly long call from Spanky. He was still in Connecticut.

"When Steve arrived," he started in, "I met him at the airport here. We had some time to kill, so we decided to go back up and fly around the local area. Steve wanted to see the layout.

"Anyway, I strapped myself in and we took off. Then Steve started zigzagging through the hillsides as we made our way over to the Angels' minor league complex.

"Boy, I'll tell ya, Red, as many times as the crew has been close to disaster over the years, it never seemed to me like we were ever on the verge of losing absolutely everything. But here we were, just me and Steve, and there wasn't a casino within a hundred miles in any direction. The way Steve was flying, though, one mistake could prove fatal.

"We finally got to the training complex, and we could see a few of the position players going through their drills on the field below. But then Steve got a wild hair up his ass, and he looked over at me with that devious gleam in his eye—you know the one I mean—and he said, 'Let's dive bomb 'em, Spank.'

"Lookin' back, I could see it was stupid, but I didn't want to question his judgment, so I told him I was all for it. Of course, I'd flown a lot of hours with Steve and I had total confidence in his skills. We'd been apart for a few months, and I was in for a little excitement.

"So what happened was, Steve tipped a wing hard to the left, and then in a flash we were zooming down towards the field. The altimeter readings plummeted—two thousand feet; fifteen hundred; one thousand feet; seven hundred...

"Then Steve pulled back on the stick and gave it full power at five hundred feet. The airplane groaned as it fought to defy gravity. After that we climbed back into the sky. At the moment, we were giggling with unstoppable glee—feeding off the fear we'd instilled in the folks on the ground, while boldly laughing at the fear we felt ourselves.

"It was a real rush.

"Then we climbed back up to three thousand feet. Steve tipped the wing again, and we were diving back for an encore, to buzz the field. We dove out of the sky, straight at the pitcher's mound—two thousand feet; fifteen hundred; one thousand feet; five hundred. And I'm here to tell you, Red, that last two hundred feet was really pushing the limit. I'm not kiddin'. My eyes were as big around as Frisbees.

"And all the time I was thinking about the force and the speed of the airplane. I was wondering if we might be past the point of its mathematical ability to pull out."

"Holy shit, Spank," I offered. My right hand was about to squeeze the telephone receiver in two while Spanky talked.

"Then Steve pulled on the stick as hard as he could," he went on. "The dive bottomed out with well less than two hundred feet to spare. The ground rushed so fast, a gum wrapper on the baseline looked like a sheet of plywood.

"Steve continued to pull on the stick—we gained

altitude at the very last instant. But before my heartbeat began to slow down, I heard Steve shout, 'Oh fuck.' And when I looked up, I could see the problem.

"A huge metal tower for a high-voltage power line that was situated on the top of the hillside had completely filled the forward windshield, and we were headed straight for it."

"Holy jumped-up Christ," I yelled. My right hand was getting numb from squeezing the receiver.

"The giant steel girders were a literal dead end," Spanky said. "But in the split second before impact, Steve veered the plane hard to the left. I heard this loud *bang*— and then we were nearly upside down. The wing had clipped the top power line.

"The funny part of it was," he said, "we almost made it. We missed the steel girder, but we were seriously out of control at that point. Steve cranked the stick all the way to the right. Then he punched the rudder. He hit it hard enough to throw the opposite wing back up—just enough to catch a little lift. It was nothing less than a miracle, Red. Then the aircraft managed to roll and stabilize. We gradually began to gain a little altitude after that."

"Goddamn it, Boss, you crazy fucker," I said to Spanky.

"The damage to the wing was extensive," Spanky continued, "but the plane was still flyable.

"But there was more to deal with than the status of the aircraft. The severed power line fell with a shower of sparks into the sun-baked, brown summer grasses below, and the hillside above the ball field burst into flames. A thick brown smoke rose in a growing column. It looked kinda like the funnel cloud of a tornado.

"Steve and I both knew we were lucky to be alive, but

we also knew that there'd be hell to pay for all of this. We'd violated some serious aviation laws.

"Steve got on the radio after that and reported the fire. Then he announced that he was coming directly in to the airport to file a report on the incident.

"'Why do that?' I asked him, wondering if we might be better off to cover our tracks.

"'Because,' Steve replied in a monotone, 'we should be fucking dead.'"

I wanted to say something reassuring, but I couldn't think of anything to say. Then Spanky went on.

"Steve knew he'd pushed every rule to the limit—he'd pushed the technology of his airplane and the unyielding mathematical formulas of gravity way beyond the point of survival. I can't tell you how lucky we were, Red."

I'd come to know the Boss very well by this time, and I knew what he must have been thinking at the time—*he'd managed to save himself and his brother, but he had pushed things way too far, even by his own standards.*

"Once back on the ground," Spanky continued, "Steve parked near the control tower and walked into the airport administrative offices to turn himself in. The FAA was notified and he was placed under house arrest until the proper officials could be contacted. The authorities met with him and reprimanded him for the incident. They revoked his pilot's license, and gave him a citation. A formal hearing was scheduled to be held in ten days.

"Steve stayed a couple more days with me," Spanky said. "Then he decided to go to Philadelphia for a week before returning for his hearing.

"Anyway, the way things worked out seemed like another miracle to me. Steve was found guilty of breaking federal aviation laws, for flying under the five-hundred-foot minimum, and for starting the brushfire. He was fined $10,000, plus the cost of the fire, but his license was reinstated.

"The authorities took into consideration the up-front way in which he'd handled things. And it seemed to be clear to the aviation officials that he had learned his lesson."

I wondered as I hung up the phone if Steve had really learned his lesson, or if he had just instinctively known the best way to handle the officials.

We had all been through some tremendous ordeals over the years—Steve, Spanky, and me—but this one seemed more than just a little over the top.

CHAPTER SIXTY

After discussing the Boss's crazy stunt, Wall and the Kid headed for Idaho. I was hoping the Kid would stumble across a few pointers while he was up there that would improve the taste of his Bitterroot chili. But, in spite of everything, I couldn't get my mind off the strange story that Spanky told me about the Boss and his miraculous airplane maneuvers. When I tried to go to sleep that night, I experienced a recurring nightmare that I was in the Boss's airplane and we were about to crash—but I would always wake up just before we hit the ground.

The worst of it was, each time I fell asleep, I'd always have a vision that we were just about to crash into something different—a mountain, a skyscraper, a giant stovepipe cactus. And I would wake up, but then I couldn't remember much about the dream.

I finally managed to trick myself to sleep by lying in bed thinking about something positive and trying to picture myself playing baseball in the big leagues.

The Boss called the following morning to inform me that he'd had a fun time with Spanky, but that his brother's ball team was on a bit of a losing streak. The funny thing about the call was, in all the time we talked, he didn't say anything about the incident with the airplane and the power line—not one word.

After that, and over the weeks that followed, I was aware that the Boss never did tell his crew, his good friends, or anyone else that I know of about the incident in

Connecticut—the incident that had almost taken his life. He didn't want us to know that he'd done such a stupid thing.

Anyway, the Boss gave me instructions over the phone that day as to where he wanted to meet after he gathered up the rest of the crew. He said he'd already lined up Fats to arm—and the way it worked out, the three of us McClouds finally met up with the Boss and Fats in Reno. But we didn't play there. Instead, we flew on to Tahoe in the Boss's airplane.

I looked the plane over pretty closely before climbing aboard, but the wing had been very professionally repaired and repainted. There was no way to tell by looking at it that our pilot had clipped a high-voltage line in one of the greatest aerial feats ever known to man—even if only two men on the face of the planet actually knew about it.

That weekend, however, turned out to be a nice reunion. The crew basked in the glow of the Boss's good mood. Fats had developed into one of our favorite arms— he was a very pleasant fellow who got along with everyone. And he'd proven himself to be loyal during his long-running time with the McClouds. In fact, by now we all pretty much considered both Fats and Toosh to be one of our own.

In any event, we enjoyed another $20,000 weekend, although we did have to hustle out of three or four unfriendly joints in a pretty big hurry. Wall was getting me out in plenty of time now, so it was nothing major.

We worked a short Sunday that weekend, and then the Boss called it off. He wanted to take his troops up to Christiana's for dinner.

Though known mostly as a ski resort, Heavenly Valley stayed fairly busy during the summer, with its five-star restaurants, and the Boss was in rare form. He was splurging on extravagant items as never before—caviar, Stoli vodka, hors de oeuvres, Chateaubriand, and, of course, scampi for Wally Gator—all of it topped off with bananas flambé for dessert.

Before the evening came to an end, the Boss called for everyone's attention, and then the crew fell silent, anticipating a moment to remember. It had something to do with the way the Boss called for all the wineglasses to come together in a toast.

There was emotion in his voice as he slowly lifted his glass in the air. "To the best damn crew one ornery boss ever had," he said.

And these were the words this group of young men longed to hear—and I knew that we all deserved to hear them. The glasses clicked together in a show of unity, and we nodded to one another. After that, we toasted each other individually, in a *ping* of ringing glass that sounded like wind chimes in a soft summer breeze.

As the night raged on, the crew and the Boss united as one. But before we all filed out of the restaurant and went our separate ways, he gathered us together one last time. As we were going out the door, the Boss told us that we might go at it again in three weeks in Vegas. We were all a little reluctant, but we all agreed anyway.

This new reduced schedule kept things from getting too hot, and we were actually still able to generate a decent cash flow. Even the Boss seemed okay with it. He didn't want to push us over the edge—and it appeared to me as though he'd decided to slack the pace a little, rather than seek the thrill of an unrelenting attack.

And to me, a three-week break before another play felt

like the very best therapy. We could savor our outstanding meal with the Boss for nearly a month before going back to work. And we all knew that when we did go back there was no guarantee we would survive the day, much less an entire weekend.

Wall and the Kid took advantage of the time off to escape back to Idaho. Wall's dad needed help separating feeder hogs for market. And I couldn't wait to take another break myself. I jumped in my Firebird Formula 400 and hit the road for Oregon, for some quality time of my own—some time for reflection. My mother had passed on eight years earlier, but I still had a father and three brothers. I never did fill them in on the details of my work. I simply didn't want to worry them.

As it turned out, though, for the first time since I'd joined the crew, I began to wonder where I might be going next. I felt like I'd been through almost every test imaginable. I'd stood up for the crew, which meant standing up to the Boss. But the way I came to think about it was that I would never have had the strength to challenge someone who I'd come to admire as much as I admired the Boss if I hadn't been able to pass every test he'd put before me first.

Still, there was a sense of change in the air—I could feel it—and I could tell the other guys were feeling it too.

I had no idea what was waiting for me beyond this little retreat in Oregon. But whatever came up, I was ready to deal with it. I had come a long way from my naive start four and a half years ago. I knew I was getting way too popular as a brain. In a sense, I was gearing myself up to take my punishment—or maybe I should just walk away. One thing was certain, though—I felt like I had a lot to be proud of, no matter what people might think of this outlandish career I'd chosen.

The question I continually asked myself was: living here in this small town, what could the locals possibly know about what I did?

But somehow things were different here. I could feel it. I knew that my off-the-mainstream career was separating me from many of the folks I'd gone to school with. Wall and the Kid, though, they didn't have to hide their part-time jobs. They were heroes back in Potlatch, Idaho—as were other crew members who would occasionally show up there for a visit. Attitudes about Las Vegas in a little, God-fearing town like Potlatch were less than favorable. Local people there simply thought gambling was a sin, and they were proud of the hometown boys who'd been able to figure out how to beat the system.

Anyway, as long as things were moving forward, it was important for me to stay in touch with the Boss. I knew he'd laid over in San Diego for a couple of days, but then I lost contact with him. He'd mentioned to Wall something about needing to take care of some West Coast business.

Like I said, though, things had changed, and everywhere any one of us went, we felt like we had to budget a little bit of time to think about the future. We all knew, instinctively, that the time in our lives had come when we would have to move beyond *the crew*. Playing time had been so scarce that new faces alone couldn't keep it going. As hard as we worked, we could see that the little chink in the *casino* armor would eventually close.

We knew too that we had drawn more blood from this bank than we ever should have. On the other hand, there was no point in turning back now. We were all dedicated to playing it out to the end—and, we all knew, one big bust would end it. But we seemed to have come to the collective conclusion that none of us had anything to lose by riding it out.

There was simply no other way to do this story justice.

Anyway, the Boss was in Arizona when he made his next contact; he simply said, "I'm going to have to delay that scheduled trip to Las Vegas."

"Okay, Boss," I dutifully replied.

There was a long period of silence on the line. I sensed that he wanted to tell me something more, but then he continued: "Some things have come up that I need to take care of."

I started to respond to this, but he went on.

"Let Wall know, will you?"

I told him I certainly would, and he hung up.

CHAPTER SIXTY-ONE

For the first time since my mother died, I found myself more worried about somebody else more than I was worried about myself—I mean, really worried. I was worried about my friends, but I was more worried about the Boss. He was up to something, and I had a real strange feeling about it. One of those things that I'd learned to read over the last few years, but I couldn't put my finger on it.

I began to spend a lot of time thinking and visiting old childhood haunts. I would walk in the park along the river late at night and ponder both the past and the future. Most of the crew and all of the arms had gone on to other things, like reliable jobs with vacation pay, paid time off, and health insurance, all to help their growing families. I supposed I would need to make the same transition in the very near future.

I was sitting around at my dad's house one day, wondering about the general state of things. The career that I'd chosen several years ago had changed me. I was a hardened young man at twenty-five years old. I had been scared to death on numerous occasions. I'd been in the back room of a casino nine times, scared every time. I've had guns stuck in my ear and cops pulling pistols on me. I'd run for my life and came out physically unscathed.

Sitting there, I couldn't believe that it was actually me who had gone through all that scary shit. I had just wanted to play baseball.

In order to get my mind onto other things, I climbed

into an old Ford Bronco that I kept around the place and drove down the Rogue River to Galice. I found the river to be relaxing, just sitting on the bank contemplating the force of the thing as it made its way to the sea—the loud, wild white water plunging through the canyons, cleaning things so thoroughly, and the calmer, flatter places where there used to be ferries before we had bridges.

I'd read in the newspaper the night before about some guy back in the 1920s who'd found an old Spanish coin just downstream from the mouth of Galice Creek. Of course, that lucky find told local historians that Spanish conquistadors—or whatever they were called back then— had made their way up the Pacific coastline to Gold Beach, and then on up the river more than a hundred years before the area had been settled by American pioneers and disgruntled, displaced gold miners from California.

I found all of that interesting, and I tried to imagine the challenge of walking up the Rogue River from Gold Beach to Galice before there were roads—or even trails. It seemed like a feat that would barely be humanly possible. It is really rough country—straight up and down and solid rock. People were a lot tougher back in those days, I suppose.

Thinking about it later, I concluded that the only way the Spanish gold piece could have been left there was if the man who was carrying it had died there. Otherwise the fellow would have moved heaven and earth until it was finally recovered. If he'd died, though, by an Indian's arrow or some other mishap, the coin would have fallen with the body of its possessor. The flesh and the bone, and the wool and leather clothing, would have dissipated into history after that, until all that was left was the gold piece.

My little excursion did manage to take my mind off of

things for a while, but when I got back home, the old anxieties returned. I thought about the Boss. As playing time in the casinos had dwindled, he was getting more than just a little bit antsy. He was desperately trying to find a source of revenue to replace the one that was rapidly going away.

The Kid and Wall had taken up jobs in Idaho. Wall, of course, went back to work on the family hog ranch. It was a large ranch and needed a lot of maintenance and upkeep. The Kid got a job plowing new phone cable into the ground. They both needed some additional income, as we all did. But, being the brain for a long period of time, I'd been able to save quite a bit of money. I put off looking for a job.

At the end of it all, I got tired of worrying. So I packed my bags and went back down to San Diego. I decided to stick it out with the Boss for a while, to see what he might come up with.

CHAPTER SIXTY-TWO

When I arrived in San Diego, I settled back in at my condo in Solana Beach. I called the Boss and talked for a short time. He told me that he'd started dating a recent acquaintance. She was a very pretty gal, about thirty years old, and I'd met her only one time before. I didn't know much about her. She and the Boss decided to take a short vacation to Belize—a former British colony, now a small independent country on the southern tip of the Yucatan Peninsula. The Boss had had many girlfriends before. One of them he fell in love with. She was a stewardess on the Pacific Southwest airliner that crashed in San Diego in 1978. He never let himself get close to a woman after that tragedy.

I gave Wall a call to let him know what was going on. All I knew about the Boss's trip was that his new lady friend was trying to find out what had happened to her husband. The husband had been missing for quite some time. She wanted to check out the last place from which she'd heard from him, and, of course, that was Belize.

Two weeks went by before I heard from the Boss. Spanky was finally finished with minor league baseball, and he was due to arrive in San Diego the next day. The Boss wanted me to come over to his condo to hook up with him and Spanky.

The minute I walked in the door at the Boss's place, he waved his hand and said, "Follow me, Red."

He was headed for the room that I used to stay in, and

when I first stepped over the threshold, I discovered the entire place had been completely rearranged. There was a large table in the middle of the bedroom, covered with maps, and there were maps plastered all over the walls. It looked like something the British Admiralty might have used to plan a military operation during World War II.

The Boss had maps of a multitude of different places, and there were red-headed pins sticking out of the surface at strategic locations.

"Here's what we've got going, Red," the Boss said, with a lot of excitement in his voice. Spanky giggled nervously, knowing what the Boss was about to say.

Then the Boss turned and produced a list of things we needed to buy. "Here, you'll need this," he said, and he handed the list to me.

Then he straightened up and said, "Red, we're going to smuggle some weed from Belize into New Mexico."

"What?" I was alarmed. "Really?"

"Yeah, Red. Here's the plan."

"Fuck, Boss, I don't know about this."

"Before you answer, hear me out."

By that point in time, I'd been with the Boss for a long time, almost five years, so I gave him the benefit of the doubt. But it really felt strange to me. The Boss had always hated having anything to do with drugs in the past. I began to wonder if he was really that desperate to get his hands on some money.

I knew it had to have something to do with the new gal that he'd met a couple of months earlier, but I sat down to listen anyway.

He began with a location out in the southern desert near Carlsbad, New Mexico. He pointed out the pins on the map where we were to set up. He talked about making our own landing strip and having a four-wheel-drive pickup with high-speed fuel pumps in the back—pumps to be plumbed into auxiliary tanks that would hold enough aviation fuel to refuel his airplane.

He anticipated that he might very well be chased by U.S. Air Force jets—which, I decided as I sat there, was a lot different than being chased out through the front doors of a casino by a bunch of bouncers—but I continued to listen.

The plan was, we would need to clear a runway area that would be just long enough for his twin-engine Cessna to land and take off again, but not long enough for a military jet to land.

"You and Spanky will need to dig a hole at the end of the runway. It will need to be four feet by five feet by two feet deep," he told me. "That will be the place where you'll have to stash the five hundred pounds of weed when I land."

Again I thought, I'd been with the Boss for a long time now, and I would normally trust his judgment, but this entire gig was beginning to sound a little iffy to me.

The Boss continued. "We will construct a cover out of plywood. I will rent a storage unit or something, so we'll have a place to work out of.

"Anyway, the plywood cover will be placed over the pit. You and Spanky will have to put dirt and sagebrush back over the cover to hide everything. While you're doing that, I'll be refueling the plane. That way, I can get the hell out of there before the feds can get a fix on us.

"Once I take off, you and Spanky will put the sagebrush on the runway so no one can tell that anything has been disturbed from the air. You'll have to rake away any signs of human activity. Then you'll jump in the truck and get the hell out of there."

He paused for a moment to study my face. He was sizing me up to see what I was thinking, but then he went on. "Then we'll come back in a week or so and get the weed."

The Boss had designed this move in a similar manner to the way we played cards—get rid of the evidence and let the jets chase him until he could find a place to land with no evidence on the plane. He figured he would probably be in some trouble, but there would be no evidence to convict him.

"That's the overall plan for the whole thing," the Boss said, "but, of course, there are a lot more details we need to go over."

We sat in silence for a few minutes, and then he asked if we were all in.

I hesitated for quite a while before I answered, but I finally told the Boss that I would help on the ground.

"But, no flying for me on this sortie," I said with a stern voice and sideways look at the Boss. And he knew why too, as he looked over at Spanky.

Smuggling drugs wasn't my thing—it really wasn't his gig either—but, in the end, my long-held respect for the Boss won out.

I told him I was in.

CHAPTER SIXTY-THREE

The following day I went out and purchased a three-quarter-ton 1972 Chevy four-wheel-drive pickup with a canopy. Spanky took me down to the car lot to pick it up. We talked extensively about the Boss's new move. We were both scared to death about it—but we were also both extremely loyal to the Boss, and we were determined to prepare for every little quirk and aspect in order to make this brainstorm a successful venture.

We purchased all of the material for the pickup that we found on the Boss's list. Then we called the Boss to let him know we were ready.

We met back at the Boss's condo to set a date on which to meet with him in Carlsbad. We pored over the maps in the spare bedroom for a couple of hours. We even took notes to be sure we were all on the same page.

Every detail was covered to the Boss's liking. We were going to meet in two weeks. Spanky and I would drive the pickup and the Boss would fly his airplane with the newly installed long-range fuel bladder.

Ten days went by pretty fast. I took the opportunity to look up some of the particulars on our destination. Carlsbad, New Mexico, turned out to be another high-desert town, like many of the ones we'd been visiting in Nevada over the years. Its elevation was about thirty-five hundred feet, and the year-round temperatures ran from minus-16 in the winter to 116 in the summer. But instead of gambling, the area's major industry was the mining of potash—most of which went to make commercial fertilizer. I wasn't expecting to find a whole lot of exciting things to do in Carlsbad.

Finally, though, D-Day was upon us. It was time for Spanky and I to hit the road. We needed enough time to drive from San Diego to Carlsbad, with a day or two to spare in the event that some unexpected contingency might pop up. The trip was uneventful, except for the nervous conversation between Spanky and I about the Boss. For the first time since we'd known him—and Spanky had known him for a very long time—we were actually worried about the Boss's mental stability. We were also worried about our future freedom and the mission that we were about to undertake.

But we were committed. "Damn the torpedoes and full speed ahead" was the nervous rallying cry for the mission. We put fear behind us, and we began going over the details of our responsibility. We wanted to make sure that we executed the plan set forth by the Boss in every single detail, to avoid any mishaps.

The crew arrived in Carlsbad and got some motel rooms. By then, the Boss had arrived at the airport and we drove over to pick him up. We were tired from all of the preparations, so we ate a nice dinner at the diner across the street, and then retired for the evening.

The next morning we went right to work. After breakfast, the Boss told us we were headed to the Ruidoso airport. We drove two hours to Ruidoso. Then we headed up the hill to the airport.

Ruidoso was nothing like Carlsbad. It turned out to be a tourist town, with camping in the summer and skiing in the winter. Some of the slopes around there ran up to the twelve-thousand-foot level.

Anyway, when we arrived at the airport, the Boss said, "Let's go, Red."

"Where to, Boss?"

"We're going to the operations room at the tower. When we arrive, I'll give you the *cool* sign. When I do that, I want you to make a disturbance. Trip and fall, kick a garbage can, bump into someone... The idea is to give me ten seconds without any attention being paid to me."

"Got it, Boss."

We arrived at the tower room, and the Boss gave me the sign. I proceeded to trip over the trash can. Then I fell to the ground. Both of the men in the room came over to see if I was all right. I stood up, brushed myself off, set the trash can upright, laughed at my clumsiness, and then headed out the door, back to the truck. When I arrived at the pickup, the Boss was right behind me.

"Get us out of here, Red. Now!" he exclaimed.

I started the truck and hit the road as fast as I could without making a scene.

"What happened?" Spanky asked.

The Boss chimed in. "I took one of their flight communication radios."

It all made sense now. The Boss needed a radio so he could monitor the heat as he flew back across the border.

With that mission accomplished, we headed back to Carlsbad. On the way, the Boss instructed me to head to the location in the desert where we would make the runway. We'd already studied the maps, and we were familiar with the roads, so we were able to drive straight to the site.

We spent the rest of the day removing sagebrush and other desert plants. It would take a couple of days to complete the task, though there wasn't really a lot of brush in the way—and after a few long days, the runway was ready.

The last step was to get the seven fifty-five-gallon drums filled with aviation fuel. That way we could get a little practice fueling the Boss's plane before he took off for Belize the next morning.

Spanky and I got very little sleep the night before. We were wide awake on adrenaline, though. We got up, cinched our belts an extra notch, took a deep breath, and headed out to meet the Boss for breakfast. We went over the final plans, finished eating, and headed for the truck.

We dropped the Boss off at the airport to get his plane. Then we headed for the makeshift runway in the desert to meet up with him out there. As we approached the runway in the pickup, we looked up to see the Boss on his final approach to the runway. By the time he'd taxied to the end of the strip, we were there waiting for him.

We fired up the pumps, hooked the ground cable to the airplane—to prevent unwanted static electricity—and then we began to fuel both tanks at the same time. The Boss monitored his watch to see how long it was going to take. When we finished fueling, the Boss said, "Awesome. That took less time than I figured."

We put everything away and went over to the Boss, where he stood out in front of his plane. I could tell he was thinking about all the last-minute preparations.

He kept looking at his watch. Then he said, "I'd better get going, Red. I'm already a half hour later than I wanted to be."

As he headed for his airplane, I said, "We'll see ya at noon tomorrow."

He waved back over his shoulder. Then he stopped, shook Spanky's hand, clapped his brother on the shoulder, and climbed into his plane.

CHAPTER SIXTY-FOUR

Spanky and I stood and watched as the Boss disappeared into the horizon. Then we headed back to town. We went to the airport and refueled all seven barrels with avgas. Then we headed back to the motel to prepare for the next day. We both worried a lot about the outcome of this mission. This was all new to us, but we'd been with the Boss for so long, we were used to his boldness. He had a larger set of balls than most.

The time dragged on. To kill some time, we headed down the street to a carnival that had been set up for the locals. It seemed like forever for darkness to come, but we finally made it back to the hotel and drifted off to sleep.

The next morning, we ate breakfast and headed to the desert. We arrived several hours early and had some extra time on our hands, so we got out our pistols and did some target shooting. As noon approached, we went to the end of the runway to wait for the Boss. We stood next to the hole we'd dug several days earlier.

Twelve o'clock rolled around, but the Boss was nowhere in sight—we waited and waited and... When four o'clock rolled around, Spanky and I looked at each other, and we both said at the same time, "Something's wrong."

With expressions of concern on both our faces, I looked at Spanky and said, "Knowing the Boss, if he didn't make it today, he'll be here the same time tomorrow." We stayed out there until we knew it was way too dark for the Boss to land. Then we headed back to the motel.

The next day rolled around and we mimicked the same routine as the day before, but the Boss didn't show up again that day. We waited until dark again. At that point, we really started to worry. Back at the motel, we tried to figure out what to do. We decided to call the Boss's San Diego attorney, Blackie.

We finally reached the man on the phone and asked him if he had heard from the Boss.

"No," he replied. "The last time I saw him, Steve told me he was headed to Vegas."

Then Blackie told us to hold on for a minute; he had another call coming in, a call that he had to take. A few minutes went by before the attorney returned to the line. Then he asked me who I was.

"A friend of Steve's," I said.

"What is your name?"

I simply told him that my name was Red and that I was currently out of town with Steve's brother.

Blackie continued on in a somber tone of voice. "I'm sorry to tell you fellows this," he said, "but the FAA just called and said that plane 5770M has crashed in Belize. The official report is that the pilot was killed on impact."

There was dead silence on the line. I couldn't respond and Spanky had a look on his face that told me he desperately wanted to know what was going on.

"I'm really sorry to have to tell you this, Red," he said. "Steve was a good man—a very good-hearted and decent man."

Spanky had moved over close to the phone, so he heard the last few sentences that Blackie uttered.

"Are you sure, Blackie?" I could feel my hand losing its grip on the phone receiver.

"It's official, from the FAA," he said.

"Fuck," I shouted. I said goodbye at that point, and then broke into tears, just as Spanky did at the same time. The Boss was dead.

I gave Spanky a hug that lasted for a full minute.

As we pulled apart, I said, "Let's get the fuck out of here."

We packed our bags, climbed into the Chevy pickup, and headed for Oregon. We cried like little babies. As we drove we talked a lot about the Boss. We couldn't believe it—we were in complete denial.

We cried some more, realizing the reality of the situation. We didn't even stop for fuel. Spanky just climbed halfway out the window, grabbed the nozzle from the barrels in the back, and pumped avgas right into the fuel tank of the truck as we drove. It was the most miserable road trip imaginable. By the time we hit Oregon, twenty-two hours had passed. Our eyes were red and swollen and we were beaten completely down to nothing.

We stayed at my dad's house for one night, and the next morning Spanky took the pickup north to Eugene, where his mother lived. He had the chore of telling her the bad news. My dad was working in Alaska on the pipeline at the time, so I was the only one at his house. The deck around the house was old and needed to be torn down. I started in on that—something to do in an attempt to relieve the sorrow that both Spanky and I felt.

There were three sets of old concrete stairs under the deck, and I proceeded to break them up with a twenty-pound sledgehammer. I swung that hammer with a vengeance for three solid days, trying to relieve the emotional pain. The blisters on my hands were so bad on the second morning, they were bleeding, and my fingers were stiff. But I grabbed that hammer and continued on until I was so tired, I couldn't pick it up.

I still had the burden of calling members of the crew to let them in on the sad news. First it was Wally Gator and then the Kid. The rest of the crew would have to come later. That was all I could handle at the moment.

I wondered around for days after that, feeling the need to put things into some kind of a logical order. Nothing seemed to fit, of course, so...

A month went by, and then two. And then it finally came to me that I couldn't simply let the Boss's scam die with him.

I called Wall and said, "Hey Gator, let's go play one for the Boss."

"Yeah, Red, let's do it." The enthusiasm in his voice left me with the impression that he too had been looking for some kind of mechanism to relieve the pain.

We gathered together a crew consisting of Skate, the Kid, Wall, Toosh, and myself to meet in Vegas on the 29th of December, 1985, to continue the Boss's quest.

ACKNOWLEDGMENTS

Sources cited:

Andersen, Ian. *Turning the Tables on Las Vegas*. New York: Vintage, 1978.

Revere, Lawrence. *Playing Blackjack as a Business*. Secaucus, NJ: Lyle Stuart, 1977.

Zamost, Scott A. "California '21' Cheaters Sought." *Las Vegas Sun*, April 3, 1982.

GLOSSARY OF TERMS

STANDARD CASINO BLACKJACK:

DEAL: To distribute the cards to start the play of a hand of blackjack.

DEALER: Casino employee who deals the cards and runs the game of blackjack from one hand to another.

DOUBLE DOWN: A player can double down by placing his/her first two cards faceup and doubling their bet to get one card down.

HAND: One round of play in the game of blackjack.

HIT: In the game of twenty-one, it is the player's option to stay on his/her first two cards or to take a card from the dealer to better his/her hand. When a player takes an additional card, it is called a hit.

PIT BOSS: A casino employee who monitors the pit area to keep everyone honest, including the players and the dealers. Pit security, in a sense.

SPLIT: When a player has two cards of the same value, he/she may turn them faceup, spread them apart, place an equal bet next to the original bet, and make two separate hands.

STAND: The act of sliding your first two cards under your chips, letting the dealer know that you are finished with your hand and won't be taking another card.

KAMMEYER BLACKJACK:

ARM: He's the high roller. He bets the crew's money and takes signals from the brain.

BRAIN: The most skilled player at the table. He catches the dealer's hole card with a mirror. He signals the arm to hit, stand, double down, or split. He plays everyone's hand at the table—except for the unsuspecting tourists'—with a slight hand movement.

CARD COUNTER: A player who can keep track of the cards in such a manner that it gives that player an advantage over the casino.

CLEANUP: A series of procedures that the crew follows to make sure nobody has been followed, tracked, or spied upon. Mainly the "arm."

CROSSROADER: Slang term for a card cheater.

FIELD MARSHAL: He's the sentry, the lookout, the eyes in the back of the brain's head. He monitors the entire scene in the casino, and he sounds the alarm via hand signals.

GAFF: Slang term for "mirror."

GAMING CONTROL AGENCY: The Nevada Gaming Control Board is the state agency that governs all gaming activity in the state of Nevada. They control the gaming licenses for casino as well as the laws for the games themselves. They are the premier gaming authority in Nevada.

GRIFFIN: An outside private detective agency that is hired by the casinos to catch card cheaters and monitor their whereabouts.

HEAT: When anyone in authority becomes aware of the crew. When detectives or the Griffin agents enter the premises.

HOUSE DICK: An employee of the casino whose job it is to monitor the casino games. Plainclothes-police-type people.

RUNNER: A player on the crew who helps set up plays and stands behind the brain to run the mirror out of the casino when the play goes sour. His job is to get the mirror out of the casino at any cost.

SCREEN: A crew member who physically blocks, with his body, anyone from seeing something that the crew doesn't want them to see. He'll block the view of the pit boss, for instance, or the dealer, or other nosey onlookers.

THE SHEET: A kind of makeshift balance sheet that the crew uses to track their profit-and-loss results as they play. The numbers and frequencies of plays are recorded, as well as the outcome of each play. The sheet is later used to divvy up the proceeds at the end of the playing period.

SHIT HITS THE FAN: When things have gone extremely bad during a play.

SPOOKING: Another way to see the dealer's hole card. Player 1 begins to play at a table. Player 2 sets up to play at a table diagonally, across the pit from Player 1. When a dealer has a ten-value card faceup, he/she always checks the hole card for a natural blackjack. At that point, Player 2 can often see the hole card and signals Player 1.

ABOUT ATMOSPHERE PRESS

Atmosphere Press is an independent, full-service publisher for excellent books in all genres and for all audiences. Learn more about what we do at atmospherepress.com.

We encourage you to check out some of Atmosphere's latest fiction and nonfiction releases, which are available at Amazon.com and via order from your local bookstore:

Chimera in New Orleans, a novel by Lauren Savoie
The Neurosis of George Fairbanks, a novel by Jonathan Kumar
Blue Screen, a novel by Jim van de Erve
Evelio's Garden, nonfiction by Sandra Shaw Homer
Difficulty Swallowing, essays by Kym Cunningham
Come Kill Me!, short stories by Mackinley Greenlaw
The Unexpected Aneurysm of the Potato Blossom Queen, short stories by Garrett Socol
Gathered, a novel by Kurt Hansen
Unorthodoxy, a novel by Joshua A.H. Harris
The Clockwork Witch, a novel by McKenzie P. Odom
The Hole in the World, a novel by Brandann Hill-Mann
Frank, a novel by Gina DeNicola
A User Guide to the Unconscious Mind, nonfiction by Tatiana Lukyanova
To the Next Step: Your Guide from High School and College to The Real World, nonfiction by Kyle Grappone
The George Stories, a novel by Christopher Gould

Breathing New Life: Finding Happiness after Tragedy, nonfiction by Bunny Leach

Mandated Happiness, a novel by Clayton Tucker

The Third Door, a novel by Jim Williams

The Yoga of Strength, a novel by Andrew Marc Rowe

Let the Little Birds Sing, a novel by Sandra Fox Murphy

Channel: How to be a Clear Channel for Inspiration by Listening, Enjoying, and Trusting Your Intuition, nonfiction by Jessica Ang

Love Your Vibe: Using the Power of Sound to Take Command of Your Life, nonfiction by Matt Omo

Leaving the Ladder: An Ex-Corporate Girl's Guide from the Rat Race to Fulfilment, nonfiction by Lynda Bayada

Letting Nicki Go: A Mother's Journey through Her Daughter's Cancer, nonfiction by Bunny Leach

Dear Old Dogs, a novella by Gwen Head

How Not to Sell: A Sales Survival Guide, nonfiction by Rashad Daoudi

Such a Nice Girl, a novel by Carol St. John

Winter Park, a novel by Graham Guest

That Beautiful Season, a novel by Sandra Fox Murphy

Rescripting the Workplace: Producing Miracles with Bosses, Coworkers, and Bad Days, nonfiction by Pam Boyd

Surviving Mother, a novella by Gwen Head

ABOUT THE AUTHOR

In 1969, I was eleven years old when my family moved to Oregon from Southern California. My three brothers and I were raised by an alcoholic father and a sweet mother. It was very difficult for my mother to cope with an alcoholic, ex-Marine husband who raised his four children with a firm hand and a loud, powerful voice. When I was thirteen years old, my parents started divorce proceedings. My mother finally had enough of the verbal abuse from my father, and we didn't blame her. During the divorce proceedings all four of us went with my mother to live. Shortly after the divorce my mother was diagnosed with terminal cancer. It was a horrible time for my brothers and I to watch, as cancer began to consume my mother.

After the divorce my father was so distraught, he moved to Alaska to work on the Alaska pipeline. I was seventeen and a junior in high school when my mother had succumbed to her illness. It was a brutal time in my life, as my family life crumbled right before my eyes. My brothers and me had nowhere to go, so my father allowed us to move into the house that we had lived in as a family a few short years earlier. It was just my three brothers and me, all teenagers, living in a house with no parental guidance. Somehow, with all the partying and teenage shenanigans, I managed to finish high school on my own.

Playing high school baseball was a saving grace. Our high school team had played in the state championship game in which I was the starting pitcher. We finished second, but the effort actually earned me a scholarship to play college baseball at Umpqua Community College. I ended up working through the summer at a local lumber mill to earn extra money for college. I had a stellar baseball career in junior college and earned another scholarship to play baseball at Portland State University. I struggled financially through college, and that's when I decided that I didn't want to live my life being poor. I really wanted to be a professional baseball player, but I was never drafted into the pro ranks.

After my senior year at Portland State and winding up a really good college career in baseball, I was planning to go to spring training in Arizona the following spring and try out for a minor league baseball team. That's when I was offered an opportunity that inspired the writing of this book.

In December 1980 a single phone call changed my life. That's when a former teammate called and offered me a job playing blackjack in Nevada. I took the offer and that started an unbelievable career in the competitive game of blackjack. That career lasted ten years before I was forced to retire from the casinos.

Shortly after my return to Oregon I met a girl. We got married and I went to work for her father's construction business. I quickly became a road building superintendent. I have been in the construction business for twenty-five years, still married and raising twin boys. I am now a corporate secretary for the same company I started with, and am writing a memoir of my experiences in Nevada.

CPSIA information can be obtained
at www.ICGtesting.com
Printed in the USA
LVHW041047021219
639121LV00004B/299/P